Sizing Up Measurement

Sizing Up Measurement

Activities for Grades 6–8 Classrooms

Ann Lawrence
Charlie Hennessy

Math Solutions
Sausalito, CA

Math Solutions
150 Gate 5 Road
Sausalito, CA 94965
www.mathsolutions.com

The publisher would like to acknowledge sources of adapted material:

page 5:   *Mini Metric Field Meet*—Although this activity has been modified many times, the original source for the idea was *Math and Science: A Solution* (Weibe 1987, 19–31).

page 29:   *Paper Angles*—This exploration is based on activities developed by Michael Serra, the author of *Discovering Geometry*.

page 44:   *About the Area of a Circle*—This lesson is adapted from a unit in *A Collection of Math Lessons: From Grades 6 Through 8* (Burns and Humphreys 1990, 109–36).

page 51:   *Square States 1*—This lesson is based on the article "Stating the Facts: Exploring the United States" (Bay-Williams, Bledsoe, and Reys 1998).

page 53:   *Square States 2*—This lesson is based on the article "Stating the Facts: Exploring the United States" (Bay-Williams, Bledsoe, and Reys 1998).

page 75:   *Building Referents for Capacity*—The diagram shown in Instruction 5 and in the "Liquid Capacity" Blackline Master was adapted from *Math Thematics Book 1* (Billstein and Williamson 1999, 354).

page 79:   *Volume Graphs*—This activity is adapted from "Fill 'er Up" from PBS's Middle School Math Project (n.d.).

page 122: *Unpumped Prices*—This lesson borrows some ideas from the lesson *Earthshine* in *Math and Literature, Grades 6–8* (Bay-Williams and Martinie 2004, 11–18).

Library of Congress Cataloging-in-Publication Data

Lawrence, Ann, 1946–
  Sizing up measurement. Activities for grades 6–8 classrooms / Ann
Lawrence, Charlie Hennessy.
    p. cm.
  Includes bibliographical references and index.
  ISBN-13: 978-0-941355-81-0
  ISBN-10: 0-941355-81-0
  1. Mensuration. 2. Mathematics—Study and teaching
(Elementary)—Activity programs. [1. Measurement.] I. Hennessy, Charlie.
II. Title.
QA465.L39 2007
372.35′044—dc22   2007018883

Editor: Toby Gordon
Production: Melissa L. Inglis
Cover design: Isaac Tobin
Interior design: Jenny Jensen Greenleaf
Composition: ICC Macmillan Inc.

Printed in the United States of America on acid-free paper
11 10 09   ML   2 3 4 5

A Message from Marilyn Burns

We at Math Solutions Professional Development believe that teaching math well calls for increasing our understanding of the math we teach, seeking deeper insights into how children learn mathematics, and refining our lessons to best promote students' learning.

Math Solutions shares classroom-tested lessons and teaching expertise from our faculty of Math Solutions Inservice instructors as well as from other respected math educators. Our publications are part of the nationwide effort we've made since 1984 that now includes

- more than five hundred face-to-face inservice programs each year for teachers and administrators in districts across the country;
- annually publishing professional development books, now totaling more than seventy titles and spanning the teaching of all math topics in kindergarten through grade 8;
- four series of videos for teachers, plus a video for parents, that show math lessons taught in actual classrooms;
- on-site visits to schools to help refine teaching strategies and assess student learning; and
- free online support, including grade-level lessons, book reviews, inservice information, and district feedback, all in our quarterly *Math Solutions Online Newsletter*.

For information about all of the products and services we have available, please visit our website at *www.mathsolutions.com*. You can also contact us to discuss math professional development needs by calling (800) 868-9092 or by sending an email to *info@mathsolutions.com*.

We're always eager for your feedback and interested in learning about your particular needs. We look forward to hearing from you.

Math Solutions.

Contents

Blackline Masters 179

Major Mathematical Contents Chart*

Lesson	Measurement Topic(s)							Other Content Strands			
	Length	Angles	Area and Surface Area	Capacity and Volume	Rates and Ratios	Similarity	Other Topic	Number	Geometry	Patterns and Algebra	Data Analysis and Probability
Building Referents for Metric Units of Length	✓										
Mini Metric Field Meet	✓		✓				✓	✓			
More Pi, Anyone?	✓								✓	✓	✓
Constant Perimeter	✓									✓	
That's Irrational!	✓							✓			
Go for the Golden 2	✓				✓	✓		✓	✓		
Building Referents for the Measure of Angles		✓						✓			
What's My Angle?		✓							✓	✓	
Paper Angles		✓							✓		
Angles in the Round		✓							✓		
Formulas from the Grid			✓						✓	✓	
About the Area of a Circle			✓				✓		✓		
Orange You Glad . . . ?			✓						✓	✓	
Square States 1			✓	✓						✓	
Square States 2			✓			✓		✓		✓	
Constant Area			✓					✓		✓	
How Do You Grow?	✓		✓	✓	✓					✓	
Chances Are			✓						✓		✓

*Includes major content of extension activities.

Introduction

Measurement is one of the very earliest forms of mathematics. For centuries people have measured quantities to cook, to build, to make clothing, to divide land, and to keep track of time and distance. In recent years, our abilities to measure have expanded dramatically; we now measure in order to travel through space, to fabricate molecular-size devices, and to create global positioning systems.

Certainly children use measurement in their daily lives, too, as they compare heights, see how far they can run and jump, keep track of how many days until their birthdays, compare their ages, and celebrate each time they need the next shoe size. As children grow older, they may become interested in sports statistics or world records involving measurement; they may use measurement to rearrange furniture or their rooms or to build items such as birdhouses or model rockets. Clearly measurement must be an important part of the mathematics curriculum, as it helps students make mathematical sense of their lives and prepares them for their future.

Unfortunately, it is easy for teachers to become overwhelmed with the abundance of measurement objectives they are asked to address; teachers often resort to dealing with those objectives by telling students what to memorize. For students who experience this kind of incomplete instruction, measurement becomes a list of terms, numbers, and facts that they easily forget.

We too have encountered the complexities of teaching measurement in our classrooms. We know that it is very easy to become overwhelmed by all that is expected of us. But we also have experienced the joys of teaching measurement in ways that help our students make sense of the mathematics they are learning. We've seen our students come away from these lessons excited about their new and deeper understandings of measurement. We've watched our students develop confidence in their ability to use measurement to understand their world rather than struggle to simply memorize rote formulas. These are the kinds of lessons we want to share with you here.

In this three-book series, Sizing Up Measurement, we have worked to create lessons that focus on essential measurement concepts that are connected to problem-solving contexts. The lessons focus on helping students

❖ identify the attribute to be measured (for example, length or weight);

- know what it means to measure—comparing the attribute of the item or situation with a unit with the same attribute: lengths must be compared with units of length, areas with units of area, and so on;
- develop an understanding of what it means to measure using standard and nonstandard units;
- select a system of measurement to be used—customary or metric;
- understand how benchmark units—such as *a centimeter is about the width of a pencil*—help determine the magnitude of specific units;
- estimate the result of the measurement, both before and after the act of measuring;
- select a measurement tool to assign a number value and determine how accurate they need to be;
- keep track of results in an organized and useful way.

As you can imagine, given the grade-level spans in this series (K–2, 3–5, 6–8), the three books deal with very different levels of mathematics, but there are commonalities among them all. Each of the books includes lessons that relate to categories of measurement important for that grade-level span, and the lessons in all three books provide meaningful contexts for students to solve problems and use their mathematical skills as they develop important vocabulary related to measurement.

Before trying these lessons, it is important to consider the natural progressions in thinking that children pass through as they develop basic concepts of measurement:

When a student lays down toothpicks to measure length and leaves gaps or overlaps the toothpicks, the student is struggling with *unit iteration*. He doesn't yet understand that the distance of the units altogether should be equal to the distance being measured.

When a student thinks that, when measuring with small units, a small total should result, the student does not yet know the *inverse relationship* between the size of the unit and the number of units—small units create a larger total and large units create a smaller total.

When a student compares the length of pencils that are not evenly lined up and thinks that the pencil that sticks out is longer, the student has not yet developed *conservation of length*—the idea that a different position does not change the length.

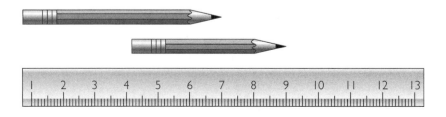

When a student knows that the marker is shorter than the pencil, and the pencil is shorter than the stick, but doesn't realize the marker therefore must be shorter than the stick, the student has yet to develop *transitive reasoning*. This is necessary in order for children to understand how rulers help us compare objects that are not side by side.

When you put a pencil against the ruler between 2 and 8, and a student thinks the pencil is 8 inches long, the student doesn't understand that the number on the ruler represents the entire distance from the "zero end" to that number.

When a student thinks an angle with longer sides has a larger measure, the student doesn't understand that the measure of an angle depends upon the spread of the angle's rays.

When a student thinks it is impossible to determine the area of an irregular polygon, the student may not understand that figures can be partitioned into shapes that have areas that she can determine.

When a student assumes that a constant perimeter always yields a constant area, the student does not understand the relationship between these two measures.

When a student depends upon a separate formula for determining the volume of each kind of prism and pyramid, the student does not understand the relationships among the volumes of such figures.

The lessons in these books are intended to provide students with opportunities to make sense of these and other critical understandings related to measurement. Through multiple experiences with length, angles, area, capacity and volume, mass and weight, ratios and rates, similar figures, temperature, and time, students learn how to measure, compare, and order. Measurement requires estimation, making comparisons, mental math, and number sense. Students need to add, subtract, multiply, divide, and perceive numerical relationships in many different ways. Measurement is a topic that deserves attention and time in every school year. We offer these lessons in the hopes that you will use and adapt them to fit your circumstances. All students need many opportunities to build their understandings, make connections to other topics, explain their thinking and procedures, and analyze and communicate their results to others. We sincerely hope that you and your students enjoy these lessons.

VICKI BACHMAN, GRADES K–2
CHRIS CONFER, GRADES 3–5
ANN LAWRENCE AND CHARLIE HENNESSY, GRADES 6–8

CHAPTER 1

Length

Introduction

Length as a measure of distance is a concept with which middle school students are familiar. This chapter aims to solidify their understanding by providing a variety of estimating and measuring activities in different contexts. The lessons focus on building measurement sense. They help students to

❖ develop personal referents for both customary and metric units;

❖ understand that as the unit of measure decreases in size, the number of units needed to express the length of an object increases;

❖ learn that many names indicate a measure of distance, such as *length, width, height, base, altitude, radius, perimeter, circumference,* and *hypotenuse;*

❖ convert, with confidence, measures of length—both customary and metric; and

❖ realize that measures of length or distance can be irrational numbers and become familiar with placing such numbers on a number line.

In the lesson *Building Referents for Metric Units of Length* (page 2), students establish personal referents for common units of length. The student who knows that his own stride is about 3 feet long can more accurately estimate that the length of the classroom is about 36 feet long than a student who has no such referent. The student who knows that she is 62 inches tall can comfortably approximate the height of a classmate, a bookcase, or the classroom door. In the lesson *Mini Metric Field Meet* (page 5), students first estimate a linear measure and then immediately use a measuring tape to find the actual measure and percent of error. In this way, students learn to make better estimates and recognize the magnitude of their measurement errors.

Also included in this chapter are lessons that engage students in new concepts and applications of length, such as

❖ finding the length of an unknown side in a right triangle—see the lessons *That's Irrational!* (page 16) and *Go for the Golden 2* (page 19)

❖ understanding what an irrational number is and where irrational lengths or distances fit with the other sets of numbers they know—see *That's Irrational!* (page 16)

❖ investigating pi through measurement and graphing—see *More Pi, Anyone?* (page 8)

❖ investigating the concept of constant perimeter—see *Constant Perimeter* (page 12)

Communication of mathematical thinking and at least one idea for extending the activity are built into each lesson.

 ## Building Referents for Metric Units of Length

Related Topic: estimation

Overview
Students estimate and measure the metric length of a variety of objects, and then they choose personal referents for the each metric unit of length.

Materials
- metric rulers or tape measures, 1 per student
- meter stick
- optional: *Millions to Measure*, by David Schwartz (2003)
- optional: decimeter paper strips for making a meter stick (see Blackline Masters), 10 per student

Vocabulary: centimeter, decimeter, meter, millimeter, referent

Instructions

1. Explain to students the importance of estimation in measurement. You might do this by reading the last half of the book *Millions to Measure*, by David Schwartz. It contains an engaging description of the metric system and how it works. It also mentions the miscalculation that the U.S. space engineers made when a spacecraft was supposed to orbit Mars but instead was lost in space forever.

   Ask the students questions to help them provide examples of situations when an estimate of length would be helpful. For example:
   - There is a dead tree in our school yard. Will the dead tree hit our school if the wind blows it over?
   - We want to play a circle game with everyone in the class. Can all the members of our class comfortably form a circle in our classroom?
   - We want to cover our classroom bulletin board with a mural. How long must the piece of paper be to cover the bulletin board?

   Solicit additional examples from the students.

2. Review the units of length in the metric system. Then ask students to think about how many decimeters long they think the board in your classroom is. Write the estimates and their range on the board.

3. Next, ask the students to think about the length of 1 decimeter and be prepared to hold up their hands to signal the length they estimate when you snap your fingers. After a few moments, snap your fingers and look around the class. Then tell the students to put their hands down.

4. Indicate to the students the range of estimates in the class, using your hands. After reminding the class that a decimeter is 10 centimeters long, have a student show the class the actual length of a decimeter on the meter stick and draw it on the board.

5. Ask the students to estimate again how many decimeters long the board measures. Write the estimates and their range on the board and have students share their strategies for estimating. Compare these new estimates with those the students gave before seeing the length of a decimeter.

6. Talk with students about the importance of having a personal referent for each metric unit of length. Explain that a personal referent is an object you see or use often, so you don't forget it. It is an object that you can think of to help you estimate the length of an unknown object. In the case of metric units of length, it is something that is as close as possible to a millimeter, a centimeter, a decimeter, or a meter in length.

7. If you wish, either in class or at home, have students create their own meter stick by cutting out ten of the paper decimeter strips including the tab, taping or gluing them together, and labeling each decimeter as shown below. After the glue is dry, have students fold their strips of paper in half lengthwise to strengthen them.

   While this activity may take a while, it is very useful for students to actually go through this process. Through this do-it-yourself experience, students are much more likely to strengthen an intuitive feel for metric units of length than by merely using a commercial measuring device.

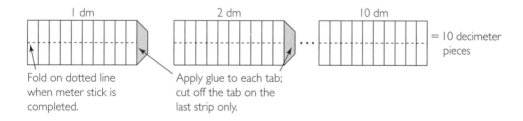

Fold on dotted line when meter stick is completed.

Apply glue to each tab; cut off the tab on the last strip only.

= 10 decimeter pieces

8. For class work or homework, assign the following:
   a. Use a metric measuring tool to find five common objects that are close to 1 millimeter in length or thickness. List them.
   b. Repeat the task above to find five common objects that are close to each of these units: 1 centimeter, 1 decimeter, and 1 meter.

9. Have students share their lists with a partner, and then have each pair share one object with the class that it thinks is a good referent for each unit of measure. Write these on the board. Suggestions may include the following:

   - millimeter: thickness of a dime; thickness of the point of a thumbtack; thickness of a fingernail
   - centimeter: thickness (or diameter) of a crayon; width of the head of a thumbtack; width of a fingernail
   - decimeter: length of a new, unused crayon; total height of a 60-, 75-, or 100-watt light bulb; length of a regular-size (about 55-gram) Snickers, Milky Way, or Twix candy bar
   - meter: width of a single front door; height of a volleyball net

10. Review that having personal referents for the metric units of measure will make estimating lengths in metric units easier. Have students choose their personal referents for each metric unit of length. When everyone is ready, tell the students that in order to become a really good estimator, they need to practice. Encourage the students to use their personal referents to make estimates of length on their own, for instance, while taking a walk, waiting for their parents in the car or a store, or doing an errand, and to check their estimates whenever possible using their paper meter sticks or a measuring tape.

11. Complete this activity by asking students to write a reflection about the importance of estimation and how their own personal referents can make it easier for them to make good estimates.

Notes to the Teacher

This activity helps students choose personal referents for most of the commonly used units of metric length. Over time, these referents should help each student become a better estimator of length.

When you use this activity with your students for the first time, you may find the following comments useful:

◈ Be sure to focus on all the metric lengths. For example, though not often stressed in classrooms, the decimeter is a common length for many crayons and candy bars. Also, remind students that the length of a long rod in a set of base ten blocks is a decimeter and the ones cube is a centimeter along each edge.

◈ Developing a feel for the size of units in any measurement system requires repeated practice. Throughout the school year, lead brief sessions during which students can engage in estimating the lengths of various objects and discuss referents.

◈ Post a list of appropriate referents for each metric unit of length on the classroom wall. Add to the list as you or students find new ones throughout the year.

Extension

Gather the following materials for each student:

- ❧ 1 decimeter of durable ribbon (wider than 1 centimeter)
- ❧ button, 1 centimeter wide and 1 millimeter thick
- ❧ needle and about 60 centimeters of thread
- ❧ pair of small Velcro squares (one hook and one loop piece)

Have students make a personal referent for metric units of length to attach to their backpack or other item by sewing the button onto the ribbon and using the Velcro for fastening the ribbon to the backpack. If a student does not want to fasten the ribbon to anything, she can use it as a bookmark.

Occasionally remind students, through questioning, that the ribbon is 1 decimeter long; the button, 1 centimeter wide; and the button, 1 millimeter thick.

 ## Mini Metric Field Meet

Related Topics: estimation, percent, percent of error, ratios

Overview

Students perform adaptations of classic field meet events. After each event, they estimate their performance in metric units and then compare that estimate to their actual performance.

Materials

- ❧ metric measuring tapes, at least 5
- ❧ procedures for the field events, 1 for each station (see Blackline Masters)
- ❧ jump ropes or pieces of rope, approximately 5–6 feet long, 5
- ❧ foam plates, at least 2
- ❧ plastic drinking straws, at least 2
- ❧ cotton balls, at least 2
- ❧ cardboard placards, each having the name of one event on it, 5
- ❧ clipboards, 1 per pair of students
- ❧ *Mini Metric Field Meet* recording sheets, 1 per student (see Blackline Masters)

Vocabulary: centimeter, estimate, meter, metric, millimeter, percent of error

Instructions

1. Set up a station for each event outside, in a gymnasium, or in a large, empty room, using the following guidelines:

    a. Lay a jump rope or other piece of rope to designate the starting line at each station.

b. Put one metric measuring tape at each station. If the tapes are less than 2 meters long, put two tapes at the stations for the standing broad jump and the standing triple jump.

c. Put plates, straws, and cotton balls at the appropriate stations.

d. Place a placard with the name of the event and a copy of the procedures for that event at each station.

2. Prepare students for this activity by conducting the lesson *Building Referents for Metric Units of Length* (see page 2) or by showing them a millimeter, a centimeter, and a meter on a measuring tape and having them suggest a referent to associate with each unit.

3. Go over the procedures for each event in the mini metric field meet. Have a volunteer demonstrate each event. Have class members make estimates and measure the actual distance.

4. Give a clipboard, two recording sheets, and a pencil to each pair of students. Instruct the class that while one student in each pair is doing the event, the other will hold the clipboard and record the partner's estimates and result. They should then swap roles.

5. Divide the students into five groups. Assign each group to a station. Explain that groups will rotate clockwise as soon as all students have completed the event in which they are participating. Let the games begin!

6. Circulate to be sure everyone is doing and recording the events correctly.

7. As soon as everyone has completed all five events, gather the materials and return to the classroom. Have each student keep her own recording sheet.

8. Ask the students to work in pairs to find their scores for each event, using the following steps:

    a. Subtract the smaller number (estimate or actual) from the larger one and record that difference on the recording sheet.

    b. Find the ratio (the difference between estimate and actual length to the actual length). Convert it to a percent. This is called the *percent of error*.

    c. Record the percent of error for each event on the recording sheet.

    d. Turn in your recording sheet.

9. On the following day, announce the medal winners—the three students with the lowest percent of error—for each event. Some teachers present cardboard medals or spray paint old musical CDs to create medals.

10. Lead the class in a discussion about the strategies the students used to make estimates, what estimating mistakes they would avoid in the future, and the meaning of *percent of error*.

Notes to the Teacher

This activity provides practice in estimating metric distances so that students can become familiar and comfortable with the basic units of length in the metric system. In addition, students work with ratios and percents as they find their scores for each event.

When you use this activity with your students for the first time, you may find the following comments useful:

❖ The scaffolding you provide before this activity is the most important ingredient for its mathematical success. Students always enjoy the activity, but having referents or benchmarks for the metric units of length is vital if they are to make reasonable estimates and improve in this area through the experience. (See the lesson *Building Referents for Metric Units of Length* on page 2 for suggestions for providing scaffolding).

❖ After students have completed the events and figured their scores, lead a class discussion about percent of error. Include questions such as the following:

  • Which indicates a better estimate: a difference of 15 centimeters between the estimate and the actual measure for the cotton ball shot put or a difference of 30 centimeters between the estimate and the actual measure for the standing triple jump? (Since a cotton ball is rarely tossed as much as a meter, while the triple jump will cover at least 3 meters, the seemingly smaller difference between the first estimate and the corresponding measure is most likely a larger percent [≥ 15 percent] of the distance covered than the same comparison for the triple jump [≤ 10 percent]).

  • Why do you think your scores were based on percent of error instead of simply the difference between the estimate and the measured length? (Percent of error is a more appropriate way to judge how good an estimate is in this situation, as illustrated in the previous paragraph.)

Extension

This experience should be one of several estimation activities with the metric system. At a minimum, there should be a similar experience with metric units of mass and volume. For example, you and your students could design an activity in which all the events related to volume. One such event could be the off-hand sponge squeeze, for which each student would do the following:

> *Reach into a bucket of water containing a sponge, using the hand with which you normally do not write. Hold the sponge full of water over an empty container and squeeze as much water as you can out of the sponge. Estimate the volume of the water squeezed out in milliliters. Ask your partner to record your estimate. With your partner, measure and record the actual volume.*

◈ More Pi, Anyone?

Related Topics: algebraic thinking, coordinate graphing, functions, slope

Overview

Students investigate the meaning of pi (π) in a graphing context. They use the diameter and circumference of cylindrical cans to construct a coordinate graph. Then they examine the points they have graphed, relating them to both the cans and the characteristics of a linear function.

Materials

◈ cylindrical cans, 1 per student

◈ centimeter grid paper, approximately 60 by 90 centimeters, 1 sheet

◈ fine-line permanent markers, 1 or 2 per pair of students

Vocabulary: circle, circumference, diameter, measures of central tendency, pi, rate of change, ratio, x-axis, x-coordinate, y-axis, y-coordinate

Instructions

1. Several days prior to this lesson, ask students to bring one or more cylindrical cans from home. Explain that the activity the class will be doing works best if there is a variety of sizes among the cans. Suggest that students look around for an unusual size to bring to class. You will also need to prepare a class assignment that students can be working on when not engaged in the activity.

2. When there are enough cans for each student to have his own (ideally, each can will also be a different size), begin the lesson by asking each student to place the can in front of him. Then work through the following questions and tasks with the class to review the mathematical understandings and terms needed for this activity.

   • What is the geometric term for the shape of a can?
   • Trace the height of the can with your finger.
   • Trace the distance around the can with your finger.
   • What is mathematical term for the distance around a can or any circle?
   • Trace the longest distance across the top of the can with your finger.
   • What is the mathematical term for the longest distance across the top of the can?
   • Through what point in a circle must the longest distance across the top of the can pass?
   • What is a ratio?
   • What is the mathematical term for the ratio of the circumference of a circle to its diameter?
   • Explain what *circumference* means in your own words.

3. Have each student use a fine-line permanent marker to make a mark about 1 centimeter long from the top rim of the can straight down the side of the can so that it will be visible when the can is laid on its side.

4. Place the large grid paper on a table or other large, flat surface and give the pre-planned assignment to the class. While the class is working on this assignment, ask students, one at a time, to bring their can to the grid paper. With each student, do the following:

   a. Briefly review the student's knowledge of coordinate graphing. Ask the student to identify the *x*- and *y*-axes on the grid and to locate one or more random points when you give the coordinates. Ask the student to identify the scale used on each axis (1 unit = 1 centimeter).

   b. Ask the student to set the can on its top with the left edge at the origin and right edge on the *x*-axis and then adjust the can until the right edge is the greatest possible distance from the origin (in other words, so that the can exactly straddles the *x*-axis), as shown in the following illustration. Be sure the student realizes that this width is the diameter of the can. Then ask the student to make a light pencil mark on the axis at this point, establishing the *x*-coordinate of the point on the graph for this can.

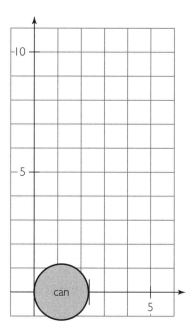

   c. Next, direct the student to turn the can so that the mark drawn earlier on the side of the can is directly in line with the *x*-axis. The mark on the can must be aligned end-to-end with the *x*-axis. The student should roll the can carefully, keeping it perpendicular to the *y*-axis until that same mark appears parallel to the *x*-axis again when the can is viewed from directly above. Then the student should carefully plot a point on the graph directly below the mark on the can.

The point should be on the same imaginary vertical line, perpendicular to the *x*-axis, as the mark the student made earlier on the *x*-axis. Also, it should be dark and large enough for the class to see when the completed graph is displayed later. Be sure the student understands that this *y*-coordinate represents the circumference of the can.

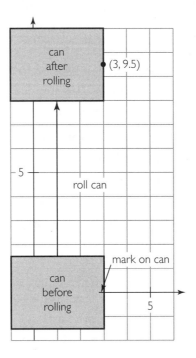

d. Ask the student to record the coordinates of the point she graphed and to find the ratio of the *y*-coordinate to the *x*-coordinate when she returns to her desk.

5. When every student has placed a point on the graph, display the graph in front of the class. Divide the class into small groups, and have each group come to the graph and work together to answer the following questions in writing:

• What does the *x*-coordinate of each point on the graph represent? Show it on the can. What is the mathematical term for this measure?

• What does the *y*-coordinate of each point on the graph represent? Show it on the can. What is the mathematical term for this measure?

• Estimate the rate of change between each pair of points on the graph.

• Use the words *diameter* and *circumference* (of the cans) to explain the rate of change between each pair of points on the graph.

• Select a few points on the graph. What are the values for the ratio of the *y*-coordinate to the *x*-coordinate for each? What is the closest whole number value to your results? Explain why this makes sense, using the attributes of the can and mathematical vocabulary.

• Where can you find pi in this graph?

6. Now lead a whole-class discussion about the answers the groups wrote. Ask follow-up questions to help clear up any misunderstandings.

7. Finally, instruct students to individually write a paragraph explaining the mathematical ideas of the activity to an imaginary student who was absent from class.

Notes to the Teacher

This activity deepens students' understanding of pi as they explore the relationship between the circumference and diameter of a circle in a new context. It also helps students establish an intuitive meaning for slope and reinforce what they have previously learned about this relationship.

When you use this activity with your students for the first time, you may find the following comments useful:

◈ If students bring to class cans that are full, encourage the class to donate the items to a food distribution center after the activity is finished. If they bring cans that are empty, remind the students to be careful with any sharp edges and to avoid distorting the cans, since this can happen rather easily once the top and the contents are removed.

◈ To ensure a variety of sizes among the cans, ask the students not to bring soup cans (someone invariably brings one anyway!). In addition, gather a few cans yourself; for large cans, try your school lunchroom or a restaurant. Also, processed meat and fruits often come in small cans.

◈ Make sure your coordinate grid is large enough to allow graphing the point for the largest can before you start the activity.

◈ If appropriate, elicit the idea that the line of points on the graph indicates a linear function ($C = \pi d$). Then ask students to describe the constant rate of change or slope of the line (this is π, since the rate of change is, $\frac{C}{d}$, which, in any circle, is always this constant value).

◈ If appropriate, tell the students to assume, for a moment, that the set of points on the graph all fell exactly on a straight line (assuming every student measured and graphed with no errors). Ask, "Would it be mathematically acceptable to connect the points on the graph?" Students should realize that connecting the points would be appropriate because the point (diameter, circumference) for any can would fall on that line, and any point on that line would represent values for a possible can. If the students seem dubious, choose a value on the x-axis for a new point, have students multiply it by pi, use the product as the y-coordinate, and observe that the point falls on the line; thus, for an arbitrary diameter, the point (diameter, circumference) falls on the line. Conversely, have students choose a new point on the line, find its y-coordinate by tracing over to the y-axis, divide that value by pi, and observe by tracing down to the x-axis that this quotient is the x-coordinate of the point; thus, the point they chose represents the values (diameter, circumference) of a possible can, and this will be true for any point they choose on the line.

Extension
Ask students to find the mean, median, and mode of the values they found for the ratio of the y-coordinate to the x-coordinate of the points they graphed. Ask them to explain whether one of these measures of central tendency is closer to the value they might expect (pi) than the others and to explain their reasoning. Looking closely at their data often helps students find possible reasons. For example, if the mode is closest to pi, the students might conclude that this is because most of the students in the class are excellent measurers! Also, if one point is very far from the rest, the value obtained for the ratio of the y-coordinate to the x-coordinate will affect the mean more than it affects the mode or the median.

Constant Perimeter

Related Topics: algebraic thinking, coordinate graphing, linear functions

Overview
Students produce different-size rectangles with a given perimeter, look for patterns, draw and graph the results on a coordinate plane, and find the function rule, which they express in both words and symbols.

Materials
◈ grid paper, any size unit length, 1 sheet per student
◈ *Constant Perimeter* instructions, 1 copy per student (see Blackline Masters)
◈ colored pencils, 1 each of two different colors per student
◈ straightedges, 1 per student

Vocabulary: altitude, area, base, coordinate graph, function rule, linear function, origin, perimeter, rectangle, T-chart, vertex

Prerequisite Concepts and Skills
Students should understand that perimeter means the distance around a figure or shape and is measured in linear units. They should be able to recognize an appropriate line of points on a coordinate graph as a representation of a linear function and know how to write a function rule from a set of points.

Alternatively, the lesson can be modified by omitting those parts that deal with functions and function rules. In this case, the lesson can be revisited after students gain these skills.

Instructions

1. Tell the students that they will investigate all the rectangles that have a perimeter of 24 units, using whole number side lengths only. Explain that they will list the dimensions, draw the rectangles on a graph, and look for patterns.

2. Ask students to offer definitions for the terms *area*, *rectangle*, *base*, *altitude*, *perimeter*, *vertex*, *origin*, and *linear function*. Verify correct answers.

3. Direct students to work in pairs to complete the steps outlined in the *Constant Perimeter* instructions. Circulate to spot problems and answer questions.

4. When all students have completed the exploration, have each pair share its findings with another pair. Then lead a class discussion about the patterns students found in both the T-chart and in the graph.

   Following are some patterns the students may notice:

   • The base plus the altitude always totals 12.
   • As the length of the base increases, the length of the corresponding altitude decreases.
   • The rectangles start off tall and skinny and get shorter until there is a square, and then they continue to get shorter and wider.
   • Each rectangle, except for the 6-by-6 square, has a "partner," that is, another rectangle with the same dimensions but reversed, for example, 1 by 11 and 11 by 1.

   After each pattern is offered, ask the students, "Why do you think this happens?" Also ask them to make a conjecture about how the pattern would change if the rectangles all had perimeters of 30 units.

5. Ask students to summarize what they learned and/or what prior knowledge was reinforced through this exploration.

Notes to the Teacher

This exploration helps students solidify their understanding of perimeter. It also connects the symbolic rule for perimeter to the data that the students generate and to the visual plot formed by the top right corners of their rectangles.

When you use this activity with your students for the first time, you may find the following comments useful:

◈ Students often include impossible rectangles, such as 2 by 12, 3 by 8, or 1 by 23, in their list. Give the students a chance to draw the rectangles on the grid paper before correcting them. When students start graphing, they usually catch this error on their own.

◈ If your students are not familiar with three-column T-charts, help them by drawing one on the board, providing the three main headings, and eliciting what kind of information needs to be provided in each column.

◈ Many students randomly fill in their T-charts, producing a jumbled set of combinations. When needed, suggest organizing the data sequentially, as shown in the following chart, to make the patterns more obvious. This also helps those students who have unintentionally omitted one or more sets of possible dimensions. Some of the different ways students may interpret the data are shown in this chart also.

Length of Base	What I See/Think	Length of Altitude
1	$\frac{24}{2} - 1$	11
2	$\frac{24}{2} - 2$	10
3	$\frac{24}{2} - 3$	9
or		
4	$[24 - (2 \times 4)] \div 2$	8
5	$[24 - (2 \times 5)] \div 2$	7
6	$[24 - (2 \times 6)] \div 2$	6
7	$[24 - (2 \times 7)] \div 2$	5
or		
8	$12 - 8$	4
9	$12 - 9$	3
10	$12 - 10$	2
11	$12 - 11$	1

◈ The graph should look similar to this:

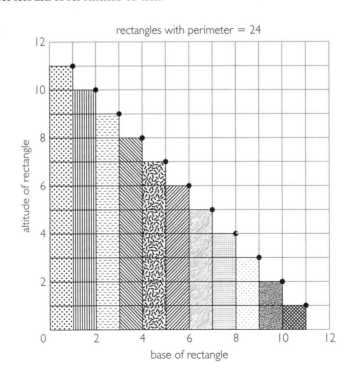

◈ Following are two of the most common descriptions that students give for the graph:

- It is a group of rectangles that overlap, starting with one having a base measuring 1 unit (making a 1-by-11 rectangle). The base of each new rectangle increases by 1 unit up to a base of 11 (making an 11-by-1 rectangle).
- It starts with a tall, skinny rectangle on the left and each one gets wider and shorter as the size of the base increases.

If needed, help the students refine the description of the graph to something like *a diagonal row of points starting with (1, 11) on the left and moving over one unit to the right and one unit down for each new rectangle {(2, 10), (3, 9), . . .} until the last point, which is (11, 1).*

◈ When they are explaining how the graph and T-chart are related, make sure the students recognize that each row in the T-chart contains the dimensions for one possible rectangle with a perimeter of 24 and shows the coordinates for the corresponding point that was graphed. Students should also notice that the left column contains all the x-coordinates for the graphed points while the right column contains the corresponding y-coordinates. Students should verbalize that the T-chart and the graph are two different representations of the same information.

◈ In expressing the function rule, some students will likely focus on the rectangles, writing something like *For each rectangle, two times the length of the base plus two times the length of the altitude equals 24.* While this statement is true, it is not complete. Since the students were restricted to whole number lengths for the sides of the rectangles, this restriction should be included. Questions about this issue can lead to a discussion of how the graph would look if any workable lengths, such as 7.3 or $\sqrt{5}$, were allowed, or more generally, when it is appropriate to connect the points on a coordinate graph and when it is not.

Other students may write, *For a rectangle with a perimeter of 24, the sum of the two whole number coordinates equals 12.* To be sure the students understand why this rule works, look for an explanation like *The sum of the two whole number coordinates equals 12 because one coordinate represents the length of the base and the other, the length of the altitude of the rectangle. Adding the two numbers together gives you half the perimeter, since each dimension is used twice to draw the perimeter.* If this thinking is not offered, ask questions to guide students to identify this generalization.

◈ In symbols, the students usually write $2b + 2a = 24$, when b equals the length of the base and a equals the length of the altitude. This fits the form of the formula for perimeter they have used in the earlier grades. Acknowledge that the rule is accurate and then encourage the students to try to find another way to write the rule, such as a rule that starts with $b = (b = 12 - a$ or $b = -a + 12)$. For students who have worked with functions, this is a nice connection with, and reinforcement of, concepts they have studied. In addition, it helps to prepare them for isolating a particular variable, which they will be required to do in both algebra and high school science.

◈ The visual pattern created by the rectangles helps students see the relationship between the length and the width (base and altitude) of rectangles with a constant perimeter. As either of these increases, the other must decrease by the same amount. This should enable students to see that the following five equations are equivalent:

$$2a + 2b = 24$$
$$a + b = 12$$
$$b = 12 - a$$
$$x + y = 12$$
$$y = 12 - x$$

Extension

Repeat this investigation with each pair of students using a different fixed perimeter. Then they look for generalizations when everyone is ready to compare results.

That's Irrational!

Related Topics: geometric construction, irrational numbers on a number line, Pythagorean theorem, radical expression

Overview

In this activity, students strengthen their understanding of irrational numbers. They use the Pythagorean theorem to help them place irrational numbers on a number line and develop a visual image of the magnitude of some irrational numbers.

Materials

◈ rulers or straightedges, 1 per student
◈ compasses, 1 per student
◈ *That's Irrational!* instructions, 1 copy per student (see Blackline Masters)

Vocabulary: coordinate (on a number line), graph (on a number line), infinite, integer, irrational number, origin, perpendicular, quotient, radical sign, real number, repeating decimal, square root, terminating decimal, unit length

Prerequisite Skills and Concepts

Students should be able to

◈ demonstrate an understanding of scale and unit length on a number line;
◈ use a compass and a straightedge to (1) construct a segment congruent to a given segment and (2) construct a line perpendicular to a given line through a given point

(A website with good instructions for such constructions is http://regentsprep.org/Regents/math/math-topic.cfm?TopicCode=construc. It also includes online videos for the constructions.); and

◈ use the Pythagorean theorem to find the missing side of a right triangle, including finding a side with an irrational number of units as its length.

Instructions

1. Ask volunteers to explain what $\sqrt{12}$ means to them. They may offer the following ideas:

   - a number that can be multiplied by itself to equal the number under the radical sign
   - a number that cannot be expressed as a terminating or repeating decimal
   - a real number that is not a rational number
   - an irrational number
   - a real number that cannot be written as an integer or the quotient of two integers
   - a number that is an infinitely long, nonrepeating decimal number

   Help students combine their ideas into a workable definition for *irrational number*. Emphasize that an irrational number is, in fact, a number, but it cannot be written as a common fraction.

2. Ask students, "Do you think each irrational number has an exact location on a number line? Why or why not?" Allow students to share their opinions, but do not provide the answer. Instead, tell the students that they will find the answer to this question by working with a number line, doing some geometric constructions, and using mathematics that they know.

3. Pass out the *That's Irrational!* instructions, rulers or straightedges, and compasses.

4. Circulate among students while they work to monitor their progress and give help as needed.

5. When everyone has completed the activity, ask students to share their responses to Steps 8, 9, and 10 in a whole-class discussion.

Notes to the Teacher

This activity provides an opportunity for students to build a stronger understanding of irrational numbers by (1) using the Pythagorean theorem to visually represent the magnitude of particular irrational numbers and (2) plotting the precise location of each of those irrational numbers on a number line.

When you use this activity with your students for the first time, you may find the following comments useful:

◈ To help them find accurate answers, have students write out all the steps when using the Pythagorean theorem with side lengths that are irrational numbers. For example:

$$a^2 + b^2 = c^2$$
$$1^2 + (\sqrt{2})^2 = c^2$$
$$1 + 2 = c^2$$
$$3 = c^2$$
$$\sqrt{3} = c$$

In particular, students often use 2 and $\sqrt{3}$ as the length of the legs when trying to construct a right triangle with a hypotenuse equal to $\sqrt{5}$. They usually do not catch their errors unless they substitute, as shown above, to verify their conjectures.

◈ Students' explanations about $\sqrt{2}$ (Step 8 on the instruction sheet) should include the information shown in Figure 1–1.

◈ For students having trouble finding the coordinate for the new point they have created on the number line, suggest that they label each side of their right triangle with its length. If they still have difficulty connecting the construction to the needed coordinate, ask them what the length of the radius of the circle is. These steps nearly always result in an *aha*.

◈ When students are comparing finished products (Step 10), help them realize that each correct number line has all the coordinates in the same relative positions and that the only difference among them is the size of the unit length.

8. First, the triangle is a right triangle since AO was constructed to be perpendicular to the number line. The length of the legs of the right triangle are each = 1 unit, so the hypotenuse is $\sqrt{2}$. Since the hypotenuse was used as a radius to construct a circle with the origin as the center, the place where the circle intersects with the number line is also $\sqrt{2}$ from the origin.

Figure 1–1 *One student's reasoning for the placement of the square root of 2 on the number line.*

◈ To be sure students understand the meaning of an irrational length, explicitly point out that every irrational number, like every rational number, has an exact location on the number line and an exact distance from the origin.

Note: Both this activity and the following extension can be done using *The Geometer's Sketchpad* or other similar software. Repeating the basics of the activity in this alternate learning environment provides excellent reinforcement of the targeted mathematical ideas of the lesson.

Extension

Ask students to plot a list of real numbers on a number line. Include at least one number written in each of the following forms: whole number, integer, positive and negative fractions (proper and improper), positive and negative decimals (terminating and repeating), percents (including those less than 1 percent and more than 100 percent), exponential expressions, and radical expressions. Include some numbers that are equivalent. One possible set of numbers is the following:

$$37.5\%, -\sqrt{3}, -2^2, 0.8\overline{3}, 1.25, 0, 0.\overline{3}, 140\%, -2^0, 100\%,$$
$$-2, -0.5, \frac{2}{3}, \sqrt{5}, \frac{5}{4}, 1.2, -1.\overline{4}, \sqrt{2}, 2^2, -\frac{1}{3}$$

 Go for the Golden 2

Related Topics: geometric constructions, irrational numbers, Pythagorean theorem, radical expressions, ratio and proportion, similar figures

Overview

Students construct a golden rectangle using the Pythagorean theorem and test that rectangle against the following definition: In any golden rectangle, $\frac{\text{length}}{\text{width}} = \frac{\text{length} + \text{width}}{\text{width}}$.

Materials

◈ compasses, 1 per student
◈ straightedges, 1 per student
◈ grid paper, 1 sheet per student
◈ *Go for the Golden 2* recording sheets, 1 per student (see Blackline Masters)

Vocabulary: congruent, construct, intersection, intersects, midpoint, parallel, perpendicular, Pythagorean theorem, radius, ratio, ray, similar figures, vertex

Prerequisite Skills and Concepts

Students must be able to do basic constructions with a compass and straightedge (two congruent segments, midpoint of a segment, and perpendicular lines).

They should also be familiar with the Fibonacci sequence (1, 1, 2, 3, 5, 8, 13, . . .) and the golden rectangle, for which the ratio of its length (longer side) to its width is approximately 1.61803, or $\frac{\text{length}}{\text{width}} = \frac{\text{length} + \text{width}}{\text{width}}$.

Instructions

1. Explain to students that they will be constructing a golden rectangle that will be used later in a survey to determine whether people actually seem to prefer its shape to that of other rectangles.

2. Distribute the recording sheets and other materials.

3. Tell students that at specific points during the exploration, as noted on the recording sheet, they will work with a partner.

4. Circulate among the students while they work to answer questions and monitor their progress.

5. When all students have completed their constructions, display them where everyone can see. Lead a class discussion to help students process the mathematics of this exploration. (Save the constructions for later use with the *Golden Rectangle Survey* activity, on page 149.)

Notes to the Teacher

This activity provides students with practice in doing basic geometric constructions and working with radical expressions. Students are required to use the Pythagorean theorem and to provide answers containing radicals such as $\sqrt{5} + 1$. At the end of the exploration, you can informally introduce the students to the golden ratio and to the concept of similar rectangles.

When you use this activity with your students for the first time, you may find the following comments useful:

❖ **Note:** You may find it more appropriate to introduce a simpler version of this activity (see *Go for the Golden 1* on page 129) before teaching this one, as the requirements and emphases are different.

❖ A website containing directions for basic constructions using only a straightedge and a compass is http://regentsprep.org/Regents/math/math-topic.cfm?Topic Code=construc. It also includes online videos for the constructions.

❖ Following are some of the patterns students should find:

   • The Pythagorean theorem enables you to find exact lengths of segments or other distances and values.

- The exact length-to-width ratio in a golden rectangle is $\frac{\sqrt{5}+1}{2}$. The decimal approximation of this golden ratio is approximately 1.61803.
- A rectangle is a golden rectangle if and only if the following is true: $\frac{\text{length}}{\text{width}} = \frac{\text{length} + \text{width}}{\text{length}}$.
- Each golden rectangle has the same length-to-width ratio regardless of the size of the chosen unit length.
- All the final rectangles are similar figures; that is, they have the same proportions, or length-to-width ratio.

If students do not find these patterns, ask questions to elicit them.

Extensions

The Fibonacci sequence and golden ratio are topics that provide a myriad of opportunities for students to work with ratios. Here are two suggestions:

◈ Have students construct, administer, and analyze the findings of a golden rectangle survey to test the conjecture that people prefer the golden rectangle to all others. (See the lesson *Golden Rectangle Survey* on page 149.)

◈ Have students create a spreadsheet, using Excel or other software, to show the ratios between consecutive numbers in the Fibonacci sequence. The first few rows of the spreadsheet should look like this:

	A	B	C	D
1	Fibonacci Sequence and Golden Ratio			
2	Rank	Fib#	Next Fib#	Ratio C:B
3	1	1	1	1
4	2	1	2	2
5	3	2	3	1.5
6	4	3	5	1.666666667
7	5	5	8	1.6

Then have students respond to the following questions:

- What do you notice about the values of the ratios in Column D?
- How does this spreadsheet relate to golden rectangles?

Students should notice the following:

- Column A contains the numbers 1–25.
- Column B contains the first twenty-five numbers in the Fibonacci sequence.
- Column C contains the Fibonacci numbers 2–26.
- Column D contains the ratio of the number in Column C to the number in Column B, or the ratio of a Fibonacci number to the previous Fibonacci number.

Angles

Introduction

The teaching and learning of measurement with angles illustrate a shift in emphases that should occur in middle school—from focusing on individual concepts to comparing, contrasting, and connecting measurement topics. For example, students usually enter middle school with some knowledge about angles, usually exposure to categories of angles based on their measures. However, in middle school, through investigations with polygons, students discover that angle measures are directly connected to many of the properties of polygons and other shapes. Similarly, they build upon their knowledge of angles and the Triangle Inequality Theorem to discover the relationships expressed by the Pythagorean Theorem and applying this new knowledge can, in turn, open the whole world of irrational numbers for them in meaningful ways. (See *Pythagoras Plus* on page 158 and *That's Irrational!* on page 16.)

Angle measurement and learning to use the protractor are often introduced in middle school. Understanding the attribute of angle size and being able to estimate the measure of angles influence the success students have in using protractors, in making scale drawings, in finding the height of an object too tall to measure directly, and in making connections among measurement topics.

The typical definition of an angle—the union of two rays with a common end point—encourages students to think of an angle as a static construct and assume that the length of the rays determines an angle's size. The lessons in this chapter take an alternative approach. They focus on an angle as a rotation of one or both rays around a common end point. From this perspective, students view angle size on a continuum; that is, they understand that as one ray is rotated farther from the other, the measure of the angle increases.

The lessons use a variety of techniques that help students learn to use a protractor correctly. In addition to describing angles as being formed by rotations of rays, students examine angles with many different orientations. They use interlocking paper plates (see *Building Referents for the Measure of Angles* on page 23) to establish mental referents for common angles and patty paper to investigate angles formed by intersecting and parallel lines (see *Paper Angles* on page 29). Other lessons target angles in polygons (see

What's My Angle? on page 26) and angles in circles (see *Angles in the Round* on page 34) and encourage students to use patterns and reasoning to form conclusions.

Communication of mathematical thinking as well as at least one idea for extending the activity are built into each lesson.

 ## Building Referents for the Measure of Angles

Related Topic: estimation

Overview

Students make an angle measurement device from paper plates. They then use it to establish angle referents. They use their referents and the device to create angles of any size.

Materials

◈ paper or foam plates, 1 each of two different colors per student

◈ rulers, 1 per pair of students

◈ protractors, 1 per student

◈ board protractor, transparent protractor, or transparency of a protractor

Vocabulary: acute angle, angle, degree, obtuse angle, referent, reflex angle, right angle, scale, straight angle

Instructions

1. Demonstrate to students the importance of estimation in measuring angles. You might do this by using a semicircular board protractor or overhead transparency of a protractor with two scales going in opposite directions. Draw a 60-degree angle and point out how a person who fails to estimate could easily read the angle as 120 degrees. You may also want to have students list activities and/or professions for which avoiding mistakes in angle measurement could be very important. Such a list could include the following examples:

architecture

astronomy

carpentry

cutting cloth and sewing quilt pieces

geography, including map reading

golfing, such as doglegs in fairways and
    angle of putts

graphic design

photography

pool or billiards

sailing

surveying

2. Tell students they will make and then use a device to help them estimate the measures of angles. Give each student two paper or foam plates of different colors. Have them use a ruler to measure and draw a radius in each plate. Then have them cut along each radius and fit the two plates together as shown below.

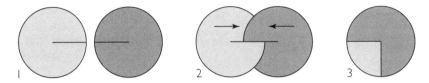

3. Have a volunteer define a *right angle*. Be sure the student mentions that a right angle contains 90 degrees and that it is shaped like a "perfect corner" or a "square corner." Suppose one of the plates is red. Ask students to hold one plate steady and rotate the other to show you a red angle that is approximately 90 degrees. Then have all the students hold their device facing you, so that you can verify that everyone has correctly shown the angle. Next have students rotate the device so that the 90-degree angle faces several different directions, as in the following examples.

Point out that a 90-degree angle is one that every student should have as a referent in her mind's eye, an image to which other angles can be compared.

4. Ask students to hold their angle device in their laps and rotate the plates to show you a red angle that is approximately 30 degrees. Again have all students hold their devices facing you, so that you can see how each student has shown the angle.

5. Without commenting on which students are showing good estimates, call on a student who has a good estimate to show the angle to the class and to explain how he decided how large a 30-degree angle is and how it should look. Often, students report that they know that a 30-degree angle is one-third the size of a 90-degree angle, so they make the angle one-third the size of the right angle they already made. Continue to call on students until you have elicited all strategies used by the class. If needed, give one of your own. Tell students that a 30-degree angle is another good referent to establish in their minds. Have students rotate their devices so the 30-degree angle faces several different directions.

6. Repeat the procedure described in Instruction 4 to have students show their estimates for an angle of 120 degrees. Point out that a 120-degree angle is a 90-degree angle plus a 30-degree angle so that they can combine the two referents they have discussed to estimate this new angle.

7. Help students establish other referents, such as 45 degrees and 180 degrees, and then ask them to estimate more challenging angles for which they can use the referents you have already discussed. For example, a 150-degree angle can be thought of as a 180-degree angle minus a 30-degree angle. Continue to have students explain their estimating strategies and rotate the angle devices to see the angles in different positions.

8. If appropriate, work with reflex angles in addition to those that are less than or equal to 180 degrees.

Notes to the Teacher

This activity helps students establish mental referents for angle measures. Such referents help students make good estimates and avoid common errors, such as reading a protractor incorrectly.

When you use this activity with your students for the first time, you may find the following comments useful:

❖ Building a bank of angle referents takes time. While this lesson helps students establish a good base, it's best to repeat the experience many times throughout the school year to firmly establish the visual benchmarks for your students.

❖ If you are able to find foam plates with thirty-six indentations around the circumference, students will eventually figure out that each indentation is equivalent to 10 degrees. Since this lesson is about learning to estimate the measure of angles by using a stored mental image of certain referent angles, these plates are helpful because students can create quite accurate angles if they use the indentations as guides. Alternatively, you may want to avoid using this "key" to force students to make their own estimates, even if they are not likely to be as accurate.

Extensions

❖ Ask students to use their angle device to show angles such as the complement of a 60-degree angle, the supplement of a 30-degree angle, or the third angle in a triangle if the other two angles measure 90 degrees and 45 degrees.

❖ The device can also be used with other topics. Ask students to show the following:
  • decimals that are less than or equal to one
  • percents that are less than or equal to 100 percent
  • fractional equivalents for decimals less than or equal to one or percents less than or equal to 100 percent
  • fractions that represent such ratios as 1 foot to 1 yard or 5 millimeters to 1 centimeter

Note: In many of these cases, the foam plates or other plates marked off in 10-degree arc angles work best if you are looking for an exact answer instead of an estimate.

What's My Angle?

Related Topics: algebraic thinking, exterior angles of polygons, interior angles of polygons

Overview

With a straightedge, students draw several different kinds of polygons. Then they use protractors to measure the interior and exterior angles of their shapes. They make generalizations about the measures and sums of such angles from the patterns they find in their data.

Materials

❖ *What's My Angle?* recording sheets, 1 per student (see Blackline Masters)
❖ straightedges, 1 per student
❖ protractors, 1 per student
❖ optional: board protractor or clear plastic protractor to use on an overhead projector

Vocabulary: decagon, diagonal, exterior angle, heptagon, hexagon, interior angle, n-gon, nonadjacent, octagon, pentagon, polygon, quadrangle, quadrilateral, septagon, 36-gon, triangle, vertex

Prerequisite Skills and Concepts

Students should know how to measure angles using a protractor. One set of online directions for this process can be found at www.ehow.com/how_12928_protractor.html and an interactive protractor is located at www.teachersfirst.com/getsource. cfm?id=6382.

Instructions

1. Ask a volunteer to define *acute angle*. Clarify the concept by using a board protractor to draw several angles on the board and asking students to identify each one as an example or a nonexample of an acute angle. Then ask each student to draw and measure an acute angle using a straightedge and a protractor. Have partners check each other's work. Repeat with another acute angle, if needed.

2. Repeat the process in Instruction 1 with obtuse angles.

3. Explain to students that they will be measuring the angles of some polygons and then looking for patterns in their results.

4. Ask a volunteer to explain what interior angles of a polygon are. To reinforce the definition, use drawings at the board to show students where the interior angles of a polygon are located and how to extend the sides of a polygon to form and measure its exterior angles. A board protractor may be used for this purpose.

5. Check to make sure all students remember definitions for *polygon, triangle, quadrangle* or *quadrilateral, pentagon, hexagon, septagon, octagon, decagon, dodecagon, 36-gon,* and n-gon by eliciting the definitions from volunteers. On the board, record the name and number of sides for each of these polygons.

6. Pass out the recording sheets.

7. As students work, circulate to see that they are correctly following directions and to answer questions.

8. When everyone is ready, lead a class discussion about the patterns the students found in their data, including generalizations about the total number of degrees in both the interior and exterior angles of any polygon.

Notes to the Teacher

This lesson provides students with practice in using a protractor in a problem-solving context. After measuring and then finding the sum of the interior and exterior angles in polygons with different numbers of sides, students look for patterns and make generalizations.

When you use this activity with your students for the first time, you may find the following comments useful:

◈ Even with students who seem proficient with measuring angles, it is often necessary to remind them that it is important to place the center of the protractor on the vertex of the angle and to line up the edge with the initial ray of the angle.

◈ Help students realize that, as a class, they have created a random sample for each type of polygon examined in this investigation, since each student chose her own side lengths for every shape. Emphasize that with such a random sample, the chances are incredibly small that they would all get the same results; however, the results do not *prove* their conjectures. Tell the class that it is the patterns they find that must be the basis for their conjectures and generalizations.

◈ If needed, use a board protractor to demonstrate for students how to measure the exterior angles in a polygon. Describe the process in this way: "Draw any polygon;

then turn it into a pinwheel shape by extending one end of each of the sides in a clockwise (or counterclockwise) pattern. In this way you will create exterior angles."

For example, each side of the polygon shown below has been extended to form an exterior angle.

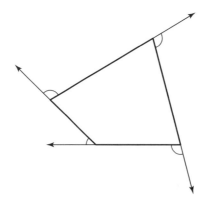

❧ Following are the correct answers for the table on the recording sheet.

Polygon Data				
Type of Polygon	Number of Sides and Angles	Total Number of Interior Triangles	Total of All Interior Angles	Total of All Exterior Angles
triangle	3	1	180°	360°
quadrilateral	4	2	360°	360°
pentagon	5	3	540°	360°
hexagon	6	4	720°	360°
octagon	8	6	1,080°	360°
decagon	10	8	1,440°	360°
dodecagon	12	10	1,800°	360°
36-gon	36	34	6,120°	360°
n-gon	n	$n-2$	$180(n-2)$	360°

❧ Be sure students discuss the visual as well as the numerical patterns that emerge, and the connections between the representations. For example:

Triangle	Quadrilateral	Pentagon	Hexagon
3 sides	4 sides	5 sides	6 sides
1 interior triangle	2 interior triangles	3 interior triangles	4 interior triangles
total 180°	total 360°	total 540°	total 720°

Visually, the total number of triangles that are formed inside a polygon increases by one each time one new side is added because there is one more vertex to connect. Numerically, the new triangle is represented by the additional 180 degrees in the interior angles that is gained each time the number of sides in the polygon increases by one.

Extension

Have students follow a format similar to the one used in this investigation to examine the number of degrees in each angle of regular polygons with various numbers of sides. This investigation works especially well when students have access to interactive software such as *The Geometer's Sketchpad*.

 ## Paper Angles

Related Topics: alternate and corresponding angles, interior and exterior angles, vertical and adjacent angles

Overview

Students use patty paper to explore the angles formed by intersecting lines, the angles formed by two nonparallel line segments and a transversal, and the angles formed by two parallel lines and a transversal. They make and test conjectures about these three different situations.

Materials

◈ patty paper, at least 4 sheets per student (**Note:** Patty paper is a waxed square paper, either 5.5 inches or 6 inches on each side, used by fast-food restaurants to separate hamburger patties. You can write on it with pencil or felt-tip pens. You can find it in the Yellow Pages under "Restaurant Equipment and Supplies," online, or from an educational company such as Key Curriculum Press [www.keypress.com].)

◈ optional: protractors, 1 per student

Vocabulary: adjacent angles, alternate exterior angles, alternate interior angles, congruent angles, corresponding exterior angles, corresponding interior angles, exterior angles, interior angles, intersecting lines, parallel, perpendicular, straight angle, supplementary angles, transversal, vertical angles

Prerequisite Skills and Concepts

The students should be familiar with the following concepts and terms before this exploration: *straight angle, adjacent angles, supplementary angles, vertical angles,* and *congruent angles.* Alternately, you can introduce the terms during the exploration, spending additional time on Instruction 2.

Instructions

1. Explain to the students that they will be using patty paper to explore the angles formed by intersecting lines.

2. Ask volunteers to offer definitions and draw examples on the board for the terms *straight angle, adjacent angles, supplementary angles, vertical angles,* and *congruent angles.* Verify correct answers.

3. Pass out three pieces of patty paper to each student. Save extra pieces for students who make errors so they can have an uncreased sheet to use for a second attempt or to compare angles as described in Instruction 8.

4. Tell the students to take their first piece of patty paper and fold the paper as shown below, making sure the crease is firm. Demonstrate.

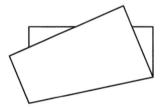

   Let students know that they do not have to match your fold exactly. Any fold that goes across the whole square is fine.

5. Next, demonstrate, as shown below, unfolding the paper and then making a second fold so that the new line intersects the first one. Unfold and have students follow the same procedure. Again, tell the students that their papers do not need to look exactly like yours.

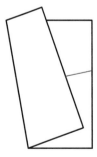 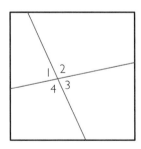

   Ask the students to number the angles as shown above.

6. Next, have students write the heading *1: Conjectures About Angles Formed by Intersecting Lines* on a piece of lined paper. Explain that they are to examine their patty paper, make and list conjectures about the angles formed by the intersecting lines, and compare their conjectures with those of their partner.

7. Have the class share and discuss the conjectures. Ask questions to elicit conjectures that students have not made yet.

8. If it does not come out in the class discussion, ask students how to verify the conjectures about congruent angles. They will most likely suggest folding the paper so that the sides of one angle fit over the sides of the other angle in the pair. Alternatively, they might say you can trace over one angle in the pair, using another piece of patty paper, and then slide or rotate it to be sure it fits exactly over the second angle.

9. Tell the students to take their second piece of patty paper and fold, unfold, and fold again to make two line segments that do not intersect. (See example on the left below.)

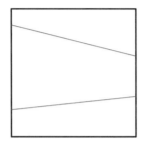 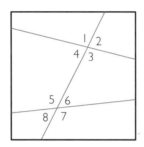

Then have them fold the paper once more to form a third line that intersects both segments, as shown in the example on the right above. Explain that this third line is called a *transversal*, and elicit a reasonable definition for this term.

10. Tell the students to number the angles as shown above. Elicit reasonable definitions for the terms *interior angles, exterior angles, alternate interior angles, alternate exterior angles, corresponding interior angles,* and *corresponding exterior angles.* You might do this by asking questions such as, "Angles three, four, five, and six are called *interior angles.* How do you think mathematicians define *interior angles?*" Write the definitions on the board.

11. Have students write a second heading on their lined paper: *2: Conjectures About Angles Formed by a Transversal Intersecting Two Line Segments.* Again, explain that they are to examine their patty papers, make conjectures about these angles, and compare their conjectures with those of their partner.

12. Have the class share and discuss their conjectures. Ask questions to elicit conjectures that student have not yet made. Be sure students verify their conjectures involving congruent angles, using one of the methods described in Instruction 8.

13. Tell the students to take their third piece of patty paper and fold it once to create a line and then unfold it. Have students fold the paper so that a new line intersects the first without being perpendicular to it.

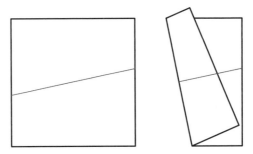

14. Ask for a suggestion for how to make a third line that is parallel to the first line. One method is shown below: Unfold the paper. Fold the bottom edge of the paper until it is aligned with the first crease and make a new crease. The new line will be parallel to the first line.

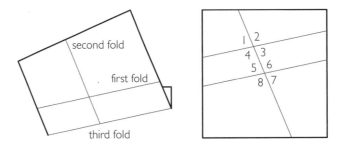

Tell the students to number the angles as shown in the example above.

15. Have the students write a third heading on their lined paper: *3: Conjectures About Angles Formed by a Transversal Intersecting Two Parallel Lines.* Again explain that they are to examine their patty papers, make conjectures about these angles, and compare their conjectures with those of their partner.

16. Have the class share and discuss their conjectures. Ask questions to elicit conjectures that students have not yet made. Be sure students verify their conjectures involving congruent angles, using one of the methods described in Instruction 8.

17. If appropriate, pass out the protractors and have students measure and record the size of each angle formed by the transversal intersecting two parallel lines.

Notes to the Teacher

This lesson provides students with an opportunity to make and test conjectures about the angles formed by intersecting lines, the angles formed by two nonintersecting, non-parallel line segments and a transversal, and the angles formed by two parallel lines and a transversal.

When you use this activity with your students for the first time, you may find the following comments useful:

❖ Conjectures about angles formed by intersecting lines (on the first piece of patty paper) should be about supplementary, adjacent, and vertical angles. For example:

 • Adjacent angles formed by intersecting lines are always supplementary.
 • There are always four pairs of supplementary angles.
 • Vertical angles are always congruent.
 • There are always two pairs of vertical angles.
 • The four angles contain exactly 360 degrees.

❖ Make a drawing on the board to elicit that a transversal is a line that intersects two *or more* other lines.

❖ Conjectures about angles formed by a transversal and two nonintersecting lines (on the second piece of patty paper) should be about supplementary, adjacent, and vertical angles. For example:

 • There are always eight pairs of adjacent, supplementary angles.
 • There are always four pairs of vertical angles.
 • Each set of four angles around a point of intersection contains 360 degrees.

❖ Most of the previous conjectures are also true for angles formed by a transversal and two parallel lines (on the third piece of patty paper). Additional conjectures for this situation should be about alternate exterior, alternate interior, and corresponding angles. For example:

 • Two pairs of alternate interior angles are supplementary.
 • Two pairs of alternate exterior angles are supplementary.
 • Four pairs of corresponding angles are congruent.

Extension

Have students use the patty paper to explore and make conjectures about the following questions:

❖ If you want to find the measures of all the angles formed by two parallel lines and a transversal, what is the fewest number of angles you actually need to measure?
❖ If the corresponding angles formed by a transversal and two lines are congruent, are the lines always parallel?

Angles in the Round

Related Topics: circles, estimation

Overview

Students explore the measure of angles inside a circle to make and test conjectures. This experience with several benchmark angles helps students better predict the measure of angles they encounter in contexts other than circles.

Materials

❧ *Angles in the Round* recording sheets, 1 per student (see Blackline Masters)

❧ optional: 24-peg circular geoboards with bands, 1 per student

Vocabulary: arc, central angle, complementary angles, inscribe, right angle, semicircle, straight angle, supplementary angles

Prerequisite Skills and Concepts

Students should know the following:

❧ A complete turn of a ray around its end point is 360 degrees, or the total of the central angles around the center of a circle is 360 degrees.

❧ In any triangle, the angles that are opposite sides of equal length have the same measure.

❧ The sum of the measures of the angles in any triangle is 180 degrees.

❧ Working definitions for *central angle*, *arc*, *right angle*, *straight angle*, *complementary angles*, and *supplementary angles*.

Instructions

1. Tell the students that they will work in pairs to investigate the measures of angles inside circles.

2. Elicit from students definitions for the terms *central angle*, *arc*, *right angle*, *straight angle*, *complementary angles*, and *supplementary angles*. Verify correct answers.

3. Pass out the recording sheets (and the geoboards, if you wish). Tell students that they are to record all their work and answers on their recording sheets. Remind them to be prepared to explain their reasoning during a whole-class discussion.

4. Circulate around the room as students work, watching and listening for the following observations and results:

   • The smallest central angle possible, using the given points, is 15 degrees.

   • Using the points on the circle and multiples of fifteen makes finding measures of angles easier.

- Using the corner of a sheet of paper or book helps determine whether an angle is right, acute, or obtuse.
- When two of the sides of a triangle are radii of the circle, those sides are congruent and, therefore, the measures of the angles across from those sides are congruent.
- Noticing that an angle is complementary or supplementary to an angle whose measure has been previously determined makes finding the measure of that angle easier.
- Any angle inscribed in a semicircle measures 90 degrees.

5. When all pairs have completed the activity, lead a class discussion about the students' findings and conclusions.

Notes to the Teacher

This activity helps students develop their sense of the size of common angles for future reference. It encourages students to notice complementary and supplementary angles, to find the missing measures of angles in a triangle, and to discover that any angle inscribed in a semicircle is a right angle.

When you use this activity with your students for the first time, you may find the following comments useful:

❧ To help students who are having difficulty finding information that is not explicit, suggest they look for "hidden information."

❧ For Question 2 on the recording sheet, help students notice that most angles to be drawn are supplementary (or complementary) to one they have just drawn. It allows students to count the number of intervals on the border of the circle required to complete 180 degrees or 90 degrees, making drawing the new angle easier.

❧ For Question 3, students must use their knowledge about radii of a circle and isosceles triangles to find the missing measures.

❧ There are several ways to find the measures of the angles in Question 4, including the following:
- Trace the triangle and place each angle of the tracing so that it is a central angle in the circle.
- Trace the triangle and use the tracing to find that Angle 1 and Angle 3 are complementary and that Angle 1 is twice the size of Angle 3.
- Extend the rays of any angle whose vertex is on the circle in Question 3 to find that the measure of such an angle is one-half the degrees along the arc cut by those extended rays. Use this information to find the measures of the angles in Question 4.

◈ As students work through Questions 4 and 5, they should realize that any angle inscribed in a semicircle measures 90 degrees.

◈ If the ideas listed here do not emerge during the class discussion, ask questions to elicit these shortcuts so that students might use such strategies in future situations.

Extension

Soon after students complete this investigation, ask each student to draw angles having the following measures, using only a straightedge.

90°	60°
45°	120°
15°	135°
30°	150°

This exercise lets students check their sense of the measures of angles they are likely to encounter many times as they study more mathematics. It is especially appropriate immediately after the *Angles in the Round* investigation, when students are most likely to recall what such angles look like, based on their experiences with angles in a circle or on a geoboard.

To best establish mental benchmarks for these angles, have students immediately measure their drawings using a protractor or have partners measure each other's angles.

The Geometer's Sketchpad and other software programs offer other ways for students to do and check such an exercise.

CHAPTER 3

Area

Introduction

Although middle school students have been taught in earlier grades that area means the "space inside" and is measured in square units, their understanding is often limited to knowing that multiplying the length and width of a rectangle gives its area. To deepen and broaden students' understanding of area, lessons in this chapter encourage covering areas with physical objects such as small squares or pattern blocks, provide experiences with surface area, and emphasize the relationship between perimeter and area.

Students must learn that a variety of terms are used to name the parts of two- and three-dimensional figures. They may encounter the dimensions of a rectangle, for example, as *length* and *width* in one place, *base* and *height* in another, and *base* and *altitude* in still another. For three-dimensional figures, they may find *length*, *width*, and *height*; *base*, *altitude*, and *height*; or even *length*, *width*, and *depth* used to label the dimensions of such figures. We believe middle school students must become flexible, able to interchange the labels and use any of these conventions comfortably. If they are familiar with only one set of labels, students can easily become confused when other terms are used, especially in dealing with three-dimensional figures. For this reason, you will find that the activities in this book do not always use the same terms; however, the use of terms within any one activity is consistent.

The activities help students build mental images of a square inch, a square foot, a square centimeter, and a square meter. Middle school students should be able to model each unit with their hands and find common objects to associate with each one. The activities also stress estimating area, using both customary and metric units.

One of the most important area topics is learning to use area formulas. It is our belief that no student should ever be asked to use a formula without participating in the development of that formula. In the lesson *Formulas from the Grid* (page 38), students derive the standard area formulas for triangles and various quadrilaterals to understand how they make sense. In *About the Area of a Circle* (page 44), students use six different methods to find the area of a circle and from their data derive the standard area formula. In the lesson *Orange You Glad . . . ?* (page 47), students derive the formula for the surface area of a sphere, using an orange and its peel.

In addition, many lessons introduce area in new contexts. For example:

◈ In *Constant Area* (page 57), students investigate different-shape rectangles all having a constant area, then look for patterns and make generalizations based on their findings.

◈ In *How Do You Grow?* (page 62), students focus on the relationship between area and perimeter as they examine a set of rectangles that grow in a specified way.

◈ In the interdisciplinary lessons *Square States 1* (page 51) and *Square States 2* (page 53), students use maps, proportional reasoning, and algebraic thinking to strengthen their skills across several strands of the middle school mathematics curriculum.

◈ In *Chances Are* (page 67), students create and analyze a game of chance in order to explore the connection between area and geometric probability.

Communication of mathematical thinking by the students is built into each lesson. Additionally, at least one idea for extending the activity is included.

Formulas from the Grid

Related Topics: attributes of parallelograms, attributes of rectangles, attributes of trapezoids, attributes of triangles

Overview

Students receive guided instruction to help them investigate and construct the area formulas for triangles, rectangles, parallelograms, and trapezoids. Once the formulas are derived, each student records on grid paper the formula and a labeled drawing for each polygon in order to create a personal reference sheet.

Materials

◈ grid paper, a variety with different-size unit lengths, 2 sheets per student
◈ colored pencils, 1 each of two different colors per student
◈ straightedges, 1 per student

Vocabulary: altitude, base, height, parallelogram, perpendicular, polygon, rectangle, trapezoid, triangle

Instructions

Note: This lesson will take at least two class periods to complete.

1. Explain to the students that they will be looking for ways to find the area of several different polygons without counting all the squares inside them. Give two sheets of grid paper to each student, making sure that you distribute paper with several different unit lengths. Also distribute the colored pencils and straightedges.

2. Tell the students that the first polygon the class will investigate is the rectangle. Ask students to each draw a small rectangle on a piece of their grid paper, using the lines on the paper as guides for perpendicular sides. (This ensures four right angles and a counting number of units for the base and the height.)

3. Ask students to count the squares, also called *square units*, enclosed by their rectangles. This step concretely establishes the size of the rectangle and reinforces the convention of measuring area in square units. Be sure students notice that the height of the rectangle can be represented by one of its sides or another segment that is perpendicular to the base. Explain that it is important that the height of any figure is perpendicular to its base because this concept applies to all area and volume formulas. (This is a common source of student errors.)

4. Ask students how they could find the area of a rectangle more efficiently than counting the squares. Most likely someone will offer "length times width" or "base times height." If not, ask questions such as, "How many square units are there in a row along the base of the rectangle? How many rows like this one are in the rectangle? What do you notice?" Ask each student to test the rule with his rectangle, since the rectangles are different sizes and shapes. Ask students whether this formula would work for any rectangle, and have them explain their reasoning.

5. Next, tell each student to record the formula *Area = base • height* with at least one labeled drawing on a second sheet of grid paper. This sheet will contain the final versions of all the formulas. As the class derives each formula, each student will add it to this sheet. Students can use color and graphics to emphasize key points in the figure and formula. For the rest of the year, this sheet can serve as a personal reference sheet. Students understand and use these sheets much better than they do a teacher-made sheet of formulas.

6. Tell the students that the second polygon they will investigate is the right-angle triangle. Ask students to draw a copy of the rectangle they created in Instruction 2 on their "working" piece of grid paper.

7. Tell students to use a straightedge to draw a diagonal that connects one pair of opposite vertices in their rectangle. This creates two right triangles.

8. Have students find the number of squares enclosed by each of their triangles. Record on the board the sizes of a few of the triangles with the estimates for their areas on the board. Then ask a volunteer to explain why her estimate makes sense. Eventually, someone will point out that you cut the rectangle in half when you draw the diagonal, so the answer must be exactly one-half of the total area for the rectangle.

9. Write the calculations suggested by the volunteer on the board, for example:

$$area = \tfrac{1}{2} (8)(10)$$

$$area = 40 \; square \; units$$

Compare this result with the student's estimate.

Again, point out that the height of the triangle, even though it is also one of the sides of the triangle, is perpendicular to the base.

10. Since the initial rectangles were different sizes and shapes, ask the students to generalize a rule that will work for any right triangle. They will usually offer area = $\tfrac{1}{2}$ (base • height) or area = $\dfrac{base \, \bullet \, height}{2}$. Tell students to record a labeled drawing and the formula on their sheet of formulas.

11. Tell the students that they will investigate a parallelogram next. Review the properties of parallelograms.

12. Ask students to draw a 10-unit line segment along one of the horizontal lines on their working grid paper. This will be the base of the parallelogram. From one end of this segment, have them draw a 6-unit segment along one of the vertical lines on the graph paper, thus establishing a *true height* (see the "Notes to the Teacher" for more information) that is perpendicular to the base of the parallelogram they are drawing.

13. To start the top base of their parallelograms, have students individually decide whether they want to move right or left from the top end point and how many units. After each student puts a point to serve as one end point of the top base, ask the class how long the top base should be. Someone will usually be able to tell you that it must be the same length as the bottom base to meet the requirements of a parallelogram. Each student should count that many units and place the second end point of the top base.

14. Ask each student to use a straightedge to connect the right and left end points of the top base to the corresponding end points of the bottom base. Again, ask students to count the number of enclosed square units. Students will find various ways to count the partially enclosed squares.

15. Have students volunteer several parallelogram sizes and the corresponding estimates for their areas. Record these on the board. Then ask the students whether they can find the area using a more exact way that will always work. Invariably, one or more students will suggest cutting a right triangle from one end of the parallelogram and attaching it to the other end to form a rectangle.

16. Have each student verify this method by shading in the triangle on one end of his parallelogram and drawing a new "matching" (congruent) one having the same

orientation at the other end of the parallelogram. Students may need to look at their classmates' results to consider whether this maneuver will work for any parallelogram. Because all of the students started with the same base (10 units) and height (6 units), some students will need to see that there are several different shapes drawn by the class and that this method works for all of them. Also, some students will need to be shown that the method also works for any size parallelogram by drawing one or more different-size parallelograms and using the method with each figure.

17. At this point, based on their work with rectangles, students usually find it easy to generate the formula for the total number of squares. Using their results from the many different parallelograms the class drew, they can conclude that the formula should again be area = base • height. If not, ask questions to elicit this formula. Remind students to record the formula and a labeled drawing on their sheet of formulas.

18. Tell students they will now investigate the general triangle. For triangles other than right triangles, students can use an approach similar to the one used for parallelograms. Ask them to start by constructing on their working paper a base having a given length, using one of the horizontal lines on the grid paper.

19. Next, ask students to choose a vertical line on their grid paper anywhere along the base and draw a dashed line (altitude or height) of a set length. The top end point of this vertical segment is one of the vertices of the triangle.

20. Then ask students to connect the new point to the end points of the base to complete the triangle. In so doing, each student creates a triangle that is already divided into two right triangles by the height of the larger triangle (the dashed line). Finding the area of these triangles by the method described for right triangles earlier (each right triangle has half the area of a rectangle with the same base and height), students can then combine the areas to get the total area of the large triangle.

21. Have students volunteer several triangle sizes and the corresponding estimates for their areas. Record these on the board. Using these results, students usually conclude that the area is the same as the product of the base and height divided by two. If not, ask questions to elicit this formula. A discussion may ensue that confirms that several common versions of the area formula for triangles are equivalent: $\frac{\text{base} \cdot \text{height}}{2}$ can also be written as $b \cdot h \div 2$ or $\frac{1}{2} \cdot bh$.

    Remind students to record the formula and a labeled drawing on their sheet of formulas.

22. The last type of polygon to be examined is a trapezoid. Because the students have seen several useful techniques by this point in the lesson, use a slightly different

approach for this shape. Ask a volunteer to draw a trapezoid on the board. Ask at least two more students to draw a figure that is still a trapezoid but that looks significantly different than the first one. Based on these drawings, ask for a definition for a trapezoid (a quadrilateral having exactly one pair of parallel sides or a quadrilateral having at least one pair of parallel sides).

23. Now ask the students to draw any trapezoid on their grid paper and count the squares to estimate its area. Have some students record their drawings with dimensions and their estimates on the board.

24. Then have students work in pairs to find a formula to determine the area of a trapezoid and be prepared to explain how and why it works for any trapezoid. You will most likely find that students use what they know about the other figures to derive different versions of the formula. For example:
   - Many pairs divide the trapezoid into three separate pieces, a rectangle in the middle with two right-angle triangles on the ends, and sum the areas.
   - Some pairs divide the trapezoid into two triangles and sum the areas.
   - Sometimes a pair starts with the two bases, averages their lengths, and then multiplies the average length by the height of the trapezoid.
   - Occasionally, a pair of students will construct two congruent trapezoids, and rotate one of them 180 degrees. Then they place them side by side to form a parallelogram, find the area of the parallelogram, and use half of that value as the area of the original trapezoid.

25. Have students share their methods. For each method, ask the rest of the students to verify whether the method works with their own trapezoids and, if it does, to write the method as a formula.

26. Have students add their own version of the formula as well as at least one alternate formula to their formulas sheet.

27. If no pair derives the standard formula, give the class time to think about it. On another day, show students the standard formula for the area of a trapezoid, $A = h\left(\frac{b_1 + b_2}{2}\right)$. Explain the notation and ask volunteers to explain how it makes sense to them. Have students add this version to their formulas sheet.

Notes to the Teacher

In this activity students derive the formulas for finding the areas of rectangles, parallelograms, triangles, and trapezoids through guided instruction. This process helps students remember the formulas and provides the mental tools to re-create them, if needed. Each student makes a personal reference sheet of these formulas.

When you use this lesson for the first time with your classes, you may find the following comments useful:

◈ Many students come to middle school with some experiences related to area. Often, however, they have simply memorized and perhaps forgotten formulas. We have found that this activity builds a sense of ownership in the students for the area formulas.

◈ This lesson is most effective if it is spread out over several days and interspersed with other explorations related to one or more types of polygons. The breaks give students time to think about the results of each investigation before going to the next one; the breaks also provide a natural way to review each formula before starting to work with the next type of polygon.

◈ This activity works best if most students figure out the patterns on their own. Sometimes it requires a good bit of time for students to make several copies of each shape, collect data, and test their ideas. Even so, this process is beneficial in the long run: testing and refining one's own ideas before coming to a conclusion too quickly is an important habit for students to establish.

◈ Finding the area by counting the small square units inside each figure verifies that students' faster methods produce correct solutions. Counting the squares also reinforces why area is measured in square units and makes the notation of area in square units, such as cm², more than an abstract label.

◈ Inviting students to share their ideas and methods for one shape often stimulates other ideas and approaches for the next shape.

◈ For each shape, reiterate that the height (or altitude) must be perpendicular to the base. To reinforce why this is necessary, have a student stand in the front doorway of the classroom, and then you can lean against the doorjamb so that you are shorter than the student. Point out that your true height in the demonstration is *not* the distance between the floor and the top of your head when leaning against the door frame, but rather the distance from the floor to the top of your head when you stand up straight, or stand perpendicular to the floor. Using the phrase "true height" to remind students that the height of a figure must be measured by a segment that "stands up straight" (is perpendicular to the base) seems to help many of them.

◈ In searching for the triangle formula, if students pick a point that is not directly above the original base, they will create an obtuse triangle. When this happens, point out how this triangle can also be viewed as half of a parallelogram so that the same formula applies.

◈ When working with parallelograms, some students may use the side of the parallel-ogram as its height since they did this for the rectangles. It helps them to see that the many different slanted sides throughout the classroom turned out to be irrele-vant in finding the actual answer. You should also remind them, if needed, that the "true height" of any geometric figure must be perpendicular to the base.

Extension

Have students use their experience in deriving area formulas to work with irregular polygons. Such polygons are usually easiest to work with after students partition them into shapes with which they are familiar. For example:

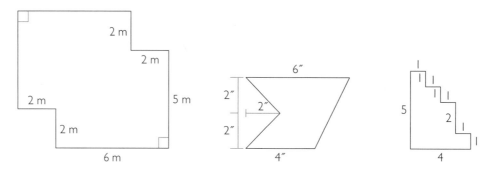

 ## About the Area of a Circle

Related Topics: areas of irregular figures, parallelograms, rectangles, and squares

Overview

Students use a variety of methods to find the area of a circle without using a formula. After sharing results, students each choose the method they think is best and explain their thinking in writing.

Materials

◈ *About the Area of a Circle* method cards, at least 3 different cards for each pair of students (see Blackline Masters)
◈ *About the Area of a Circle* instructions, 1 per student (see Blackline Masters)
◈ pan balances, at least 2
◈ linoleum circles with 10-centimeter radius, at least 1 per pair using Method Card 4
◈ 1-by-10-centimeter linoleum rectangles, at least 32 per pair using Method Card 4
◈ 1-by-1-centimeter linoleum squares, 9 per pair of students using Method Card 4
◈ compasses, 1 per student or pair of students
◈ protractors, 1 per student or pair of students
◈ rulers, 1 per student or pair of students
◈ centimeter grid paper, 1 sheet per each pair of students using Method Card 1 (see Blackline Masters)

◈ circles with 10-centimeter radius, 1 per pair of students using Method Cards 2, 3, 5, and 6 (see Blackline Masters)

◈ bags of beans, 1 per each pair of students using Method Card 6

◈ 2-by-63-centimeter strips of cardboard, with ends taped to form a circle with a radius of 10 centimeters, 1 per pair of students using Method Card 6

Vocabulary: approximate, area, circle, circumscribe, congruent, inscribe, radius

Prerequisite Skills and Concepts

Six different methods for finding the area of a circle are used in this lesson. For Methods 2, 3, 5, and 6, students must be able to do basic constructions with a compass and straightedge, including those required for inscribing a square in a circle or circumscribing a circle with a square.

Instructions

1. Prior to the lesson, duplicate and cut out the method cards.

2. To begin, have students describe methods they might use to find the area of a square, a rectangle, and a parallelogram. Then ask students how finding the area of a circle is like finding the area of these figures and how it is different. Explain that this investigation will involve using methods other than a formula to find the area of a circle.

3. Ask students to offer definitions for terms from the vocabulary list that have not yet come up during the discussion. Verify correct answers.

4. Tell the students that you will give each pair three different method cards for finding the area of a circle. Explain that pairs are to carry out each method and record their work.

5. Distribute the method cards. Give each student a copy of the instructions.

6. When all students have completed their assignments, lead a whole-class discussion about their findings, the challenges they faced, and the mathematics they used. Record the results obtained for each different method on the board as you discuss it.

7. Have students respond in writing to the reflection question in Step 4 of the instructions. Make it clear that students can choose any of the six methods as the best in their reflection even if they did not investigate that method with their partner.

Notes to the Teacher

This activity provides students with hands-on experiences and/or explanations of several methods for finding the area of a circle without using a formula.

When you use this lesson for the first time with your classes, you may find the following comments useful:

◈ Using several methods for finding the area of a circle supports two important mathematical understandings: (1) the area of a circle is always an approximation, and (2) it is possible to approximate the area of circles and other figures without using a standard formula.

◈ It usually takes students longer to complete Method 1 and Method 6 than the other methods. Keep this in mind when assigning methods to pairs.

◈ As stated earlier, for Methods 2, 3, 5, and 6, students should do the basic constructions with a compass and a straightedge. If the students do these constructions without compasses, you will need to emphasize the importance of checking the corners of the squares to make sure that each measures exactly 90 degrees.

◈ Some students may be bothered by the curvy parallelogram since it is not a polygon. Ask these students to imagine cutting the circle into more and more sectors. Point out that the smaller the sectors were cut, the less curvy the long sides of the parallelogram would become, so that, with very "skinny" sectors, the shape would approximate a parallelogram very closely.

◈ For students who know the formula for finding the area of a circle, the emphasis of this lesson often shifts. They focus on how close the result of each method is to 314 square centimeters. The potential for applying the methods used in this lesson to find the area of irregular shapes is usually clear and exciting to these students.

◈ Both Methods 5 and 6 provide nice springboards for students to derive the formula for finding the area of a circle at a later time.
  • If you use Method 5 to introduce the area formula, color a band about 1 centimeter wide around the inside of the circle's boundary and show this to the class before cutting the circle into wedges. This makes it easy for many students to look at the curvy parallelogram and realize that the length of the parallelogram's base is equal to one-half the circumference ($\frac{1}{2}\pi \cdot d$ or $\frac{1}{2}\pi \cdot 2 \cdot r$ or $\pi \cdot r$). Then, since the height of the curvy parallelogram is r, its area equals $\pi \cdot r \cdot r$ or $\pi \cdot r^2$.
  • If you use Method 6 to have students derive the area formula, you will need to remind the students what this method entailed, and you may need to ask them to give an expression for the area of each small square in terms of the circle. Since the side length of each square is equal to the radius of the circle, the area of each square is r^2. Thus the area covered by the beans in the rectangle equals a little more than $3r^2$. By approximating the extra area covered by the beans as about $\frac{1}{7}$ of the fourth square, the students can conclude that the area

covered by the beans, and hence, the area of the circle, is approximately equal to $3\frac{1}{7} \cdot r^2$.

Extension

Present students with several irregular shapes having some curved parts along the perimeter. For example:

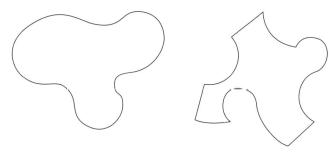

Have each student use the method she chose as most effective way to determine the area of a circle to find the area of each irregular shape.

Lead a discussion during which students report their findings and compare them to decide which method(s) seems best to use.

 Orange You Glad . . . ?

Related Topic: surface area of a sphere

Overview

Students investigate and construct the formula for the surface area of a sphere using an orange. Using such a model to physically discover how many square units it takes to cover the surface of a sphere helps students to understand the formula, and, if needed, to re-create it.

Materials

◈ oranges (as spherical in shape as possible), 1 per small group of students
◈ paper towels or other absorbent paper, approximately $1\frac{1}{2}$ square feet per small group of students
◈ *Orange You Glad . . . ?* recording sheets, 1 per student (see Blackline Masters)
◈ plastic trays or countertops that can be easily cleaned, approximately 2 square feet of surface space per small group of students
◈ knife sharp enough to cut an orange in half
◈ blank overhead transparencies, 1 per small group of students
◈ overhead pens, 1 per small group of students
◈ optional: 6-inch pieces of string, 1 per small group of students
◈ optional: rulers, 1 per small group of students

Vocabulary: great circle, pi, radius, sphere, surface area

Prerequisite Skills and Concepts

Students should be familiar with finding the area of a circle and using the formula $A = \pi r^2$.

Instructions

1. Before class, cut the oranges in half, keeping the two halves of each orange together. Alternately, help students cut the oranges once you have modeled the activity and distributed the materials and recording sheets.

2. Ask students to offer definitions for the terms *surface area*, *radius*, and *great circle* of a sphere. Verify correct answers. Then have the students relate their definitions to an orange.

3. Explain that each small group of students will use an orange to investigate and make a conjecture about the formula for finding the surface area of a sphere.

4. Demonstrate the main steps of the investigation:

   a. Using a whole, uncut orange, make the orange model a sphere: squeeze and roll the fruit into a shape as close to a sphere as possible.

   b. Cut the orange into two hemispheres to reveal a great circle of the orange. Ask a volunteer to point out to the class the great circle.

   c. Draw a great circle of the orange on a paper towel by tracing around the circular face of either hemisphere.

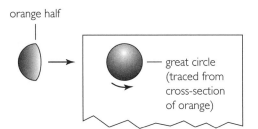

   Ask students to individually estimate how many great circles can be covered with the pieces of your orange peel. Ask for volunteers to share their thinking. Tear off pieces of the orange peel, each about $\frac{3}{4}$ to 1 square inch in size. Place the pieces, one at a time, in the great circle you drew, pointing out that you are being careful not to overlap pieces or leave gaps. Fill at least three-fourths of your circle. Emphasize that each circle must be covered entirely with no gaps or overlaps. Ask each student to reconsider his or her estimate silently.

5. Provide students with the recording sheets, which include instructions for the activity and questions that they should answer in writing. Emphasize that each student should be prepared to explain the group's findings and thinking in a whole-class discussion. Tell them to leave the display of their findings until the class discussion has been completed.

6. Allow small groups of students time to set up their work space with the appropriate materials. Have students wash their hands if you intend to let them eat the oranges at the end of the investigation. Distribute the cut oranges or help groups prepare their uncut oranges.

7. Each group performs the investigation, including writing responses to the questions.

8. Have each group summarize its findings and conclusions on an overhead transparency.

9. When everyone is ready, have groups share their findings and conclusions. Discuss any differences among the groups and help students to reconcile those differences.

10. Consider allowing students to eat their oranges before cleaning up their work space. They *always* want to eat some or all of their oranges!

Notes to the Teacher

Research shows that students commonly have difficulty remembering formulas unless they discover those formulas themselves. This activity offers students the opportunity to find the formula for the surface area of a sphere through a guided investigation.

When you use this activity with your students for the first time, you may find the following comments useful:

❖ Student definitions for surface area should include the following:

• Surface area is the number of square units needed to cover the entire outside of a solid figure.

• The correct unit of measure for surface area is square units.

• Several partial surface areas can be added to find the total surface area for a solid. (If necessary, use a rectangular solid as an example to illustrate this point: surface area = $2ba + 2bh + 2ah$, or the total surface area is the sum of the surface areas of all the faces.)

If these ideas are not volunteered, ask questions to solicit them.

❖ Help students realize that the surface area of the orange equals the surface area of the peel. If they do not discover this on their own, ask questions to elicit this understanding.

❖ Help students realize that the radius of a great circle of a sphere is the same as the radius of the sphere itself. With an orange, the radius of a great circle is also the radius of the orange. If they do not discover this on their own, ask questions to elicit this understanding.

❖ To reveal a great circle of an orange, students need to cut the orange exactly in half. To help them do this, suggest that they cut through the "equator" of the orange to create two hemispheres. Students can use a piece of string to find the largest measure around the orange to increase their accuracy.

◈ If students cut their orange into two significantly unequal pieces, they can trim the larger piece to approximate half the original orange, but they still need to use all the pieces of the peel to cover the circles they draw.

◈ If a group comes up with the wrong formula, such as surface area $= 3\pi r^2$, help them find their error. Most often students leave gaps between pieces of peel or overlap them. Waiting until after the class discussion to clean the work space will allow them to see and correct their mistake.

◈ A quick way to determine whether students understand how to use the formula they have derived is to have each group find the surface area of its original orange. Ask the group to use a ruler to determine the radius of the great circles they have drawn and then substitute it in their formula to find the numerical value for the surface area of their orange.

Extension

To confirm the validity of the formula students discovered, use a foam sphere and a ball of thick yarn, about 1 centimeter in diameter, to do the following:

1. Place one end of the yarn on the sphere. Stick a straight pin into the sphere and wind the yarn to form concentric, touching spirals until the surface of the sphere is covered. Elicit from the students that the "square units of yarn" covering the sphere represents its surface area.
2. Cut the yarn so you have only the piece used for covering the sphere and unwind it. Disregard the remainder of the yarn.
3. Cut the sphere in half.
4. Starting in the center of the great circle of the sphere, pin down the yarn and wind it in the same way as before. Put a mark on the yarn when the great circle is completely covered.

sphere

great circle

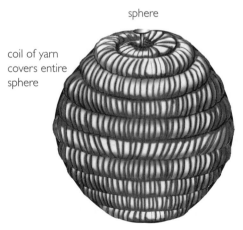

coil of yarn covers entire sphere

Area of yarn = length required to cover outside surface of sphere; this amount = SA of sphere.

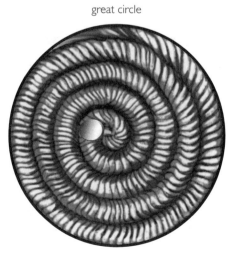

Area of yarn × 4 = SA of sphere ($4\pi r^2$). Yarn will cover ≈ 4 great circles.

5. Place the mark on the yarn in the center of the great circle of the sphere. Pin it down and wind until the great circle is again completely covered with yarn.

6. Put another mark on the yarn. Repeat Step 5 until you have used the entire piece of yarn.

The students are always surprised at how close the yarn comes to covering exactly four great circles.

Square States I

Related Topics: algebraic thinking, interpreting maps, using proportional reasoning

Overview
Students estimate the relative size of various states in the United States, compare their estimates with the actual sizes of the states, and write equations to represent relationships between or among the states.

Materials
◈ small maps of the United States, including Alaska and Hawaii, 1 per pair of students (See website information in "Notes to the Teacher" section on page 53.)

◈ large map of the United States, including Alaska and Hawaii (See website information in "Notes to the Teacher" section on page 53.)

◈ lists of areas of the states in the United States, ranked by size, 1 per pair of students (See website information in "Notes to the Teacher" section on page 53.)

◈ 3-by-18-inch strips of paper, at least 3 per pair of students

◈ optional: calculators, 1 per pair of students

Vocabulary: area, estimate, referent, round, scale

Prerequisite Skills and Concepts
Students should be able to estimate, round numbers, use a scale on a map, and write simple equations to represent situations.

Instructions

1. Explain that this exploration will be about the relative sizes (areas) of all the states in the United States and will involve estimating, using the scale on a map, and writing equations related to the areas of the states.

2. Display a large map of the United States where everyone can see it. Ask a volunteer to explain how to estimate the area of a particular state, using the scale on the map. Ask other volunteers to offer their ideas until the class agrees on a reasonable method.

3. Pass out a small map of the United States to each pair of students. Ask each pair to use the map to estimate (1) the ten states that have the largest area, in order from largest to smallest, and (2) the ten states that have the smallest area, in order from smallest to largest. Tell them to list their estimates on paper.

4. As pairs complete their lists of estimates, give them each a list of the states' actual areas and direct them to compare their estimates with the actual rankings.

5. When everyone is ready, ask each pair to identify the state whose area is nearest to 10,000 square miles (Vermont) and the state whose area is nearest to 100,000 square miles (Colorado). Lead a discussion about how these facts can be used as benchmarks or referents when making comparisons between or among states about their relative sizes. For example, since Louisiana looks about half the size of Colorado on the map and/or about five times the size of Vermont, its area might be about 50,000 square miles. This estimate is quite good, since the area of Louisiana is 51,843 square miles.

6. Now ask each pair of students to find at least three other relationships comparing the areas of different states. For each one, tell them to write a statement in words and then to express the relationship using mathematical symbols. Show an example, like this:

Nevada is about ten times the area of Maryland.

n = area of Nevada; m = area of Maryland

$n \approx 10m$ or $m \approx n/10$

Discuss why these two equations have the same meaning.

Tell students to write each of their statements on a 3-by-18-inch strip of paper and post it on the bulletin board.

7. Have the students share and discuss their findings and equations.

8. At a later time, check whether students have grasped the idea of using referents for areas on a map. To do this, show them a map of North America, Central America, and South America. Cover up the scale and see what conjectures they can make about the areas of some of the other countries in the Americas.

Notes to the Teacher

In this activity, students estimate the relative size of different states in the United States, compare their estimates with the actual sizes, and write equations to represent relationships between or among the states. This experience helps students build a sense of the size of land areas and increases their ability to make reasonable comparisons of those areas.

When you use this activity with your students for the first time, you may find the following comments useful:

❖ If appropriate, tell each pair of students to determine their "estimation score" by giving themselves a point for each correct state in their list and half a point for every time they estimated a state exactly between the correct two states on the actual list. The pair with the highest score could be named State Size Estimators Extraordinaire.

❖ The following website has a U.S. map that can be copied and pasted into a word-processing document: http://travel.yahoo.com/p-map-191501863-map_of_ united_states-i. Note that this map has a different scale for Alaska and Hawaii, which provides an added challenge. U.S. maps are available in almanacs and encyclopedias as well.

❖ A website that lists the states, ranked by area and total area, is www. enchantedlearning.com/usa/states/area.shtml. Again, such lists occur in almanacs and encyclopedias as well.

❖ The following website has a map of both North America and South America as well as Central America: http://www.wall-maps.com/Continents/NGamericas-over.jpg.

Extension
Teach *Square States 2* (see below).

 ## Square States 2

Related Topics: algebraic thinking, similar figures, square roots

Overview
Students use a specific scale factor to construct paper squares that accurately represent the states. They use these squares to predict the relative and actual areas of the states.

Materials
❖ small maps of the United States, including Alaska and Hawaii, 1 per pair of students (See website information in "Notes to the Teacher" section above.)
❖ list of the areas of the U.S. states ranked by size, 1 per pair of students (See website information in "Notes to the Teacher" section above.)
❖ rulers, 1 per pair of students
❖ protractors and/or compasses, 1 per pair of students
❖ calculators, 1 per pair of students
❖ 12-by-18-inch construction paper, 1 sheet per pair of students

Vocabulary: area, scale, scale factor, square root

Prerequisite Skills and Concepts

Students should know that different shapes can have the same area. They should have experience using both scales on a map and scale factors. It is helpful if they have had experience finding the side length of a square when its area is given.

Instructions

1. Explain that this exploration is a follow-up to *Square States 1* (page 51) and involves estimating area and using scale factors.

2. Ask students to offer definitions or explanations for the meaning of *square root, scale on a map,* and *scale factor.* Verify correct answers.

3. On the board, write the area in square miles of your home state. Ask each pair of students to find the dimensions of your state if its area stayed the same but the state were shaped like a square. Ask for volunteers to share their answers and to explain how they found them. Verify the correct answer and procedure (finding the square root of the area), and then ask another volunteer to explain why this procedure makes sense.

4. Next, tell each pair of students to find an appropriate scale to create a square representing your state that will fit on a sheet of blank $8\frac{1}{2}$-by-11-inch paper. Tell them to show their calculations on lined paper, use a protractor or compass to draw the square on the blank paper, and then cut the square out. For example, see Juan and Liz's work in Figure 3–1.

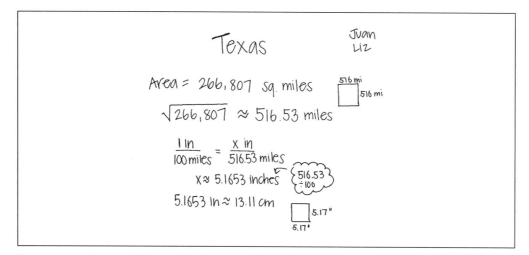

Figure 3–1 *Juan and Liz made a square with a side length of 13.11 centimeters (scale: 1 inch = 100 miles) to represent Texas.*

5. Pass out paper, rulers, calculators, protractors, compasses, and scissors and set students to work. As students finish, post their squares where all can see them. When everyone is ready, ask different pairs to explain the scale factor and method they used to determine the size of the square they made.

6. Explain that the class will now make a square to represent each state so that those squares will show the relative areas of the states. Ask what will be necessary for these squares to be useful for such comparisons. Students usually offer that the same scale must be used for all states. If they do not express this idea, elicit it through questions, such as "Why were the squares created by different pairs of students to represent our state different sizes?" and "How could we have made sure all the squares were the same size?"

7. Challenge each pair to come up with a scale so that (1) the square for Alaska will fit on a 12-by-18-inch piece of paper, (2) the square for Rhode Island will be large enough to see, and (3) the scale will be "friendly" (easy to work with). Have students share their ideas with the class to determine the scale to be used by everyone. (**Note:** The scale 1 inch = 100 miles works well.)

8. Pass out a list of all the states with their actual areas, and one sheet of 12-by-18-inch paper to each pair of students. Assign states to pairs of students. Have each pair do one large and one small state or two medium-size states to make sure they have enough paper to do both. Ask students to write the name of the state on the back of each square as they complete it.

9. Next, have each pair exchange squares with another pair of students and do the following:
   a. Use the list of states and their areas to guess which state each square represents before looking at its back.
   b. Check that the side of the square is the correct length for the given area.

10. Once all state squares have been made and checked, have students post the appropriate squares with the equations the class wrote during the *Square States 1* lesson. By doing this, students can see the proof for their equations. For example, since Nevada is about ten times the area of Maryland, students might have written $n \approx 10m$ (n = area of Nevada and m = area of Maryland) in *Square States 1*. Now, with the squares posted, the students can see that the square representing Nevada is ten times larger than the square representing Maryland.

11. At some point, ask the class how the squares would change if the state areas were given in square kilometers instead of square miles. This question can serve as a good assessment of the depth of understanding the students have for proportional reasoning and scaling.

Notes to the Teacher

This activity is designed as a follow-up to *Square States 1* (page 51).

When you use this activity with your students for the first time, you may find the following comments useful:

◈ If students are struggling to find the size of a square with the same area as your home state, stop and offer a simpler problem. For example, have the students think about answering the question for a state with an area of 100 square miles.

◈ Your students may decide upon a different scale than 1 inch = 100 miles (they may even choose a metric scale!). As they are deciding, encourage them to find the largest scale that seems both possible and reasonably simple to use as this will allow them to notice more easily small differences in areas among their squares.

◈ When checking another pair's work, students work backward. Reversing a sequence of steps is good practice for later work in algebra.

◈ Extra copies of the squares for some states may be needed when posting squares with the equations from *Square States 1* since some states will most likely appear in more than one equation.

◈ An important aspect of this lesson is its real-world context. When learning how to find square roots of numbers, students often wonder about when that process would be used in real life.

◈ Posting the equations or other problems that use the squares the students created for several days or weeks significantly increases the impact of both this lesson and that of *Square States 1*, especially for the students who struggled with one or more concepts during the lessons.

Extension

Post the squares for Colorado and Vermont as referents.

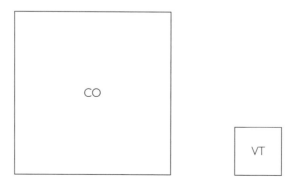

Then post other squares to show true equations. For example, you could post *square for Oregon* (slightly smaller than Colorado) + *square for North Carolina* (slightly bigger than half Colorado) = *square for Montana* ≈ 1.5 × Colorado), as shown below. Ask students to try to identify the states in the equation, with or without measuring the sides of the squares.

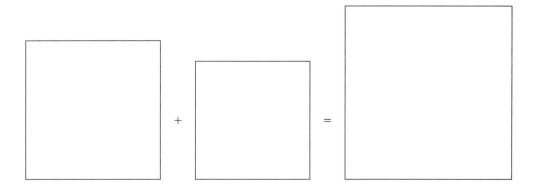

When appropriate, let students design and post their own equations for other students to solve.

Constant Area

Related Topics: algebraic thinking, coordinate graphing, inverse variation, patterns

Overview
Students draw rectangles with a given area, examine and graph the numeric data to find patterns, and derive generalizations about the rectangles from the patterns.

Materials
◈ grid paper with any unit length, such as 1 centimeter or 1 inch, 1 sheet per student
◈ colored pencils, 1 each of two different colors per student
◈ straightedges, 1 per student

Vocabulary: altitude, area, base, coordinate graph, domain, height, origin, range, rectangle, vertex

Prerequisite Skills and Concepts
Students should understand that *area* means a measure of the size of the interior of a two-dimensional figure or shape and is measured in square units. They should be familiar with rectangles and coordinate graphing.

Instructions

1. Have students work in pairs to list the dimensions of as many rectangles as they can that have an area of 24 square units, using whole number side lengths only. Explain that pairs are to compare their results and make any needed changes for each step of this activity.

2. Instruct students to each draw every rectangle in their list on grid paper, using a straightedge. Direct them to use the origin as the bottom left vertex of each rectangle to create a coordinate graph.

3. Have each student organize the measures of the bases and heights of the rectangles into a T-chart.

4. Ask students to describe on lined paper any patterns they noticed in both their T-charts and their graphs.

5. Next, have students make a point at the top right vertex of each rectangle they graphed, using a different-colored pencil than the one used to draw the rectangles.

6. Ask students to describe in writing the pattern made by the marked points and to explain how their answer makes sense when compared with the T-chart.

7. Finally, have students write a rule in words and/or symbols for the marked points and explain how the rule makes sense for all rectangles with an area of 24 square units.

8. As students finish, have partners practice how they will explain their findings to the rest of the class so that their explanation will show an understanding of both the area of a rectangle and their rule.

9. Have each pair conference briefly with another pair to compare understandings or to clarify details. When all pairs have finished conferencing with at least one other pair, lead a class discussion about the investigation.

Notes to the Teacher

In this lesson, students experience how a symbolic rule or common formula is generated from a set of examples. Instead of just solving an abstract equation for a given variable, they have an opportunity to make connections between the rectangles they have drawn, the numeric data they have collected from these rectangles, the visual plot of the top right corners of their rectangles, and the symbolic rule.

When you use this activity with students for the first time, you may find the following comments useful:

❖ Adjust the lesson according to your students' familiarity with patterns and functions. For students who are new to linear functions, the visual pattern created by these rectangles should help them see the relationship between the base and height (length and width) of rectangles with a constant area. As either of these quantities increases, the other must decrease, but the increases are not a constant amount. This should enable students to derive one of these three equivalent equations:

$$a \times b = 24 \quad \text{or} \quad ab = 24$$
$$x \cdot y = 24 \quad \text{or} \quad xy = 24$$
$$y = 24 \div x \quad \text{or} \quad y = \frac{24}{x}$$

◈ Sometimes students mistakenly start their list of rectangles by finding solutions that give a constant perimeter of 24, such as 1 by 11, 2 by 10, and so on. Consider letting them continue without commenting, because when they start to draw the rectangles on the coordinate graph, they usually see that these pairs do not give a constant area of 24 and benefit from finding their own error.

◈ Encourage students to double-check their drawings by making sure each of their rectangles encloses 24 small squares on the grid paper. This also helps reinforce for students why area is measured in square units.

◈ Students often create a random T-chart of jumbled information and cannot see significant patterns. Suggest to these students that they reorganize their data sequentially, as in the following chart, since patterns become clearer in an organized list.

Length of Base	Length of Height
1	24
2	12
3	8
4	6
6	4
8	3
12	2
24	1

◈ If students omit one or more sets of possible dimensions, suggest they look for "partner rectangles" (rectangles with the same dimensions but reversed, such as 2 by 12 and 12 by 2).

◈ Following are some of the patterns the students may notice:
  • The base times the height always has a product of 24 square units.
  • As the length of the base increases, the length of the corresponding height decreases, but not always by the same amount.
  • The rectangles start off tall and skinny and get shorter and wider.
  • Each rectangle has a partner rectangle.

◈ Ask the students why each pattern makes sense to them. Have students make a conjecture about what would happen similarly or differently if the rectangles all had areas of 36 square units.

◈ The students' graphs should look similar to the one shown below.

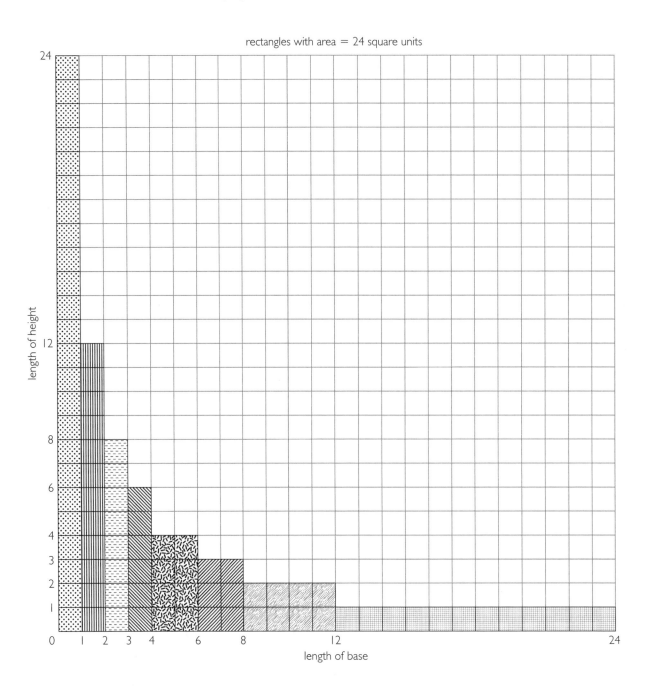

rectangles with area = 24 square units

◈ The most common description for the graph is something like *A group of rectangles that overlap, starting with one that has a base measuring 1 unit (making a 1-by-24 rectangle) with the base increasing by 1 unit each time up to a base of 24 (making a 24-by-1 rectangle)* or *It starts with tall, skinny rectangles on the left and they get wider and shorter as the size of the base increases.*

◈ Verbally describing the set of points is not easy for many students. The visual image is clear, but students often have a hard time finding the right words. Look for a version of the following main idea in their descriptions: *As the base increases, the height decreases by a smaller amount each time.*

◈ When the students are explaining how the graph and T-chart are related, make sure they recognize that each row in the T-chart contains the dimensions for one possible rectangle with an area of 24 and shows the coordinates for a corresponding point that was graphed. They should notice that the left column contains all the x-coordinates for the graphed points while the right column contains the corresponding y-coordinates. Students should recognize that the T-chart and the graph are two different representations of the same information.

◈ When students are expressing the function rule, some students will focus on the rectangles, writing something like, *For each rectangle, the base times the height will always give the product of 24.* The important idea is to note that the graph is not linear and it is reflected in a different type of function rule ($xy = 24$).

◈ If appropriate, challenge students to determine whether whole number solutions are the only ones that will fit the function rule. Ask them to use the graph to find the dimensions of a rectangle in which the length of the base is the same as the length of its height. Tie the answer to approximating the square root of 24. Also, you may ask the students about negative numbers in the rule, such as -6×-4. This discussion highlights the importance of a given domain.

◈ In symbols, the students usually write the rule as $xy = 24$, $hb = 24$ (b = length of base and h = length of height), or $l \cdot w = 24$. If appropriate, challenge them to rewrite the rule to isolate one of the variables so that they come up with $b = \frac{24}{h}$ or $y = \frac{24}{x}$. The idea of doing and undoing is important to success in algebra.

Extension

Repeat this investigation with each pair of students using a different fixed area, such as 30 or 60. Challenge the class to find generalizations among all the rectangles. For example, students can notice that an investigation of any fixed area produces the following patterns, among others:

◈ As the length of the base increases, the length of the corresponding altitude decreases, but not always by the same amount.
◈ The rectangles start off tall and skinny and get shorter and wider.
◈ The graph of points is not a line, but a curve.

They should also discover that some patterns do not occur every time. For example, all rectangles with a fixed area do not always have a partner rectangle for every pair of dimensions (when the fixed area is a perfect square).

◈ How Do You Grow?

Related Topics: algebraic thinking, numerical patterns, perimeter, ratios

Overview

Students look for patterns as they investigate a particular set of growing rectangles. They find the expressions for the base, perimeter, and area for any stage of the pattern and analyze their findings.

Materials

❖ *How Do You Grow?* recording sheets, 1 per student (see Blackline Masters)
❖ 1-inch color tiles, at least 24 per pair of students
❖ grid paper, 1 sheet per student
❖ colored pencils, 1 each of two different colors per pair of students

Vocabulary: altitude, area, base, linear function, perimeter, stage, T-chart

Instructions

1. Tell the students that they will investigate the perimeters and areas of a particular set of rectangles in order to find patterns and make generalizations.

2. Ask students to offer definitions for the terms *rectangle, perimeter,* and *area.* Verify correct answers.

3. Give students the following guidelines for completing the recording sheet:

   a. Use color tiles to build each stage.
   b. Draw one three-column T-chart for perimeter and another one for area, like the ones shown below.

Perimeter		
Stage	**What I See**	**Perimeter**

Area		
Stage	**What I See**	**Area**

c. Fill in the data. Look for patterns in the perimeter data and a different, but consistent, pattern in the area data.

d. Enter the data from your T-charts for each stage into the appropriate columns in the table on your recording sheet.

e. When you and your partner have completed the table, compare and discuss your findings.

f. Work together to answer the questions in Part 2.

4. In a whole-class discussion, have students share their findings and answers to the questions. Discuss any differences and help students reconcile those differences.

Notes to the Teacher

This activity provides an experience with both perimeter and area. It reinforces the differences between the two measures, focuses on looking for patterns, and strengthens students' algebraic thinking and problem-solving skills.

When you use this activity with your students for the first time, you may find the following comments useful:

◈ Making drawings for the early stages of patterns is an important step. Making the drawings and putting the values in the first three rows of the table remind students what the terms *base* and *height* mean and help them recall the definitions for *perimeter* and *area*.

◈ Creating separate three-column T-charts provides opportunities for the class to discuss equivalent expressions, as shown below. Specifically, $2 \times 2n + 2 \times n$, $2(2n + n)$, $4n + 2n$, and $6n$ are equivalent.

STUDENT A

	Perimeter			
Stage		**What I See**		**Perimeter**
	Base	**Height**	**Calculations**	
1	2	1	$2 \times 2 + 2 \times 1$	6
2	4	2	$2 \times 4 + 2 \times 2$	12
3	6	3	$2 \times 6 + 2 \times 3$	18
…	…	…	…	…
n	$2n$	n	$2 \times 2n + 2 \times n$	$4n + 2n$ or $6n$

Stage	What I See			Perimeter
	Base	*Height*	*Calculations*	
1	2	1	2(2 + 1)	6
2	4	2	2(4 + 2)	12
3	6	3	2(6 + 3)	18
...	...	...	...	...
n	2n	n	2(2n + n)	4n + 2n or 6n

If your students are not familiar with three-column T-charts, help them by constructing the columns, providing the three main headings, and eliciting what kind of information needs to be provided in each column.

Having each student build his own T-charts honors each student's way of interpreting the pattern. This approach also increases the chances for every student to make sense of the expressions for the nth stage of the patterns.

◈ Patterns students find in the table about perimeter and area should include the following:

- The length of the base for each stage is two more than the length of the base in the previous stage.
- The length of the base is twice the stage number (2n).
- The length of the height for each stage is one more than the length of the height in the previous stage.
- The length of the height is the same as the stage number (n).
- The perimeter of each stage is six more than the perimeter for the previous stage.
- The perimeter of any stage is two times twice the stage number plus two times the stage number [2(2n) + 2n].
- The amount of increase in perimeter between consecutive stages is 6, for example, 6, 12, 18, 24, ...
- The area of any stage is twice the stage number times the stage number (2n)(n).

◈ Student explanations for how the patterns fit with what they know about perimeter and area should include the following:

- Both perimeter and area grow from stage to stage because a larger base and a larger height increase the distance around the rectangle (perimeter) and the number of square units needed to cover it (area).
- Perimeter grows by 6 for each stage. The base grows by 2 and the altitude by 1, but since there are two bases and two heights in a rectangle, the perimeter actually increases by 4 and 2, respectively, for a total of 6.

- Area does not grow by the same amount for each new stage. Since you multiply (old base + 2) • (old height + 1), the area will grow at an increasing rate; for example, 2, 8, 18, 32 for Stages 1 through 4, with the amount of change increasing by 4 between each pair of consecutive stages. This makes sense because any time you keep increasing the value of both factors, their new product will increase more for each stage. This can be seen in the drawings as well: more small squares must be added for each new stage. Unlike perimeter, which is additive, area is multiplicative, so it becomes bigger faster.

- Area grows faster than perimeter. When the base and the height of a rectangle change, the perimeter increases by the units added along the four edges, whereas the area increases by an entire row of square units added along the length and another added along its width.

❧ Student graphs for base versus perimeter and base versus area should approximate the one shown below.

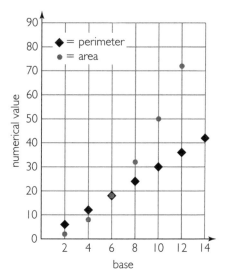

❧ Students' patterns and explanations related to the graph for perimeter should include the following:

- The graph for the perimeters of this set of rectangles is a linear function since the points form a straight line.
- The rate of change for perimeter is constant (from one point to the next consecutive point, the x-coordinate moves to the right one unit while the y-coordinate moves up six units) since the increase in perimeter between consecutive pairs of rectangles is always six.

❧ Students' patterns and explanations related to the graph for area should include the following:

- The graph for the areas of this set of rectangles is a not a linear function because the points do not form a straight line.

- The rate of change is not steady because area is multiplicative: the rectangle in Stage 1 has an area of 1×2, or 2 square units. The rectangle in Stage 2 has an area of 2×4, or 8 square units. The rectangle in Stage 3 has an area of 3×6, or 18 square units, and so on. Thus, from one point to the next consecutive point, the x-coordinate consistently moves to the right 2 units while the y-coordinate moves up 6 units, then 10 units, then 14, then 18, and so on.

◈ Have students explain their strategies for finding the missing values for Question 5 on the recording sheet. Such sharing helps students see the advantages of a strategy they did not use.

Extensions

◈ Help students define a new group of rectangles with a different growing pattern for the base, height, or both. After the students complete an exploration similar to this one, have them compare similarities and differences between their findings in this activity and those with the new rectangles.

◈ Distribute the following table to each student along with color tiles. Tell the class to build each pair of rectangles, simplify all ratios, and answer the questions following the table. For the original rectangle, suggest they build a 1-by-2 rectangle. Have students work in pairs and share their thinking.

Dimensions for the Two Rectangles	Ratio of Dimensions	Ratio of Perimeters	Ratio of Areas
Original : Both dimensions doubled	1:2		
Original : Both dimensions tripled			
(Predict, then check) Original : Both dimensions quadrupled	Prediction	Prediction	Prediction
	Actual Ratio	Actual Ratio	Actual Ratio
Original : Both dimensions multiplied by any factor, f			

Questions

1. When the side lengths of a rectangle are doubled, how does the ratio of corresponding sides of the two rectangles compare with the ratio of their perimeters? Why does this make sense?

2. When the side lengths of a rectangle are doubled, how does the ratio of corresponding sides of the two rectangles compare with the ratio of their areas? Why does this make sense?

3. What pattern do you find in the data in the Ratio of Dimensions column? Why does this make sense?

4. What pattern do you find in the data in the Ratio of Perimeters column? Why does this make sense?

5. What pattern do you find in the data in the Ratio of Areas column? Why does this make sense?

6. What pattern do you find between the ratios in the Ratio of Perimeters and the Ratio of Areas columns? Why does this make sense?

7. What patterns do you predict you would find if you repeated this investigation with triangles or pentagons?

 Chances Are

Related Topic: probability

Overview

Each student creates a simulation of a dart game involving two boards containing geometric shapes. The student then finds the theoretical probability for each game board by comparing the areas of the shapes and analyzing the game for fairness. Finally, students work in pairs, playing a classmate's game to determine whether it is fair.

Materials

◈ $8\frac{1}{2}$-by-11-inch construction paper with 2 9-by-9-centimeter squares, as shown, 1 per student

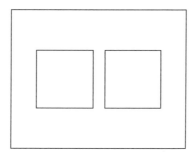

◈ 9-by-9-centimeter squares of $1\frac{1}{2}$-centimeter grid paper in various colors, 2 sheets per student

◈ transparencies of $1\frac{1}{2}$-centimeter grid paper, 1 per student and 4 for the teacher

◈ metric rulers, 1 per student

◈ dice, numbered 1 to 6, 1 each of two different colors per pair of students

◈ optional: calculators, 1 per student

Vocabulary: area, coordinates (on a coordinate plane), experimental probability, fair game, theoretical probability

Prerequisite Skills and Concepts

Students need to understand theoretical and experimental probability and have some experience finding areas of irregular geometric shapes. It would be helpful, but not necessary, if they had some experience with geometric probability (probability involving geometric figures).

Instructions

Note: This lesson will require more than one regular class period to complete.

Before Class

1. Create the transparencies needed for Instructions 2 and 7. On a clear transparency, draw two squares, each 9 by 9 centimeters. In one square construct a parallelogram and in the other, a star, as shown below.

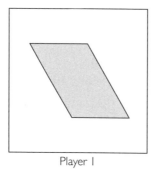
Player 1

Player 2

2. Cut two 9-by-9-centimeter squares from a transparent $1\frac{1}{2}$-centimeter grid. Label the squares, both vertically and horizontally, from *1* to *6*, as shown below.

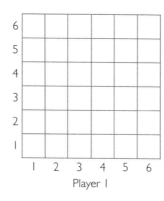
Player 1

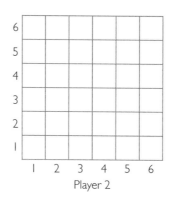
Player 2

Day 1: Making a Game of Chance

1. Ask students to define *probability* and to explain what it means for a game to be fair. After briefly reviewing these concepts, explain to the students that each of them will design a game of chance, analyze its fairness, and then play and analyze a partner's game.

2. Ask students to imagine a dart game in which the game boards are the two squares shown below. Explain that each player is to throw the same number of darts at her game board and, with each throw, try to hit the inside of the dark shape to score a point.

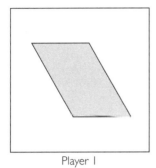

Player 1

Player 2

Ask the students whether they think the game is fair and, if not, which player they believe has the advantage, assuming the players have equal skill. Take a poll. Then ask how they could prove whether the game is fair or not. Some students may suggest playing the game for a long time to see which player hits inside the dark shape more times. Others may suggest finding the areas of the two dark shapes to see which is larger. Remind the class that the first suggestion deals with experimental probability, that is, collecting and analyzing the results (data) from many games, and that the second suggestion deals with theoretical probability, that is, finding out which shape has the largest area, and thus, the greater chance of being hit.

3. Next, tell students that they will each construct a game similar to the one they have been discussing. On chart paper or an overhead transparency, write the following guidelines for constructing the game.

a. Make a sketch before you start to draw the actual game board. Make the shapes more interesting than a simple parallelogram. Be sure that it is not obvious whether the game is fair. Also, keep in mind that you must be able to find the areas of the shapes you create.

b. Use your ruler to draw your two target shapes on your squares of grid paper. Cut out the shapes.

c. Trace around each shape on a sheet of lined paper and label its dimensions. Find its area, showing your formulas and work.

d. Verify whether your game is theoretically fair and explain why in writing. Include the results of your calculations in your explanation.

e. Turn the shapes over so the gridlines don't show. Glue each shape inside one of the squares on your sheet of construction paper.

4. Distribute the materials. As students work, circulate to answer questions and help when necessary.

5. As they finish, tell the students to trade game boards with a partner, check each other's work, and fix any errors.

6. Have the students turn in their papers and save them for the next day.

Day 2: Analyzing a Game of Chance

1. Pass the papers back to the students. Have each student pair up with a new partner. Talk through or post the following directions:

    a. Start a new section on your lined paper. Look at your partner's game. Write your impression as to whether the game seems fair or not.

    b. Play the game with your partner:

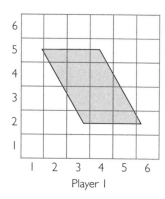 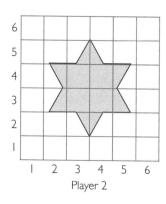

Player 1   Player 2

        1. Place a transparent grid over each game board (as shown above).

        2. Designate one die to indicate the horizontal square and the other, the vertical square. Decide who is Player 1 and who is Player 2. For the first round, Player 1 rolls the dice and finds the square that corresponds to the roll. For example, for a roll of (3, 2), Player 1 identifies the square in column 3 and row 2. If that square contains any of the shaded area, as in this example, Player 1 gets a point. Then Player 2 rolls, following the same procedure. This ends Round 1.

        3. Play fifty rounds. Keep track of the score.

        4. After fifty rounds, the person who did not design the game records the results and writes a conclusion about whether the game appears to be fair from the experimental data.

    c. Now play the other partner's game, following the same procedures outlined above.

    d. Next, find the theoretical probability of winning your partner's game.

        1. On your lined paper, find the area of your partner's target shapes.

        2. Include a sketch of each shape with measurements and show your calculations.

3. For each game board, find the ratio of the area of the dark shape to the area of the square. This is the theoretical probability of scoring with a dart.

4. Write a conclusion about the fairness of the game.

2. Lead a class discussion. Have each pair who played together show their game boards to the class and describe how they found the areas of the target shapes. Have other students suggest alternative ways those areas could have been found. Then discuss the probabilities of the games and any surprises or questions the students may have encountered.

Notes to the Teacher

In this activity, students construct irregular geometric shapes and calculate the areas of such shapes. They also determine experimental and theoretical probabilities to draw conclusions about the fairness of a game created by a classmate.

When you use this activity with your classes for the first time, you may find the following comments useful:

❖ If your students have not encountered geometric probability, this activity can serve as an introduction to this concept. In this case, you will need to spend some extra time discussing how geometric probability works in general before considering the context of the games the students are creating and analyzing in this activity.

❖ If your students need to review finding the area of an irregular shape, have them work with the shape shown below.

1. Measure all segments.

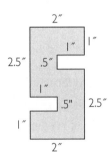

2. Partition the shape into familiar shapes.

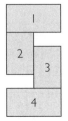

3. Find the area of each part, showing formulas and steps. Then add their areas.

Rectangles 1 and 4

$$A = b \cdot h$$
$$A = 2 \cdot 1$$
$$A = 2 \text{ sq. in.}$$

Rectangles 2 and 3

$$A = b \cdot h$$
$$A = 1 \cdot 1.5$$
$$A = 1.5 \text{ sq. in.}$$

$$\textbf{Total Area} = 2(2) + 2(1.5)$$
$$= 4 + 3$$
$$= 7 \text{ sq. in.}$$

Be sure to have students suggest alternative ways to partition the irregular shapes and go through the steps for each.

Here are some other ways to partition the irregular shape:

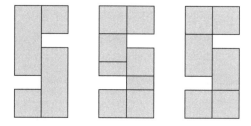

❖ If appropriate, have students construct for themselves the two game boards on a blank sheet of paper instead of providing the construction paper with squares. In this case, they will need protractors and/or compasses.

❖ If calculators are available, the students should use transparent grids that have smaller squares and are numbered like the coordinate plane to find the experimental probability. Then, rather than rolling dice for each turn, the student can use the calculator to generate a pair of numbers that will serve as the coordinates for a point. If a point lies inside the target area, the player gets a point. This method should produce results that are closer to the theoretical probability.

Extension

If *The Geometer's Sketchpad* or other similar software is available, have students create games like the ones in this activity. With this software, students can animate a point to move randomly inside each square. In addition, the game creator can put notes to the student who is testing the game for fairness in the sketch with a Hide/Show button, as shown below.

If appropriate, ask students to devise a way to make unfair games fair by changing either the figures or the points awarded, as illustrated in the following example.

Student sketch before clicking on Show button:

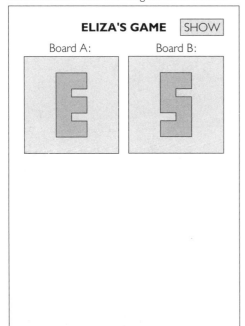

Student sketch after clicking on Show button:

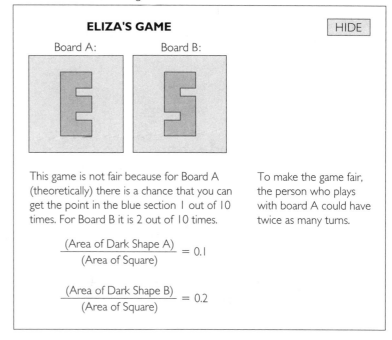

This game is not fair because for Board A (theoretically) there is a chance that you can get the point in the blue section 1 out of 10 times. For Board B it is 2 out of 10 times.

$$\frac{\text{(Area of Dark Shape A)}}{\text{(Area of Square)}} = 0.1$$

$$\frac{\text{(Area of Dark Shape B)}}{\text{(Area of Square)}} = 0.2$$

To make the game fair, the person who plays with board A could have twice as many turns.

CHAPTER 4

Volume

● ●

Introduction

Similar to the study of length and area, the study of volume or capacity should first include an understanding of what it measures. The *volume* of a solid object is the amount of space something takes up, or, if it is hollow, the amount of space contained within its boundaries. The *capacity* of a container is the amount of space into which a liquid can be poured or another material placed. In actuality, people often use *volume* and *capacity* interchangeably.

In the lessons in this chapter, measurement sense continues to be an emphasis. Students develop personal referents for units of volume and capacity. They estimate and verify volume and capacity in many contexts, and as a result, understand why the unit of measure for each must be three-dimensional. They learn that volume is measured in cubic units such as cubic inches, cubic feet, and cubic centimeters, whereas ounces, cups, gallons, milliliters, and liters, for example, are used to measure capacity.

Very important in the study of volume is the development of standard formulas and the connections among them. Typically, middle school students think of the volume of a prism as its length times its width times its height. In the lesson *Bigger and Bigger* (page 95), students consider the volume of a rectangular prism as a set of stacked, congruent layers of cubes for which the number of layers determines its height. By looking at many kinds of prisms from this same perspective, students will be able to generalize that the volume of any prism is the product of the area of its base and its height, or $V = Bh$ (B = area of base layer, h = height of prism).

Next, students must transfer this core understanding to other shapes, for example, cones and pyramids that do not consist of congruent layers. Students need to compare the volumes of pairs of solid figures, such as a cylinder and a cone with the same base area and height. In *Fishing for Formulas* (page 84), students derive the formula for the volume of a pyramid by comparing it with a prism that has a congruent base and the same height. In *The Difference an Angle Makes 2* (page 104), students investigate cylinders and cones that have congruent bases and the same heights. By filling both three-dimensional figures with beans, rice, or water, students discover that the volume of the cylinder is always three times that of the cone, and conversely, that the volume of a

74 ■

cone is one-third the area of its base layer times its height, or $V = \frac{1}{3} Bh$. Thus, they can derive the generalized formula for the volume of any point solid, volume $= \frac{1}{3} \cdot$ area of base layer $\cdot$ height of solid.

These generalized formulas, coupled with internalizing the connections they imply, free students from having to memorize a different formula for each kind of solid figure.

Finally, in *On the Ball* (page 90), students determine the general formula for the volume of a sphere by applying what they've learned about its surface area and the volume of a pyramid.

This chapter also targets new ways for middle school students to investigate volume and capacity. It includes the following lessons:

❖ *Volume Graphs* (page 79) is an investigation about the relationship between the shape of a container and the height of water it contains as equal increments are added.

❖ *Blocks of Cheese* (page 92) is an investigation about minimizing surface area for a given volume within the context of a cheese factory.

❖ *The Difference an Angle Makes 1* (page 87) is an investigation about the effect of removing different-size sectors from a circle on the volume of the resulting cone.

❖ *Bigger and Bigger* (page 95) calls for algebraic thinking to find, graph, and compare growth patterns of the surface area and volume of a particular set of prisms.

❖ *Cylinder Mystery* (page 100) involves changing the dimensions of a cylinder and comparing the effects those changes have on the volume of the new cylinder.

Communication of mathematical thinking is built into each lesson. Additionally, at least one idea for extending the activity is included.

 ## Building Referents for Capacity

Related Topics: algebraic thinking, estimation

Overview
Students estimate the relationships among several nonstandard containers. They verify the relationships and express them using equations containing variables. Later they use the equations to find the number of each type of container that would be needed to supply drinks for a party and establish everyday referents for customary units of liquid capacity.

Materials
❖ sets of 4 irregularly shaped empty containers that are familiar to the students with capacities of 1 cup, 1 pint, 1 quart, and 1 gallon, 1 set per small group of students

❖ sets of 4 standard-shape empty containers with capacities of 1 cup, 1 pint, 1 quart, and 1 gallon, 1 set per small group of students

❖ pitchers of colored water, 1 per small group of students

- ❖ paper towels, a few sheets
- ❖ labels for irregularly shaped containers, 2 per container
- ❖ large poster or transparency of liquid capacity graphic (see Blackline Masters)
- ❖ optional: copies of liquid capacity graphic (see Blackline Masters), 1 per student

Vocabulary: capacity, cup, gallon, ounce, pint, quart, referent, volume

Prerequisite Skills and Concepts

Students should have some prior experience using variables to express known relationships, for example, expressing the relationship between a foot (f) and a yard (y) as $y = 3f$ and $f = \frac{1}{3}y$.

Instructions

1. Prior to the lesson, for each set of irregularly shaped containers, label each with a variable. Write each variable w, x, y, and z on a separate label. Affix label w on the container with a capacity of 1 gallon, x on the container with a capacity of 1 cup, y on the container with a capacity of 1 quart, and z on the container with a capacity of 1 pint. Cover the capacity of each container if it is provided on the container. Prepare a second set of labels, this time using the customary unit for each container.

2. Explain to the students that the principal needs their help. Give the following details: The principal is having a party and wants to be sure to have enough drinks for each person that comes. Since juices and other drinks come in containers of many different sizes and shapes, the principal is wondering how many of each type of container will be needed to provide 24 ounces of liquid for each of the thirty-six guests invited to the party.

3. Show one set of irregularly shaped containers to the students. Have them work in small groups to make estimates for the relationships between their capacities. For example, ask, "How many times would you need to fill and pour the contents of Container z into Container y to completely fill it?" or "What fraction of the capacity of Container y is the capacity of Container x?"

4. Tell the groups to record their estimates in equation form, such as $y = 2z$. When most groups seem ready, let each group share an estimate with the class and verify it by having a student pour colored water from one container into another. Record correct equations on the board.

5. Display the graphic shown on the following page and ask volunteers to explain the information it represents. (The 8 stands for 8 ounces, the C for cup, the P for pint,

the Q for quart, and the G for gallon; also implied are the following equivalents: 8 ounces = 1 cup, 2 cups = 1 pint, 2 pints = 1 quart, and 4 quarts = 1 gallon.)

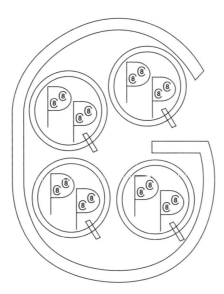

6. When everyone in the class seems comfortable interpreting the graphic, have students work in their small groups to write equations that show the relationships among the customary units of liquid capacity, referring to the graphic, if needed. Allow them to use their set of standard containers to pour colored water from one container to another in order to verify their equations. Have paper towels handy for cleaning up any spills.

7. Have students share and analyze their equations in a whole-class discussion.

8. Inform the class that each of the irregularly shaped containers actually has a capacity equal to a customary unit of liquid capacity. Ask for volunteers to try to name the standard units for the containers. Verify correct answers and have students in each group attach a second label to each irregular container, giving its liquid capacity (for example, add a label reading "1 gallon" on the irregular container with the label w when a student correctly identifies the capacity as a gallon.)

9. Ask students to solve the problem presented at the beginning of the class. They should use their equations to determine how many of each kind of the irregularly shaped containers would be needed for a party if the principal would like to have 24 ounces of liquid for each of thirty-six guests.

Notes to the Teacher

This lesson provides hands-on experience to build familiarity with customary units of liquid capacity and their relationships to each other. It also helps students build familiar referents for these units.

When you use this lesson for the first time with your classes, you may find the following comments useful:

❖ Use irregularly shaped containers that are familiar to the students, such as popular brands of juice and soda, household cleaners, or paint cans. After the lesson is completed, leave the labels on these containers and continue to keep them in view in your classroom to encourage students to use them as personal referents for customary units of liquid capacity.

❖ The first part of the activity can help students strengthen their estimation skills with volumes of liquids. Once the actual capacities and relationships between the containers are known, the students reinforce the learning from the first part of the lesson, emphasizing the relationships among customary units of capacity and using variables to write equations, both within a real-word context.

❖ Writing equations like those required by this activity is no simple task for many middle school students. It is important to provide concrete experiences for students to help them use variables to write formulas that express known relationships. For example, even though most middle school students know that there are 3 feet in a yard, use three 1-foot rulers and a yardstick to show the relationship. Write *1 yard* = _____ on the board and hold up the yardstick next to the three rulers. After the students say "three feet," convert the words into $y = 3f$. Then reverse the action. Write *1 foot* = _____, hold up a 1-foot ruler, and iterate it along the yardstick. After the students respond "one-third of a yard," convert the expression to $f = \frac{1}{3}y$ or $f = \frac{y}{3}$. This kind of experience helps prepare students for algebra and science classes in which they will be asked to write equations in terms of a particular variable.

❖ It is helpful to give each student a copy of the graphic used during the lesson.

❖ You can vary this lesson by asking each group to come up with a shopping list for the principal, listing the types of drinks and the number of containers of each type that they suggest he buy for the party, including the mathematics to show that this list would provide the amount of liquid the principal wanted for each guest at the party.

❖ A few days after this lesson, ask each student to list familiar containers that will serve as her personal referents for units of capacity. Have students share these referents, so they have the opportunity to refine or add to their list with options offered by their classmates.

Extension

Use another version of this activity, substituting familiar containers that each have a capacity that is a friendly number of metric units, such as 1 liter, 500 milliliters, 200 milliliters, and 75 milliliters. Include a discussion of the cubic centimeter. The equations that show the relationships among the containers in this lesson will involve decimals, thus providing practice with another set of skills that many middle school students need to reinforce.

 Volume Graphs

Related Topics: graphing on a coordinate plane, length, rate of change or slope, spatial reasoning, spatial visualization

Overview
To increase their understanding of both volume and rate of change, students investigate the relationship between the shape of a container and the height of the water in the container as equal measures of water are added.

Materials
- ❧ clear empty bottles or vases in various sizes and shapes, 1 per small group of students plus a few extras
- ❧ pitchers or other large containers filled with colored water or rice, 1 per small group of students
- ❧ graduated cylinders, 1 per small group of students
- ❧ metric rulers, or meter sticks, 1 per small group of students
- ❧ fine-line markers, 1 per small group of students
- ❧ 2 grid paper, 1 $8\frac{1}{2}$-by-11-inch sheet per small group of students, plus 2 extra sheets
- ❧ sheet of newsprint or a blank transparency

Vocabulary: capacity, cubic centimeter, meniscus, milliliter, scale (on a graph), volume

Prerequisite Skills and Concepts
Students should be familiar with plotting points on a coordinate plane.

Instructions

1. Before class, select two containers with distinctly different shapes. Prepare graphs for them. To do this, pour 25 milliliters of water into one of the containers. With a fine marker, draw a dash on the container to show the height of the water. Add another 25 milliliters of water and again mark the container. Continue this process until the container is filled. On one sheet of the large grid paper, draw coordinate axes and label the *x*-axis *Amount of Water* and the *y*-axis *Height of Water (to the Nearest Tenth of a Centimeter)*. Decide on a specific length for each of the axes (for example, 25 centimeters for the *x*-axis and 20 centimeters for the *y*-axis) and plot

the points. Repeat this process with the other container. Draw the graph on a new piece of grid paper but make the axes the same lengths as those in the first graph. Wipe away the marks on the containers.

Write the following directions on a transparency or newsprint.

a. Pour 25 milliliters of colored water from a graduated cylinder into your container.

b. Use a fine-line marker to draw a small dash on the container to show the height of the water.

c. Continue adding water in increments of 25 milliliters, marking the new height of the water until the container is full.

d. Carefully measure and record the height of each mark on the side of the bottle to the nearest tenth of a centimeter.

Set out all the containers, including the ones for which you made the graphs, so that everyone in the class can see them.

2. To begin the activity, ask students to offer definitions for the terms *volume* and *capacity*. Verify correct answers.

3. Choose one of the containers for which you have prepared a graph. Show it to the class and demonstrate pouring 25 milliliters of the colored water at a time into the container. Do this step three or four times. Be sure you do not completely fill the container.

4. Ask each student to create a mental image of a graph in which each point represents the amount of water in the container (*x*-coordinate) and the height of the water in the container (*y*-coordinate) as increments of 25 milliliters are added to the container until it is full. Pause to give students time for this visualization.

5. In small groups, have students discuss what the graph would look like; then have the groups share their predictions.

6. Show the students the two graphs you prepared ahead of time. Do not tell the students which graph is which or identify the second container, which should be on display with the others.

7. Instruct students to discuss in their small groups which graph represents the original container and prepare to explain their reasoning. After they share their thinking, tell the class which graph goes with the container. If needed, go through the process step-by-step for the class, discussing each part of the graph as you proceed.

8. Next, ask each group to choose the container from the display that they think is represented by the other graph. Again have them share their thinking, and then identify the correct container. If needed, have students demonstrate the steps for the second container and discuss how the graph shows what is happening.

9. Distribute the materials to the groups. Display the newsprint or transparency that you prepared ahead of time with the directions. Tell the class to use the same procedure you did to gather data about their container and then construct a graph on a large sheet of grid paper.

10. Have students post their graphs and return the containers to the table. Label each graph with a letter and each container with a number in random order.

11. Direct each group to try to match each container with the correct graph.

12. When all groups are ready, lead a discussion. Have students share their predictions for matching containers and graphs and explain their reasoning. Allow groups to adjust their predictions, and then have each group identify its container and the matching graph.

13. In a whole-class discussion, have students identify the pattern of rates of change in each graph and explain how the differences reflect the shapes of the containers.

Notes to the Teacher

This activity provides students hands-on experience with increasing volumes of water in containers having irregular shapes. As they graph the data that compare the amount of water with its height in the container, students think about the different rates of change in their graph and how those rates correspond with the shape of the container, thus deepening their understanding of both volume and slope.

When you use this activity with your students for the first time, you may find the following comments useful:

❖ When choosing containers, make sure that the shape of each one is distinct from all the others that have similar capacities. However, if two containers are similar in shape but have very different capacities, include them to add another dimension to the activity. If possible, include a cylindrical and an almost spherical container.

❖ As you demonstrate the procedure for gathering data to the class, emphasize guidelines for measuring, including the following:
  • When measuring liquid in a graduated cylinder, you must decide whether to read from the lowest or highest point of the meniscus; either is acceptable, but you must be consistent.
  • Be sure you are at eye level with whatever you are measuring.
  • Choose the unit of measure (nearest tenth of a centimeter) and use the same unit for every measurement.
  • Be sure the ruler is perpendicular to the tabletop or desktop, not slanted, when you make each measurement.
  • Be sure the zero mark on the ruler is even with the bottom of the container.

- Two group members should make every measurement. If they disagree, they should measure a third time.

❖ To ensure measurements that are as accurate as possible and participation by all, in each group, assign a role to each person. For example, when pouring water, one student can pour from the graduated cylinder into the container, another student can make the mark on the container, and a third student can verify that both are accurate. When measuring the height of the marks, one student can hold the ruler perpendicular to the work surface and the others can agree on the height of each mark and record the data. Because it is important for the ruler to remain stationary, the student holding the ruler should record the data after the other students have finished measuring.

❖ Using the same length for all x-axes and all y-axes on every graph focuses students on matching the shape of the graphs to the correct containers rather than on the numbers or individual points. This restriction also requires students to use additional skills during the lesson. First, students must find an appropriate scale to use in order to make their data fit in the graph they make. Second, when interpreting the graphs of other groups, students must use their estimation and spatial skills to help them match containers and graphs correctly despite a variety of scales.

❖ When students interpret the graph for a container, be sure they relate the steepness of each portion of the graph to both the shape of the bottle (the amount of change in the height of the water for an added 25 milliliters of water) and the rate of change (the steepness of the graph). They should realize that both are greatest when the container is "skinny" or "becoming skinnier," that is, when the surface area of the water is smaller or becoming smaller. For example:

Amount of Water	Height of Water
25	1.5
50	2.3
75	2.9
100	3.4
125	4
150	4.5
175	5.2
200	6.5
225	7.8
250	8.4
275	10.7
290	15.6

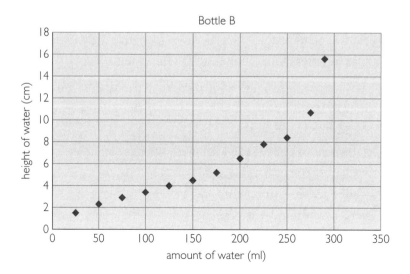

For the vase below, the rate of change (slope) is not steady as water is added in equal measures. For intervals in which the vase becomes thinner, the rate increases, whereas for the intervals in which the vase becomes wider, the rate decreases. For two sets of intervals, both the vase and rate of change stay about the same.

For the vase below, the rate of change is not steady as water is added in equal measures. However, the graph is almost symmetrical as the height of the water increases more rapidly, then less rapidly, then more rapidly again. Notice the distance between consecutive points on the graph is greatest between the first two points and the last two points, which corresponds with the rates at which the shape of the vase changes fastest.

Amount of Water	Height of Water	Amount of Water	Height of Water
25	1.5	350	6.5
50	2.3	375	6.8
75	2.8	400	7.1
100	3.3	425	7.5
125	3.7	450	7.9
150	4	475	8.3
175	4.4	500	8.8
200	4.8	525	9.4
225	5.2	550	10
250	5.5	575	10.7
275	5.8	600	11.4
300	6	625	12.2
325	6.2	650	13.2

❖ Through questioning, help students understand that the graph does not reflect uneven changes in the volume of water; the increase is always 25 milliliters per interval. The graph simply shows the height of the water in the container. Thus, at each interval, the volume of the water in the container increases 25 milliliters. Some groups may need to graph this linear function as well.

◈ If appropriate, pose the question, "Do the graphs represent functions?" This query will allow you to introduce your students to step functions.

Extension

Have students follow a procedure similar to the one used in this lesson to explore another relationship—that of weight. As before, the students add water in 25-milliliter increments to the container, marking, measuring, and recording the height of the water after each addition. The students also weigh the empty container before any water is added and again after each additional 25 milliliters of water, recording the total weight each time, until the container is filled.

Have students, using the same container, repeat the steps using rubbing alcohol instead of water.

Have students create two graphs for each liquid: the first graph should display amount of liquid in the container (*x*-coordinate) versus height of liquid in the container (*y*-coordinate), and the second graph should display amount of liquid in the container (*x*-coordinate) versus weight of the container plus the liquid (*y*-coordinate).

Except for inevitable differences in measurement, the shape of the first graph for each liquid should be identical to the one that would be produced in this lesson and approximate a coincidental function. The second graph for each liquid will approximate a linear function; however, the rate of change in the graph for alcohol will be less than that in the graph for water.

Students will discover that a given volume of alcohol weighs less than the same volume of water. This extension serves to reemphasize that adding equal increments of a liquid into a container increases the volume by equal amounts. This relationship remains steady despite the variations in height of the liquid measures due to the irregular shape of the containers. Once students see this constant relationship between mass and volume for each liquid, they can focus on what sets these two graphs apart—the difference in the density of the two liquids.

 ## Fishing for Formulas

Related Topics: linear measurement, Pythagorean theorem, ratio, spatial visualization

Overview

Students construct a net and a model for either a cube or a rectangular prism. They then construct a pyramid having a base that is congruent to and a height that is the same as their first figure. Finally, they compare the volumes of their figures to derive the formula for finding the volume of a square or other rectangular pyramid.

Materials

◈ centimeter grid paper duplicated on tagboard or very thick paper (see Blackline Masters), 2 sheets per student

◈ jumbo paper clips or small pieces of wire the same thickness as a paper clip, 1 per pair of students

◈ small lumps of clay, 1 per pair of students

◈ washable fine-line markers, 1 per pair of students

◈ rulers, 1 per pair of students

◈ rice or sand, approximately 600 milliliters per 1 or 2 pairs of students

◈ *Fishing for Formulas* instructions, 1 copy per student (see Blackline Masters)

◈ optional: models of prisms and pyramids, 1 of each

Vocabulary: apothem, base of a prism or pyramid, cube, cubic centimeter, height of a prism or pyramid, milliliter, net, prism, pyramid, rectangular prism, rectangular pyramid, slant height, square pyramid

Prerequisite Skills and Concepts

Students should know the basic properties of rectangular prisms including cubes, and rectangular pyramids including square pyramids. Students should have had experiences working with cubes to find the volumes of rectangular prisms. It will be helpful if the students know how to use the Pythagorean theorem to find a missing side length in a right triangle.

Instructions

1. Explain to the students that they will construct nets and models to compare the volumes of two solid figures.

2. Ask students to offer definitions for *prism, rectangular prism, cube, rectangular pyramid, square pyramid, base of a prism or pyramid,* and *height of a prism or pyramid.* Be sure the discussion includes the number of faces, the shapes of the faces, which face(s) serve as the base, and how the height is measured for each kind of figure. It is very helpful to have models available to help students clarify misunderstandings.

3. Pass out the instructions for the activity. Answer any questions students have about the investigation.

4. As the students begin working, post on the board the following headings for a class data table: Names, Dimensions of the Rectangular Prism, Volume of the Rectangular Prism, Volume of the Pyramid, and Ratio of the Volume of the Prism to the Volume of the Pyramid.

5. When all students have completed the investigation and posted their results, lead a whole-class discussion about their findings, observations, and conclusions.

Notes to the Teacher

This activity provides experience in constructing a prism and a pyramid with congruent bases and equal heights, finding the volume of both figures, and using patterns in the class data to derive a formula for the volume of a square pyramid or other rectangular pyramid.

When you use this activity for the first time with your students, you may find the following comments useful:

❧ Allow student pairs to choose whether they will construct a cube or a rectangular prism, but make suggestions to ensure that there is a variety of shapes and sizes among the class's rectangular prisms.

❧ The following two websites have information about nets: www.ams.org/featurecolumn/archive/nets.html and http://argyll.epsb.ca/jreed/math8/strand3/3102.htm.

❧ To view some sample nets of cubes and other rectangular prisms, go to www.google.com, click on Images, enter "rectangular pyramid net" in the text box, and click on Search Images.

❧ When students measure the height of their pyramids directly, the following technique works well: Use a jumbo paper clip straightened out or another piece of wire of similar thickness. Stick the wire into a small lump of clay on a tabletop so that it is perpendicular to the table and one end of the wire is touching the table. Fold back the base of the pyramid so that the pyramid is hollow, and then lower the pyramid (point upward) carefully so that the wire goes through the point of the pyramid. Press down slightly on the pyramid to be sure all the bottom edges are touching the table. Use a washable fine-line marker to make a mark on the wire at the tip of the pyramid. Remove the pyramid, and measure the length of the wire from its bottom to the mark. The other member of the pair should repeat the process to ensure accuracy.

❧ Students can use the Pythagorean theorem to produce a pyramid with the same height as the prism. They can easily determine the slant height of the pyramid (the hypotenuse) by measuring or counting the center column of square centimeters on any of its triangular faces. Since one leg of the triangle is half the length of the adjoining base, the missing leg is the height of the pyramid.

slant height of pyramid = 15 cm
$\frac{1}{2}$ base of pyramid = 7 cm

$$c^2 = a^2 + b^2$$
$$15^2 = 7^2 + b^2$$
$$b \approx 13.3 \text{ cm}$$

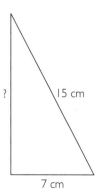

- If you want your students to use the Pythagorean theorem to make sure the heights of their pyramids match that of their prisms, you may want to suggest to them that they pick dimensions for their prisms that set up Pythagorean triples, for example, a 10 × 10 base, making the apothem 5 and a height of 12, yielding a slant height of 13; or a 12 × 12 base, making an apothem of 6 and a height of 8, yielding a slant height of 10. Pythagorean triples provide friendly numbers for finding the volume.

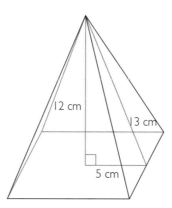

Extension

Have students carry out a similar investigation using other prisms, such as triangular, pentagonal, hexagonal, and octagonal prisms, to verify that the formula for any right pyramid is volume $= \dfrac{\text{area of base level} \cdot \text{height}}{3}$

 The Difference an Angle Makes I

Related Topics: algebraic thinking, functions, proportional reasoning

Overview

Students construct related pairs of cones and cylinders. Then, using rice, they find the volume of each solid and graph and analyze their results to discover the formula for finding the volume of a cone.

Materials

- *The Difference an Angle Makes 1* recording sheets, 1 per student (see Blackline Masters)
- grid paper, 1 $8\frac{1}{2}$-by-11-inch sheet per student
- rice, about 300 milliliters per pair of students
- thick paper or thin tagboard containing a circle with a diameter of either 9 centimeters or 12 centimeters, with one or more diameters drawn, 1 sheet per pair of students
- protractors, 1 per pair of students
- metric rulers, 1 per pair of students
- graduated cylinders or beakers, 1 per student
- calculators, 1 per student

- jumbo paper clips or small pieces of wire the same thickness as a paper clip, 1 per pair of students
- small lumps of clay, 1 per pair of students
- washable fine-line markers, 1 per pair of students
- optional: compasses, 1 per pair of students
- optional: models illustrating the following concepts: solid, central angle, slant height, sector, and base and height of a cone and cylinder

Vocabulary: base of a prism or cone, cubic centimeters, central angle, height of a cylinder or cone, milliliters, net, sector, solid, volume

Prerequisite Skills and Concepts

Students should be familiar with finding the volume of a cylinder and know how to apply the Pythagorean theorem.

Instructions

1. Tell the students that they will work in pairs to find and analyze patterns in the volumes of pairs of related cones and cylinders. Using models or drawings, introduce or review the following terms: *solid, central angle, slant height, sector* of a circle, and *base* and *height* of a cone and cylinder.

2. Demonstrate how to make a cone from the paper circle by removing a sector of a particular size (see recording sheet for instructions).

3. Discuss making a net for a cylinder on the leftover tagboard and constructing the cylinder from the net.

4. Distribute the recording sheets and outline the following procedures:
   a. For each step, one of you will do the construction and measuring. Your partner will check the work for accuracy.
   b. Switch roles with your partner for each new step.
   c. Make a paper funnel out of a used piece of paper to pour the rice from a cone or cylinder into the graduated cylinder.
   d. Record all data on your recording sheet.

5. Explain that the graduated cylinder is for measuring the quantity of rice to determine the volume of each solid.

6. Pass out the materials and circulate as the students work to spot problems and answer questions.

7. When all students have completed the investigation, lead a class discussion based on their findings, observations, and conclusions.

Notes to the Teacher

This activity provides hands-on experience in constructing a cone and a cylinder that have congruent bases and the same heights, finding the volume of both solids, and using patterns in the class data to discover a formula for finding the volume of a cone.

When you use this activity with your students for the first time, you may find the following comments useful:

◈ Alter or omit one or more parts of this investigation when it is not appropriate for the level of your students. For example, you might have all student pairs work with same-size circles. Or you might omit the graphing component.

◈ Be sure each sector size listed in the table on the recording sheet is assigned to one or more pairs of students for each of the two circle sizes. If your class is too small to do this, ask students who finish early to construct a second pair of solids.

◈ Caution students to save the remainder of their tagboard or paper after cutting out their sector; they will use it for drawing the net for their cylinder.

◈ To measure the height of the cones, suggest the following technique: Use a jumbo paper clip straightened out or another piece of wire of similar thickness. Stick the paper clip or wire into a small lump of clay on a tabletop so that it is perpendicular to the table and one end touches the tabletop. Lower the cone carefully so that the paper clip or wire goes through the point of the cone; press down slightly on the cone to be sure the entire circumference is touching the table. Use a washable thin-line marker to make a mark on the paper clip or wire at the tip of the cone. Remove the paper clip or wire, and measure its length from its bottom to the mark.

◈ Students can use the Pythagorean theorem to find the height of their cone since the slant height of the cone always equals the radius of the starting circle and one leg of the right triangle is the radius of the cone. Thus, the missing leg is the height of the cone. The example below is for a circle with a 90-degree sector removed. The circle had a diameter of 12 centimeters.

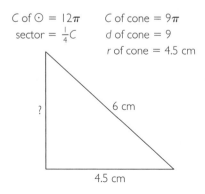

C of $\odot = 12\pi$ C of cone $= 9\pi$
sector $= \frac{1}{4}C$ d of cone $= 9$
           r of cone $= 4.5$ cm

?

6 cm

4.5 cm

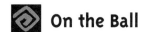 **On the Ball**

Related Topics: surface area of a sphere, volume of a pyramid

Overview

Students find the formula for the volume of a sphere by using a model to physically break down a sphere into pyramids. Through this experience, students' understanding of the formula deepens, and if needed, they can usually re-create the formula by thinking back to this investigation.

Materials

◈ foam or clay balls, 3 to 4 inches in diameter, 1 per small group of students

◈ putty knives or other implements to cut the balls, 1 per small group of students

◈ Snap Cubes or other manipulatives in the shape of a cube, at least 36 per small group of students

◈ *On the Ball* recording sheets, 1 per student (see Blackline Masters)

◈ blank overhead transparencies, 1 per small group of students

◈ overhead pens, 1 per small group of students

Vocabulary: apex, great circle, hemisphere, pi, pyramid, radius, sphere, surface area

Prerequisite Skills and Concepts

Students need to know the formulas for the surface area of a sphere, the volume of a rectangular pyramid, and the area of a circle and how to use them.

Instructions

1. Ask students to offer definitions for the terms *apex*, *surface area*, *radius*, and *great circle* of a sphere. Verify correct answers. Review the formulas for the surface area of a sphere and the volume of a pyramid.

2. Explain that each group of students will use a ball to investigate and make a conjecture about the formula for finding the volume of a sphere.

3. Demonstrate the beginning steps of the investigation:

   a. Cut the ball into hemispheres. Ask a volunteer to point out to the class the radius of the sphere.

b. Now cut a piece out of one hemisphere so that it is shaped as much as possible like a square pyramid with a bulging base, as shown below.

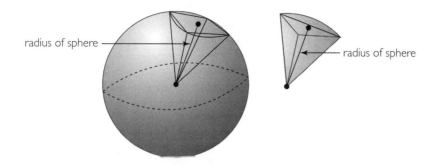

Explain that each group should cut several such "pyramids" from the sphere, always making sure that the base of each "pyramid" is part of the surface area of the sphere and that the apex of the pyramid is at the center of the sphere.

4. Provide students with the materials and the recording sheets, which include directions for the steps they should follow and the questions that they should answer in writing. Emphasize that each student should be prepared to explain the group's findings and thinking in a whole-class discussion.

5. Have each group of students summarize its findings and conclusions on an overhead transparency.

6. When everyone is ready, have groups share their findings and conclusions. Discuss any differences among the groups and help students to reconcile those differences.

Notes to the Teacher

Research shows that students commonly have difficulty remembering formulas unless they investigate and construct those formulas themselves. This activity offers students the opportunity to find the formula for the volume of a sphere through a guided investigation.

When you use this activity with your classes for the first time, you may find the following comments useful:

◈ It is often difficult for students to cut the small "pyramids" from the sphere. If each group has at least one example that closely approximates the desired shape, the group can use that "pyramid" to think about what would happen if the entire sphere were cut into congruent shapes. The most important result of this part of the investigation is that each group realizes that (1) the height of each "pyramid" has the same measure as the radius of the sphere and (2) the sum of the areas of the bases of the "pyramids" is the same as the surface area of the sphere.

◈ The last piece of the puzzle is for each group to realize that this situation is like the rectangular prisms in Part 1 of the recording sheet. That is, the volume of the sphere can be found by adding the volumes of all the "pyramids":

$$\text{volume of each pyramid} = \frac{\text{area of base} \cdot \text{radius}}{3}$$

volume of sphere = sum of the volumes of all the "pyramids"

$$\text{volume of sphere} = \frac{\text{area of base} \cdot \text{radius}}{3} + \frac{\text{area of base} \cdot \text{radius}}{3}$$
$$+ \frac{\text{area of base} \cdot \text{radius}}{3} \ldots$$

Since the sum of the areas of all the bases $= 4\pi r^2$, volume $= \frac{4\pi r^2 \cdot r}{3}$ or volume $= \frac{4\pi r^3}{3}$

Blocks of Cheese

Related Topics: spatial visualization, surface area

Overview
In this activity, students imagine that a cheese company is seeking advice about the most economical shape for the blocks of cheese it manufactures, each of which has a volume of 36 cubic units. Students build models and draw nets of all possible rectangular prisms with this volume. Each group then makes recommendations to the company.

Materials
◈ Snap Cubes or other small cubes, 36 per pair of students
◈ grid paper with unit length matching the side length of the cubes, at least 2 sheets per student
◈ rulers, 1 per student

Vocabulary: cubic units, dimensions, net, prism, rectangular prism, square units, surface area, volume

Instructions

1. Ask the students to imagine that they have been asked to make a recommendation to a company that sells cheese in the shape of rectangular prisms. Each identical block of cheese contains 36 cubic centimeters and is covered with red wax. The

company wants to know what is the most economical shape to manufacture, that is, what dimensions would be most profitable.

2. Ask students to offer definitions for the terms *prism*, *rectangular prism*, and *volume*. Verify correct answers or provide them, if needed.

3. To model the task, give the class a simpler problem to work on in pairs. Hand out the materials and ask students to suppose that the company wants each block of cheese to be a rectangular prism with a volume of 8 cubic centimeters. Tell the pairs to build such a prism with their cubes.

4. When everyone is ready, ask volunteers to describe what they have built. Point out that the volume of a prism can be thought of as rectangular layers of the same number of cubes stacked like a tower. This concept of volume seen as layers is a powerful one and one of the main learning objectives of this lesson.

5. Now ask volunteers for the dimensions of the base of their prism and the number of layers of cubes in the prism. Record examples on the board, as illustrated below.

Base	Number of Layers	Volume
1 cm × 4 cm	2	8 cm³
2 cm × 4 cm	1	8 cm³
1 cm × 1 cm	8	8 cm³
1 cm × 8 cm	1	8 cm³
2 cm × 2 cm	2	8 cm³

Notice that a base of 4 × 1 and others are not included since they are equivalent to dimensions in the list.

6. When all possibilities have been listed, ask students to offer a definition for *net*. Work together to draw an appropriate net for the first example on the board, as shown below.

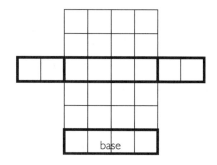

Using grid paper, make, cut, and fold the net to show that it exactly covers the rectangular prism having a base of 1 cube by 4 cubes and two layers. Have students figure out the area of the net. Explain that this net represents the red wax that covers the cheese and that its size, 28 square centimeters, is the surface area of the block of cheese. Ask if a different-looking net could exactly fit around the same prism. Give students a chance to find one and share their results.

7. Now ask the following questions: "Can the net we made together fit exactly around any other prism in our list?" (yes) and "Will all the nets that fit around a rectangular prism with a volume of eight cubic centimeters contain twenty-eight square centimeters?" (no).

8. Return to the original problem of finding different shapes for cheese blocks with a volume of 36 cubic centimeters. Explain to the students that they are to work in pairs to determine how many different rectangular prisms are possible that contain 36 cubic centimeters. Give the following directions:
   a. Build each rectangular prism with thirty-six cubes.
   b. For each prism, record the dimensions of the base, the number of layers of cubes it contains, and its volume.
   c. Draw an appropriate net and find its area.
   d. Use your findings to decide which rectangular prism is the best shape for the cheese company to manufacture.
   e. Compose a letter to the owner of the cheese company that includes your recommendation and your rationale. Include drawings and calculations.

9. When everyone is ready, have groups share their recommendations with the class and summarize the mathematical ideas of this lesson.

Notes to the Teacher

This activity provides a hands-on experience in which students build all possible rectangular prisms of a specific volume. The mathematical focus is on thinking of the volume of a rectangular prism as identical layers in a tower. Students also create nets for the prisms they build and compare their surface areas.

When you use this activity with your students for the first time, you may find the following comments useful:

❧ The sample problem illustrates that the prisms in this lesson are defined by the dimensions of their base and *not* by the way they are oriented. For example, if you list a prism with a 1-by-4-centimeter base with two layers and then another student offers a 4-by-1-centimeter base with two layers as a different prism, turn the original prism so the students can see that the base remains the same. Later, when the nets are drawn, have students show that every net that will work for a 1-by-4-by-2-centimeter prism will also work for a 4-by-1-by-2-centimeter prism.

❖ Drawing, cutting, and testing the various nets requires a lot of time. You may want to assign each pair a specific number of nets or have students finish this part of the lesson as homework, especially if they have prior experience with making nets.

❖ Be sure to discuss the following mathematical ideas as the students share their recommendations:

- The volume of any rectangular prism can be thought of as a rectangular base with congruent layers of cubes stacked to form a tower. This way of thinking of volume as successive layers can be applied to all prisms.
- Knowing the volume of a rectangular prism does not tell you its surface area. Likewise, knowing the surface area of a prism does not tell you its volume.
- For prisms with the same volume, the surface area can vary significantly.
- For prisms with the same volume, the surface area will be smaller as the dimensions get closer to each other (or as the shape of the prism gets closer to a cube).
- Making or drawing a net for a prism is one way to find its surface area.
- Rectangular prisms with the same dimensions always have the same volume and surface area. This is true for all prisms.

Extension

Tell students that the cheese company again wants their advice. The red wax the company buys to cover each 36 cubic centimeters of cheese comes in sheets that are 200 centimeters by 200 centimeters. Which net is the most economical for the company to use—that is, which net will give the least amount of waste? Tell students to be prepared to demonstrate and explain the mathematics that supports their choice.

 ## Bigger and Bigger

Related Topics: algebraic thinking, numerical patterns

Overview

Students find patterns for a particular set of growing rectangular prisms. They then find values for the base, altitude, height, surface area, and volume for some of the prisms and analyze their findings to make generalizations about the entire set of prisms.

Materials

❖ *Bigger and Bigger* recording sheets, 1 per student (see Blackline Masters)
❖ cubes, any size (as long as each pair of students uses the same size), at least 36 per pair of students
❖ quadrille grid paper, 1 sheet per student
❖ colored pencils, 1 each of two different colors per pair of students

Vocabulary: altitude, base, height, linear function, prism, rectangular prism, surface area, volume

Instructions

1. Explain to the students that they will investigate the surface areas and volumes of a particular set of rectangular prisms to find patterns and make generalizations about the set.

2. Ask students to offer definitions for the terms *rectangular prism*, *surface area*, and *volume*. Verify correct answers.

3. On the board, create a table like this:

Surface Area				
Stage	**Base Layer**		**height**	**What I See**	**Surface Area**
	Length	*Width*			

4. Then, using two cubes, build a rectangular prism like this:

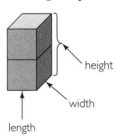

Explain that this is the first stage in a set of rectangular prisms that have a particular growing pattern, and write *1* in the first column of the table. Ask volunteers to provide the length, width, and height of the model and fill in those values.

Surface Area				
Stage	**Base Layer**		**height**	**What I See**	**Surface Area**
	Length	*Width*			
1	1	1	2		

5. Explain that the next column, "What I See," is very important because it will show how each of them finds the surface area for each stage. Add that the information written for each stage must follow the same pattern as Stage 1. Explain that they should not worry if their partner uses a different method since there is more than one way to find the surface area of a rectangular prism. Finally, count the number of exposed cube faces and enter *10* in the last column.

6. Distribute the cubes and recording sheets and instruct the class to carry out the investigation as directed on the recording sheets. Circulate while students are working, offering help when needed.

7. When all pairs have completed the investigation and shared their findings, lead a whole-class discussion. Discuss any differences and help students to reconcile those differences.

Notes to the Teacher

This activity reinforces the differences between surface area and volume and gives students practice in finding patterns. Looking for patterns in a particular set of rectangular prisms helps students extend their thinking about relationships between surface area and volume and strengthens their algebraic reasoning and problem-solving skills.

When you use this activity with your classes for the first time, you may find the following comments useful:

◈ Building the early stages of the rectangular prisms is an important step and should not be skipped. It helps students hone their visualization skills while finding the asked-for values for the models they build. It also helps them clarify their definitions of *length*, *width*, *height*, *surface area*, and *volume*.

◈ Creating separate expanded T-charts provides opportunities for the class to discuss equivalent expressions. Equivalence can be demonstrated through simplification, as shown below, or by substituting different stage numbers for *n* in the last expression in the following table.

STUDENT A

Stage	Base Layer		height	What I See	Surface Area
	Length	Width			
1	1	1	2	$2 \times 1^2 + 4(1 \times 2)$	10
2	2	2	4	$2 \times 2^2 + 4(2 \times 4)$	40
3	3	3	6	$2 \times 3^2 + 4(3 \times 6)$	90
4	4	4	8	$2 \times 4^2 + 4(4 \times 8)$	160
5	5	5	10	$2 \times 5^2 + 4(5 \times 10)$	250
10	10	10	20	$2 \times 10^2 + 4(10 \times 20)$	1,000
100	100	100	200	$2 \times 100^2 + 4(100 \times 200)$	100,000
n	n	n	$2n$	$2 \times n^2 + 4(n)(2n)$ or $2n^2 + 8n^2$ or $10n^2$	$10n^2$

STUDENT B

Surface Area					
Stage	**Base Layer**		**height**	**What I See**	**Surface Area**
	Length	*Width*			
1	1	1	2	$(4)(2 \times 1) + 1^2 + 1^2$	10
2	2	2	4	$(4)(4 \times 2) + 2^2 + 2^2$	40
3	3	3	6	$(4)(6 \times 3) + 3^2 + 3^2$	90
4	4	4	8	$(4)(8 \times 4) + 4^2 + 4^2$	160
5	5	5	10	$(4)(10 \times 5) + 5^2 + 5^2$	250
10	10	10	20	$(4)(20 \times 10) + 10^2 + 10^2$	1,000
100	100	100	200	$(4)(200 \times 100) + 100^2 + 100^2$	100,000
n	n	n	$2n$	$(4)(2n \times n) + n^2 + n^2$ or $8n^2 + 2n^2$ or $10n^2$	$10n^2$

Having each student build her own T-charts honors each student's way of interpreting the pattern. It also increases the chances for every student to make sense of the expressions for the nth stage of the patterns.

◈ Following are some of the patterns often found by students (in response to Question 1 on the recording sheet):

- The length of the base for each stage is one more than the length of the base in the previous stage.
- The length of the base layer is the same as the stage number.
- The length of the base layer for each stage is one more than the base layer in the previous stage.
- The width of the base layer is twice the stage number.
- The width of the base layer for each stage is two more than the width in the previous stage.
- The height is the same as the stage number.
- The pattern of increases in surface area between consecutive stages is 30, 50, 70, and so on. These increases grow by a constant increment of 20.
- The surface area of any stage is two times the stage number squared plus eight times the stage number squared ($2n^2 + 8n^2$ or $10n^2$).
- The pattern of increases in the volume between consecutive stages is 14, 38, 74, 122, and so on. These increases grow by 24, 36, 48, and so on. Thus, these increases grow by a constant increment of 12.
- The volume for any stage is the stage number squared times twice the stage number [$(n^2)(2n)$ or $2n^3$].

If the students do not find any of these patterns, elicit them with questions. In addition, students will most likely find other patterns not mentioned here.

◈ Student explanations for how some of the patterns fit with what they know about surface area and volume (in response to Questions 1, 2, and 3 on the recording sheet) often include the following:

- Both surface area and volume grow from stage to stage because as each dimension of a prism is increased, the number of units needed to cover it (area) and the number of cubic units it will contain (volume) must also increase.
- Surface area does not grow by the same amount for each new stage. Instead, it grows at an increasing rate. This makes sense because for each face, the area must include the entire strip of square units added along the top and the strip of new square units running down one side. You can see this in the drawings as well: more small squares must be added on each face for each new increase in the stage number.
- Volume grows at an increasing rate because whenever the value of all three factors is increased, the new product will increase. You can also see this in the drawings: more small cubes must be added for each new increase in the stage number.
- Volume grows faster than surface area because, for surface area, you are adding *rows* of new squares whereas for volume, you are adding whole *layers* of new cubes. You can see this in both the drawings and the models.

◈ In response to Question 3, student graphs for relating length to surface area and length to volume should approximate the following example.

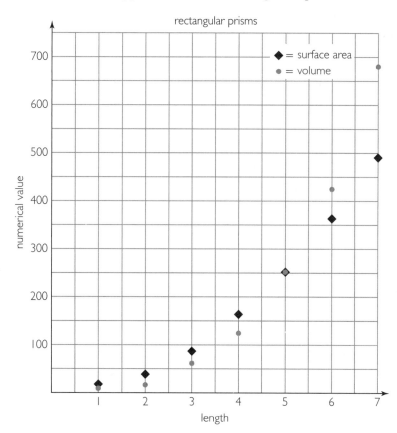

❖ Students should observe that neither the graph for surface area nor the one for volume for this set of rectangles is a linear function. Each set of points falls on a curve, indicating that the growth pattern is not constant. This observation fits with the drawings, values in the table, and rules the students find for these rectangular prisms.

❖ The graph for volume of this set of rectangular prisms grows at a faster rate than the graph for surface area. The points representing volume have lower y-values for the first few stages, but the y-values become larger than those for surface areas with the same x-values since the growth rate for volume continues to increase at a faster rate. Again, this observation fits with the drawings, values in the table, and rules the students find for these rectangular prisms.

❖ Students may have difficulty understanding that these patterns would not hold for any set of rectangular prisms. If so, have them work with the first few stages for a new group of rectangular prisms with a different growing pattern for the length, width, height, or any combination of these dimensions to see the differences between their old and new data.

❖ Have students explain their strategies for finding the missing values for Question 5 on the recording sheet. Such sharing can lead to other students seeing the clarity or efficiency of a strategy they did not use.

Extension

Have students enter data from this investigation into a spreadsheet, using Excel or another software program, and change the growth patterns to see what happens with different sets of rectangular prisms. While there will be differences in the results as the dimensions change, the new expressions for surface area and volume will always be related to the familiar formulas for surface area and volume of rectangular prisms, and the growth patterns for surface area and volume will always be increasing.

 ## Cylinder Mystery

Related Topics: algebraic thinking, area, circumference, patterns

Overview
Students make six different cylinders and fill them with popcorn to gather data and compare their volumes. They then find patterns and make generalizations about the relationships between changes in the dimensions of their cylinders and the changes in their volumes.

Materials

❖ *Cylinder Mystery* recording sheets, 1 per student (see Blackline Masters)
❖ Sets of tagboard that include 2 8.5-by-9-inch pieces, 1 16.5-by-3-inch piece, 1 24.5-by-3-inch piece, and 2 8-by-8-inch pieces, 1 set per pair of students
❖ 24-inch strips of masking tape, 1 per pair of students
❖ popcorn (popped), approximately 3 cups per pair of students
❖ zip-top plastic bags to hold popcorn, 1 per pair of students
❖ rulers, 1 per pair of students

Vocabulary: circumference, cylinder, diameter, dimensions, factor, height, radius, volume

Prerequisite Skills and Concepts

Students should know the volume formula for cylinders and how to use it. They should be able to find the diameter, radius, and area of a circle when given its circumference.

Instructions

1. Prior to the lesson, prepare a tagboard cylinder or choose a container (a gallon zip-top bag works fine) to hold the popcorn that you will pour from the cylinder you will construct during the demonstration portion of the lesson (see Instruction 3).

2. Explain to the students that they will be making several cylinders of specified sizes and comparing their volumes in order to find patterns and make generalizations about the relationships between the dimensions and the volume.

3. Demonstrate the method students should use to construct and fill each cylinder. Use a different-size piece of tagboard than those the students will be using, such as 4 inches by 6.5 inches. Explain to the students that they first need to determine which piece of tagboard should be used to construct a particular cylinder and check its measurements. Demonstrate measuring and recording the dimensions of the tagboard that you are using. Identify which edges are to serve as the height and which are to serve as the circumference. In this example, the edge for height could be 4 inches and the edge for circumference, 6.5 inches.

4. Along either *height* edge of the tagboard, draw a line that is 0.5 inch from the edge and parallel to it. Explain that this 0.5-inch strip will serve as the overlap for taping the tagboard into a cylindrical shape. Thus, the circumference equals 6 inches.

5. Form a tube, overlapping the 0.5-inch strip, and tape firmly along the seam. Point out that this shape is a cylinder with no top or bottom.

6. Place an 8-by-8-inch square of tagboard beneath the tube to serve as the bottom of the cylinder and demonstrate holding the square firmly in place while filling the topless cylinder with popcorn and then pouring it into another container.

7. Ask students to work in pairs to find the volume of the cylinder you just constructed, using only the measures you recorded on the board (the original dimensions of the tagboard). Have them explain procedures, including the following steps:

   a. identifying the height of the cylinder (4 inches) on the model and relating it to the sides of the original piece of cardboard (4 inches)

   b. identifying the circumference of the cylinder (6 inches) on the model and relating it to the sides of the original piece of cardboard (6.5 inches)

   c. working from the measure of the circumference to find the radius:

$$C = \pi \cdot d$$
$$6 = \pi \cdot d$$
$$\frac{6}{\pi} = d$$
$$\frac{6}{2\pi} = \frac{d}{2}$$
$$\approx 0.96 \text{ inches} = \text{radius}$$

   d. finding the approximate volume of the cylinder in cubic inches by using the volume formula:

$$V = \pi r^2 h$$
$$V \approx 3.14 \cdot (0.96)^2 \cdot 4$$
$$V \approx 11.6 \text{ cubic inches}$$

8. Pass out the materials and recording sheets to the class and go over the directions, if necessary.

9. While the students are working, circulate to spot problems and to answer questions.

10. When all groups have completed the investigation, lead a whole-class discussion about their findings, generalizations, and understandings. Be sure the discussion includes an explanation for *why* the patterns of change when increasing the height of a cylinder are different from the patterns of change when increasing the circumference.

Notes to the Teacher

This activity provides the framework for students to discover that multiplying the height of a cylinder by a particular factor and multiplying the radius of the same cylinder by the same factor have different effects on the cylinder's volume. Students can discover that doubling the height of a cylinder, for example, only doubles the volume of the original cylinder, whereas doubling the radius of the cylinder quadruples its volume.

When you use this activity with your classes for the first time, you may find the following comments useful:

◈ If your students need practice planning, measuring, and cutting pieces of tagboard of specific sizes, you can provide each group with two pieces of 12-by-25-inch tagboard instead of precutting the sizes listed in the "Materials" section.

◈ Some students need to label the appropriate sides of the tagboard rectangles with the measures of the height and circumference for each cylinder before they begin constructing the cylinders. This is especially true for the cylinders with a height of 6 inches and those with a height of 9 inches. This helps them avoid errors in using these dimensions as the circumferences of the cylinders.

◈ Students often have difficulty understanding the underlying reason for *why* two different patterns emerge when multiplying the height of a cylinder by a given factor and multiplying the radius of the same cylinder by the same factor. If this confusion arises, have your students make a two-column table as shown below. In the first column, have them write the formula for the volume of a cylinder and then substitute the original height, the height doubled, and the height tripled. In the second column have them write the formula for the volume of a cylinder and then substitute the original radius, the radius doubled, and the radius tripled. For example, for an original cylinder with a height of 3 inches and a circumference of 8 inches:

Original Height	Original Radius
$V = \pi r^2 h$	$V = \pi r^2 h$
$V \approx 3.14 \cdot 1.27 \cdot 1.27 \cdot 3$	$V \approx 3.14 \cdot 1.27 \cdot 1.27 \cdot 3$
Doubling Height	**Doubling Radius**
$V = \pi r^2 h$	$V = \pi r^2 h$
$V \approx 3.14 \cdot 1.27 \cdot 1.27 \cdot 6$	$V \approx 3.14 \cdot 2.55 \cdot 2.55 \cdot 3$
Tripling Height	**Tripling Radius**
$V = \pi r^2 h$	$V = \pi r^2 h$
$V \approx 3.14 \cdot 1.27 \cdot 1.27 \cdot 9$	$V \approx 3.14 \cdot 3.82 \cdot 3.82 \cdot 3$

Without working through the calculations, students can often observe that changing the height affects only one factor in the equation whereas the changing the radius affects two factors. When the height is doubled, the new volume is two times the original volume, and when the height is tripled, the volume is three times the original volume. On the other hand, when the radius is doubled, the new volume is four times the original volume, and when the radius is tripled, the volume is nine times the original volume.

If needed, the students can do the calculations to help reinforce the numerical difference that these two changes make.

Extension

Have students predict and then compare the results they found in this investigation about the growth patterns of volume with those when the dimension(s) of a rectangular prism, pyramid, cone, and/or sphere are changed in ways similar to those required in this investigation.

 ## The Difference an Angle Makes 2

Related Topics: algebraic thinking, nonlinear functions, patterns

Overview

Students work in pairs to construct cones by repeatedly removing sectors from a circle. Using rice, they find the volume of each cone and graph and analyze the results.

Materials

◈ *The Difference an Angle Makes 2* recording sheets, 1 per student (see Blackline Masters)

◈ quadrille grid paper, 1 sheet per student

◈ uncooked rice, about 350 milliliters per pair of students

◈ containers to hold the rice, 1 per pair of students

◈ thick paper or thin tagboard containing a circle with a diameter of 18 centimeters, with the center and one diameter drawn, 1 per pair of students

◈ metric rulers, 1 per pair of students

◈ protractors, 1 per pair of students

◈ graduated cylinders or beakers, 1 per pair of students

◈ optional: compasses, 1 per pair of students

◈ optional: models that can be used to demonstrate the concepts of central angle, sector diameter, circumference, and slant height

Vocabulary: adjacent angles, angle, central angle, circumference, diameter, sector, slant height, vertical angles, volume

Instructions

Note: This investigation may take longer than one class period.

1. Tell the students that they will work in pairs to find and analyze patterns when different-size sectors are removed from the same circle and the remaining part of

the circle is made into a cone each time. Ask students to define *vertical angles* and *adjacent angles*. Using a model or drawing, introduce or review the terms *central angle*, *sector*, *diameter*, and *circumference* of a circle, and *slant height* of a cone.

2. Using a circle with an arbitrary sector removed, demonstrate how to make a cone.

3. Distribute the recording sheets and outline the following procedures:

   a. For each step, one of you draws the angle, and the other checks the work for accuracy.

   b. Switch roles with your partner for each new step.

   c. Before making any cuts, exchange your circle with another pair to check the accuracy of your work.

   d. Make a paper funnel out of a used piece of paper to pour the rice from a cone into the graduated cylinder.

   e. Record the data for each cone in the table on the recording sheet before making the next cone. This is important because you will no longer have that cone once you begin to make the next one.

   f. Look for patterns and think about relationships in the data as you do the investigation.

4. Pass out the materials and circulate as the students work so that you can spot problems and answer questions.

5. When all students have completed the investigation, lead a class discussion based on their findings, observations, and conclusions.

Notes to the Teacher

In this activity students practice drawing and measuring angles, construct variously sized cones by removing sectors from a circle, and gather data. Then they graph the data, find and analyze patterns in the data, and explore a cubic function.

When you use this activity with your students for the first time, you may find the following comments useful:

◈ Alter or omit one or more parts of this investigation when it is not appropriate for the level of your students. For example, you might require each pair of students to make only one or two of the cones and then have everyone share all the sets of cones to gather data.

◈ Most students are surprised to find that the volume of a cone made after cutting out a 60-degree sector is actually larger than the volume of a cone made after cutting out a 30-degree sector. Have an extra set of cones available for students who, after having gathered and graphed all their data, want to verify a set of their volume data, such as this one.

◈ Ask students who finish early to make cones with a different central angle for the removed sectors. Students most often choose to investigate sectors with 45 degrees and/or 75 degrees.

Extensions

Distribute one square sheet of grid paper to each student in the class. Tell them to remove one unit square from each corner of the sheet and fold the paper to make an open box. Have each student find the volume of the box and share the results. Then tell them to experiment by removing squares with larger and larger side lengths to find the box that has the largest volume.

After repeating this activity with several different-size paper squares, you can extend the exploration by allowing the students to use side lengths for the removed squares that are not whole numbers and/or you can have the students investigate this same problem using rectangular sheets of paper of different sizes.

Graphing the data adds to the power of this investigation as students can see the largest volume in the graph.

Rates and Ratios

● ●

Introduction

Ratios and rates, along with proportional reasoning, represent a shift in thinking from additive reasoning to multiplicative reasoning. Imagine presenting the following problem to your middle school students.

> On Tuesday, I noticed that two plants in the office were flowering. One had 6 blooms on it; the other had 12. On Wednesday, I noticed that the plants had 8 and 15 blooms, respectively. Which plant had the greatest increase in blooms?

Students using additive reasoning will choose the second plant, explaining that its increase was one more than that of the first plant since its blooms went from twelve to fifteen and the first plant went from six to eight. Students using multiplicative reasoning will choose the first plant, responding that on Wednesday, the first plant had $1\frac{1}{3}$ times as many blooms as on Tuesday while the second plant had only $1\frac{1}{4}$ times as many blooms. Alternatively, they may express the idea conversely, saying that the first plant had $\frac{2}{6}$ or $\frac{1}{3}$ more blooms on Wednesday than it did on Tuesday, while the second plant had only $\frac{3}{12}$ or $\frac{1}{4}$ more blooms.

The activities in this chapter help students learn to find, express, and explain part-to-part ratios, part-to-whole ratios, rates, and unit rates, based on data they gather. They also help students realize that using proportions is a powerful problem-solving tool. In the lesson *If I Were a . . .* (page 108), students use facts from a popular book to set up equivalent ratios about themselves and an animal. In *Exploring Rates* (page 112), the students perform three tasks—reading a designated passage, shooting hoops, and tracing stars. They determine their personal rate for each task, and then they find the average rate for the class. In the activity *Hello, Proportions* (page 116), students are introduced to proportions through verbal analogies, an effective alternative to the typical textbook method.

Other lessons in this chapter continue to engage students with ratios, rates, or both, in a wide range of contexts.

❖ In *Unpumped Prices* (page 122), students predict the unit price of a variety of liquid products, and convert the actual price to cost per gallon to compare the prices.

- In *Go for the Golden 1* (page 129), students analyze the patterns in ratios of successive Fibonacci numbers and construct a near-golden rectangle.
- In *Could It Be?* (page 125), students use a fictional journey from an adolescent novel to deepen their understanding of the relationships among distance, rate, and time.
- In *Swinging Rates* (page 134), students apply their knowledge of circles and the relationships among distance, rate, and time to investigate the rates of swinging pendulums.
- In *What's with the Factor?* (page 132), students discover what happens to both the ratio of length to surface area and the ratio of length to volume as the dimensions for a rectangular prism are multiplied by the same factor.

Communication of mathematical thinking as well as at least one idea for extending the activity are built into each lesson.

 ## If I Were a . . .

Related Topics: area, distance/rate/time, length, mass/weight, proportional reasoning, volume/capacity

Overview
Students read unusual facts about an animal, use one of the facts to form equivalent ratios about the animal and themselves, and then solve for the unknown value. Finally, they make the analogy clearer by using a real-life unit of measure.

Materials
- *If I Were a . . .* instructions, 1 copy per student (see Blackline Masters)
- *If You Hopped Like a Frog,* by David M. Schwartz (1999)
- *Biggest, Strongest, Fastest,* by Steve Jenkins (1995)
- *Actual Size,* by Steve Jenkins (2004)
- 11-by-17-inch paper, 1 sheet per student
- variety of measuring tools such as rulers, yardsticks, meter sticks, measuring tapes, scales, trundle wheels, and measuring cups, enough for students to share
- optional: sources of information for finding the measures of common objects, such as the Internet, almanacs, and other reference books
- optional: colored pencils or fine-line markers, enough for students to share
- optional: calculators, 1 per student

Vocabulary: customary units of measure, metric units of measure, proportion, rate, ratio

Instructions

1. Explain to the class that you will be reading aloud a book that contains unusual facts about animals when they are compared with a person who is about $4\frac{1}{2}$ feet tall and weighs about 60 pounds. Tell them to listen for facts that are most interesting to them and to jot down the animals involved.

2. Read one or more of the books in the "Materials" list to the class at a fairly slow pace so that the students can get the general impact of each comparison and record those that interest them. Then circulate the book(s) among the students.

3. Write this fact on the board: *A 3-inch-long frog can hop 5 feet.* Ask a volunteer to set up a ratio that would compare the length of the frog to the length of its hop. Remind students that the units of measure must be the same. Elicit the ratio 3:60 or 1:20. Ask students to explain what each number represents.

4. Ask a volunteer what his height is. Have a classmate verify the measure, using a yardstick or tape measure. Now write the ratio between the volunteer's height and the distance he could jump if the volunteer were a frog, using *d* for the variable. Ask the class what the *d* stands for and point out that the order is the same as in the ratio for the frog. Ask students for ways to find the value of the variable.

5. Tell the students that each of them will make a poster on which they compare themselves to an animal of their choice. Show them examples to help them understand the rest of the assignment and make clear the quality of the work and the amount of detail that are expected. Be sure you explain (1) that a proportion is not the only way to find the missing value (remind students of the various strategies they used to solve the example problem) and (2) the requirement that the answer must be explained using a real-life "unit of measure." (See Figures 5–1 and 5–2.)

6. Distribute the instruction sheets and other materials and circulate to answer appropriate questions and help with problems.

7. As students finish their posters, have them meet in small groups to pose their problems to each other and/or to present their posters and respond to other students' comments and questions.

8. After all students have met in small groups, lead a class discussion focusing on the mathematics they used and interesting information that they discovered.

Notes to the Teacher

This lesson provides three types of experiences within one activity. It offers (1) an appealing context in which each student creates a pair of ratios and applies mathematical reasoning to make a comparison between them, (2) an opportunity for students

Mathematical Statement: **If I Were a Whooping Crane . . .**

A whooping crane that is 4 feet tall has a 16 inch neck. If I were built like a whooping crane, I would have a neck $23\frac{2}{3}$ inches long. My neck would be nearly as long as a stack of five soda cans!

Mathematical Reasoning:

Setting up My Proportion:

I decided to do all my calculations in inches. Since there are twelve inches in a foot, an average whooping crane of four feet is 4 × 12 or 48 inches tall, and the ratio of its height to its neck is 48:16 (or 3:1 simplified). I am 5′11″ tall which is 5 × 12 + 11 or 71 inches tall. The ratio of my height to my "whooping crane neck" would be 71:x. Since I wanted the ratios to be equivalent, I could use the proportion $\frac{3}{1} = \frac{71}{x}$ to solve my problem.

Solving My Proportion:

Since the whooping crane's ratio was so simple, I needed only to find the scale factor that would change 3 to 71. Since 71 ÷ 3 = $23\frac{2}{3}$, and 1 × any number is that number, my neck would be $23\frac{2}{3}$ inches long if I were built like a whooping crane.

Making Sense of My Answer:

Although $23\frac{2}{3}$ inches is pretty easy for me to imagine since it is so close to two feet, if I were trying to help someone understand how long that measure is in an everyday way, I measured a soda can and found it to be $4\frac{3}{4}$ inches tall. Since $23\frac{2}{3} ÷ 4\frac{3}{4} = 4\frac{56}{57}$, which is, of course, very close to 5, my neck would be nearly as long as a stack of five soda cans.

Figure 5–1 *Building measurement sense through mathematical analogies: student sample 1*

to better understand the importance of order and units when comparing ratios, and (3) an experience that uses familiar objects to build meaning for the size of quantities such as a distance of 100 feet or a weight of 200 kilograms.

When you use this activity with your students for the first time, you may find the following comments useful:

◈ Read the endnotes in *If You Hopped Like a Frog* and share them with the class in some way. Students will need some of the information provided in those notes to set up their ratios. Also, the notes always seem to increase students' motivation to find good examples of well-known objects to make the measure they find more understandable to their classmates.

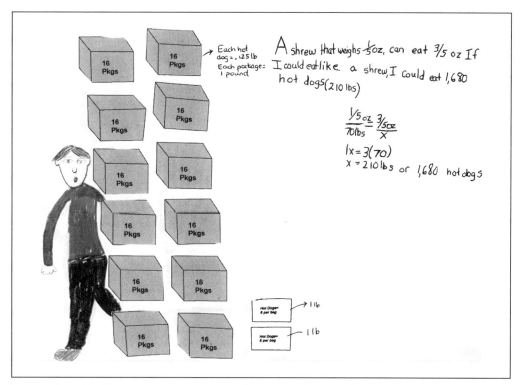

Each hot dog = .125 lb
Each package = 1 pound

A shrew that weighs 5 oz, can eat 3/5 oz If I could eat like a shrew, I could eat 1,680 hot dogs (210 lbs)

$$\frac{1/5 \, oz}{70 \, lbs} = \frac{3/5 \, oz}{x}$$

$1x = 3(70)$
$x = 210 \, lbs$ or $1,680$ hot dogs

Figure 5–2 *Building measurement sense through mathematical analogies: student sample 2*

◈ Using the books *Biggest, Strongest, Fastest* and *Actual Size*, by Steve Jenkins, as resources gives students more choices for their individual ratio comparisons. Extra fact finding will be required by students using *Biggest, Strongest, Fastest*; thus, this book provides a way to differentiate instruction within a class. The illustrations in *Actual Size* are visually stunning because they have a 1:1 ratio with the real creatures that are discussed.

◈ If you want your class to focus on either the metric or the customary system of measurement, you can require that all students convert, when needed, any measures as their first step in this activity. Alternatively, you can ask *every* student to convert the measure given in the book to the other system to provide everyone practice with this skill.

◈ If your students are not proficient with ratios, have them work in pairs to check each other at several points during the lesson:
  • after writing down their two ratios (Is the information correct? Are the ratios consistent in order and units of measure?)
  • after finding the missing measure (Is the method used a sound one? Is the answer correct? Can the person clearly explain her thinking and procedures?)
  • after finishing the comparison of their solution to a well-known object (Does the chosen object actually make the solution easier for most people to understand? Is the comparison mathematically correct? Can the person clearly explain his thinking and procedures?)

◈ If, after you show the sample student work, your students need further clarification about using a real-life unit of measure to help others understand the magnitude of their answer, present the following example to them: "Suppose your conclusion is 'If I could jump like a frog, I could jump twelve hundred inches, or one hundred feet.' You could do research to find that a basketball court is fifty feet wide and then explain on your poster, 'A basketball court is fifty feet wide, so if I could jump like a frog, I could jump the width of two basketball courts.'"

◈ Look for opportunities to increase the depth of students' understanding of ratio through the students' work. For example, in *If You Hopped Like a Frog,* the author states that a 1-foot-long chameleon has a tongue 6 inches long. In *Actual Size,* the author states that a 7-foot-long anteater has a tongue that is 2 feet long. Ask students which statement is more amazing and why. They should be able to reason that the ratio of body length to tongue length is 2:1 for the chameleon whereas the same ratio for the anteater is 7:2. Thus, despite the fact that the anteater has a longer tongue, the chameleon's tongue is proportionally longer for its body length. In fact, if the anteater's tongue were in the same ratio to its body as the chameleon's, the anteater would have a tongue 3 feet 6 inches long!

This kind of questioning can also arise from the student comparisons to well-known objects.

Extensions

◈ If appropriate, ask students to take another student's original ratio, convert it to a different system of measure (customary to metric or vice versa), and complete the steps of the lesson using the other student's personal measurements but a different well-known object for comparison. This can help students get a better sense, for example, that 100 feet and about 305 decimeters represent the same distance and that both can be thought of as either the twice the width of a basketball court or the height of fifty fire hydrants.

◈ Have students, in small groups, share their posters with other math classes that meet at the same time—in the same grade or in another grade, as appropriate. Hearing the presentations is beneficial for both your students and the students in the other classes.

 Exploring Rates

Related Topic: measures of central tendency

Overview

Students perform three familiar tasks in timed trials to determine individual rates of performance. Students then make conjectures about their results and share them in a class discussion.

Materials

❖ *Exploring Rates* recording sheets, 1 of each per student (see Blackline Masters)
❖ *Rows of Stars* sheet, 1 per student (see Blackline Masters)
❖ colored pencils, 1 each of two different colors per student
❖ clocks or watches with a second hand, at least 2
❖ books or passages (approximately 1,200 words) from a book, 1 copy per student
❖ real or toy basketball hoop and ball, at least 1 set

Vocabulary: average, mean, median, mode, per, range, rate, ratio, unit rate

Instructions

1. Explain to the students that each of them will be performing three tasks to help the class determine the rate at which an average person might complete each one. There are two versions of each task.

2. Ask students to offer definitions for the terms *ratio*, *rate*, and *unit rate*. Verify correct answers.

3. Before starting the first task, talk through the task with the whole class so that students will understand what is expected of them.

    a. Tell students to think about the task of running 100 meters forward and that of running the same distance backward.

    b. Ask students which they expect to be larger, the numerical value for yards per second or that for seconds per yard and why.

    c. Next, ask the students to mentally calculate the four rates (one at a time) that correspond with those asked for in the upcoming tasks. Tell them that a person ran the distance forward in 10 seconds and have them find the number of yards per second and the number of seconds per yard. Then tell them the person ran the distance backward in 20 seconds and again have them find the number of yards per second and the number of seconds per yard. Do not discuss at this time how students arrived at their answers; allow each student the opportunity to find the ratios in a way that makes sense to her.

4. Distribute the recording sheets for the first task, reading rates. Explain to students that their first task will be to find and compare their reading rate when reading silently with their reading rate when reading aloud. Further explain that you will give them all the same passage to read and that you will time them.

5. Distribute what they are to read, directing them to put the copy facedown until you say, "Start," or to open their books to the page you have chosen but not to read until you say, "Start." Tell students that when you say, "Start," they are to begin reading silently and continue until you say, "Stop," at which time they will

mark the last word that they have read. When everyone is ready to begin, say, "Start." At the end of 140 seconds, say, "Stop."

6. Now write the number of words in the passage or list each page number of the book on the board with the number of words on it. Announce to the students that they are to count the number of words they read, write it on the recording sheet, and find the two rates that are listed. Then they should share methods and check calculations with a partner.

7. For the second part of this task, repeat the procedure. This time tell the students to read the same passage aloud using an audible, but subdued, voice. Then have students complete the recording sheet by explaining in writing the meaning of the two numerical rates they have determined.

8. Lead a class discussion in which students share the methods they used to find each rate and explain the meaning of each expression, such as *0.3 seconds per word*. Have the class draw a conclusion about which form of the rate (words/second or seconds/word), if any, seems more suitable for each part of the task and make a conjecture about which task people usually do faster, read silently or read aloud.

9. Next divide the class into two groups. Ask one group to do the tracing stars task (using a different colored pencil with each hand) while the other group does the shooting hoops task. Before they perform the tasks, the students should make conjectures about which version of each task people usually do faster. Have at least two students do the timing for each group. When everyone has finished, have the groups switch tasks. If one group finishes before the other, those who have finished can begin doing their calculations until the other group completes its task. (**Note:** If your school has a gym or playground with several basketball hoops, take your students there: the shooting hoops task will go much faster.)

10. Have students share their results in a whole-class discussion.

11. If appropriate, have students determine the class average for each task to see whether their conjectures are supported by the data. You may want to collect the students' papers, compile the data (without using student names) for each task into a list, and have the students do the data analysis on another day.

Notes to the Teacher

This activity provides firsthand experience in determining the rates at which certain tasks can be done. Students share and discuss their methods, make conjectures, and see whether the class data support their thinking.

When you use this activity with your students for the first time, you may find the following comments useful:

❖ Having students share the ways they arrived at their rates for the first task can help students who are finding the rate by rote division without understanding the meaning of the procedure. (See Figure 5–3.)

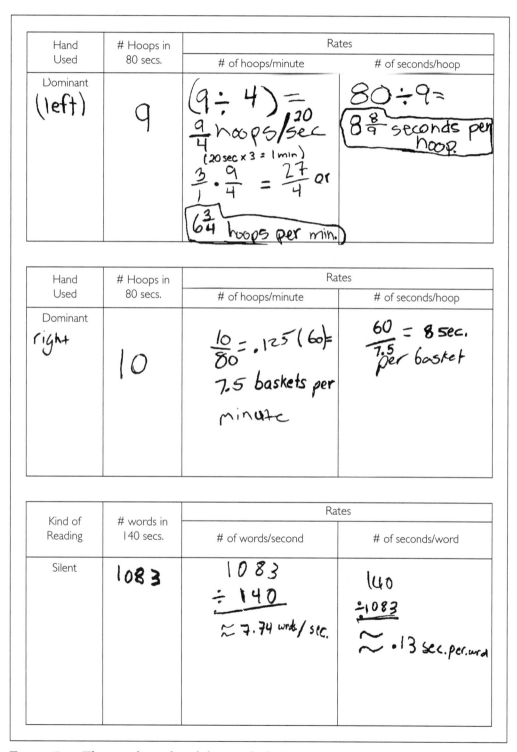

Figure 5–3 *Three students shared their methods for arriving at rates for the tasks.*

- For the tracing stars task, it is helpful to let students trace a few stars with their non-dominant hand, using the bottom row of stars, before starting the timed task.

- Finding the rates is more difficult for tracing stars and shooting hoops than for reading rates because one rate uses seconds and the other, minutes. Circulate among students to help those who do not notice that the unit of time is not the same for these tasks.

- Before determining the average rates for the class, have volunteers review the meanings of *range*, *mean*, *median*, and *mode*. Before doing the calculations, ask the class to choose which of the three averages they believe best describes the data for each task and why. Ask this question again after the class has found all averages.

Extension

Have students work in small groups to devise an investigation similar to this one that can be done outside of school. For example, they could determine rates for doing jumping jacks or copying a paragraph. Each group gathers, compiles, and analyzes the data. Then the groups report their findings to the rest of the class.

Hello, Proportions

Related Topic: proportional reasoning

Overview

Students are introduced to proportions through verbal analogies. They then work with problems to write and solve appropriate proportions.

Materials

- *Hello, Proportions* recording sheets, 1 per student (see Blackline Masters)

Vocabulary: analogy, equivalent, equivalent fractions, proportion

Prerequisite Skills and Concepts

Students should understand the following ideas:

- Equivalent fractions, such as $\frac{2}{4}$ and $\frac{1}{2}$, represent the same amount.
- Multiplying or dividing both the numerator and the denominator of a fraction by the same number results in an equivalent fraction, such as $\frac{2}{3} \times \frac{4}{4} = \frac{8}{12}$.
- The number 1 can be represented by a fraction with the same numerator and denominator, such as $\frac{2}{2}$, $\frac{8}{8}$, and $\frac{25}{25}$.

Instructions

Note: This lesson will take two days to complete.

Day 1

1. Write the following on the board:

$$dog : bark :: cat : \underline{\hspace{2cm}}$$

   Ask if anyone knows how to read this statement. If no one volunteers, explain that a statement written in this form is called an *analogy* and is read, "Dog is to bark as cat is to . . . what?" Ask for volunteers to fill in the blank with a word that makes sense and to explain their reasoning. For example, a student might respond, "'Since the noise a dog makes is a bark, you fill in the blank with the noise a cat makes, 'meow.'"

   All explanations should include the idea that the *relationship* between *dog* and *bark* is the same as the relationship between *cat* and *meow*.

2. Offer more analogies, such as the following examples, until the class seems comfortable with the construct.

   cook : stove :: photographer : <u>camera</u>

   large : small :: cold : <u>hot</u>

   triangle : three :: pentagon : <u>five</u>

   ton : mass :: inch : <u>length</u>

   As the students respond to these examples, point out that the relationship between the pairs stayed the same and that the order in each pair of words remained the same. For example, it would not be correct to write *triangle : three :: five : pentagon*.

3. Return to the first analogy, dog : bark :: cat : meow. Have students discuss with a partner whether the analogy bark : dog :: meow : cat expresses the same relationship.

   Most students will agree that the two analogies are the same and understand that reversing the words in *both* parts of the analogy preserved the relationship, that is, both analogies are still about an animal and the sound it makes. They can also see that, though the original order is different, it remains consistent in both parts.

   Put the following illustration on the board to help students see that the two analogies are equivalent.

$\dfrac{\text{sound 1}}{\text{animal 1}}$ $\downarrow$	$\dfrac{\text{sound 2}}{\text{animal 2}}$ $\downarrow$	
$\dfrac{\text{bark}}{\text{dog}}$	$\dfrac{\text{meow}}{\text{cat}}$	→ sound 1 : sound 2 → animal 1 : animal 2

Point out that there are actually two sets of relationships that appear when the analogy is written in this way. Vertically, there is the sound-to-animal relationship, while horizontally, there is the sound-to-sound and animal-to-animal relationship.

4. Ask students to work in pairs to write the original analogy (dog : bark :: cat : meow) in as many different ways as possible that preserve the equivalence. Here are some possibilities:

cat : dog :: meow : bark   meow : bark :: cat : dog

bark : dog :: meow : cat   dog : cat :: bark : meow

cat : meow :: dog : bark   meow : cat :: bark : dog

Draw or have a student draw a diagram similar to the one shown previously for each of the arrangements that is offered, and ask the students to identify both the vertical and horizontal relationships they see.

5. It is likely that someone will suggest dog : meow :: cat : bark or cat : bark :: dog : meow. If not, suggest it. Draw the diagram below and have students fill in the missing words.

In doing this, students will be able understand that the analogy is not equivalent to the others since vertically the animals are matched with the wrong sounds and, horizontally, the order is reversed.

Tell the students that they will connect analogies to mathematics on the next day.

Day 2

1. Begin by asking students to define an analogy and describe the big ideas they learned the previous day. Next write the following analogy on the board:

2 roses : $4 :: 6 roses : $12

Ask a student to read the expression aloud. Verify that "Two roses is to four dollars as six roses is to twelve dollars" is the correct way to read the expression.

Ask students to discuss with a partner, then share with the class (1) how the analogy compares with the analogies discussed on the first day and (2) whether the analogy is true and why. Most likely, students will point out that the analogy is like the others because it relates the number of roses to the cost, but different because it involves numbers.

They will reason that the analogy is true in a variety of ways. Some might say, "It's three times as much money for three times as many roses." Others might find a unit rate of $2 per rose and multiply by 6 to get $12. Though rare, someone might explain that 2 roses is $\frac{1}{3}$ as many as 6 and $4 is $\frac{1}{3}$ as much as $12.

2. Remind students that it is often helpful to rewrite an analogy in a different form. Write on the board:

$$\frac{2 \text{ roses}}{\$4} = \frac{6 \text{ roses}}{\$12} \quad or \quad \frac{2}{4} = \frac{6}{12}$$

Explain that the second statement is read, "Two is to four as six is to twelve," and contains only numbers. It is called a *proportion*, and it can be thought of in the same way as the analogies that contain only words.

Define a proportion as a mathematical statement that indicates two fractions, ratios, or rates are equivalent. Verify that when two-fourths is multiplied by three-thirds, it becomes six-twelfths. In this context, the number of roses was tripled, or multiplied by three, so the price was also tripled. Thinking in a "vertical" way, point out to students that both denominators are twice their numerators, or that the cost of the roses is always twice the number of roses. The following diagram can help reinforce these ideas.

$\frac{\text{number}}{\text{price}}$ ↓	$\frac{\text{number}}{\text{price}}$ ↓	
$\frac{2 \text{ roses } ↓}{\$4}$	$\frac{6 \text{ roses } ↓}{\$12}$	→ numbers (2 : 6) → price ($4 : $12)

3. Explain to students that proportions can be used to solve many math problems. Ask them to consider the following situation related to the proportion the class has been considering:

> *Suppose 2 roses cost $4. Set up a proportion to find how much 10 roses would cost at the same rate, and then solve it.*

Have students share their results. All should have a proportion equivalent to $\frac{2 \text{ roses}}{\$4} = \frac{10 \text{ roses}}{d \text{ dollars}}$ or $\frac{2}{4} = \frac{10}{d}$. Applying what they know about fractions, they should reason that $\frac{2}{4} \cdot \frac{5}{5} = \frac{10}{20}$ and, thus, $d = \$20$. Often students will point out that they did not need a proportion to solve this problem. Respond that they are correct. Explain that you are teaching them how to use a proportion because it is a tool that will be very helpful in solving more complex problems.

Have students practice using proportions to solve the following problems. Encourage them to check their answers by using methods they already know.

If 2 roses cost \$4, how much will 24 roses cost?

If 2 roses cost \$4, how many roses can be bought for \$28?

If 12 roses cost \$36, what will 3 roses cost?

4. Now that you have linked proportions to analogies and illustrated how to solve proportions, have students use proportions to solve measurement problems.

Ask them to work with a partner to write the following relationship as equivalent ratios and to look for relationships that appear both vertically and horizontally.

1 inch on a map : distance of 6 miles :: $2\frac{1}{2}$ inches on the map : distance of _____ miles

When pairs are ready, have them share their thinking. Using the proportion $\frac{1 \text{ inch}}{6 \text{ miles}} = \frac{2.5 \text{ inches}}{x \text{ miles}}$ or $\frac{1}{6} = \frac{2.5}{x}$, review that the relationship between distance on a map and actual number of miles appears vertically on each side of the equals sign and the relationship between inches and actual miles appears horizontally. Emphasize that any mathematical proportion that is true will show similar relationships.

Next have students solve their proportions and share their strategies for the missing distance.

5. Distribute the recording sheets. As students work, alone or in pairs, circulate to spot problems and give help when needed.

6. When everyone is ready, have students share their solutions in a whole-class discussion. When two correct proportions are offered, validate both and ask whether one seems easier to understand than the other and why. Emphasize that either horizontal or vertical relationships can be used to solve for an unknown value in a proportion.

Notes to the Teacher

This activity uses verbal analogies to introduce proportions. It helps student recognize the importance and usefulness of both vertical and horizontal patterns within proportions. Students practice writing and solving proportions related to situations involving measurement.

When you use this lesson for the first time with your students, you may find the following comments useful.

◈ Sometimes students have difficulty understanding how an analogy shows a relationship. Leading questions can help. For example, for the introductory analogy used in this lesson, ask questions such as: "Are you saying that the pair of words *dog* and *bark* go together in the same way that *cat* and *meow* go together? Do you mean that each is a pair of words that includes an animal and the noise it makes?" Follow that up with "So could we say that the relationship between *dog* and *bark* is the same as the relationship between *cat* and *meow*?"

◈ When appropriate, remind students that when solving a proportion, it is sometimes easier to rewrite it in a different form.

◈ As soon as you feel they are ready, ask students what would happen if they simplified either side of a numerical proportion before solving it. Trying this for themselves helps students see that simplifying first, if possible, yields the same solution and makes it easier to compute with the numbers.

◈ Eventually, you want all students to understand that there are four correct ways to set up a proportion for a given relationship. For example, using the first problem on the student activity sheet, 6 miles : 40 minutes :: _____ miles : 100 minutes, any of the following proportions is appropriate:

$$\frac{6}{40} = \frac{m}{100} \qquad \frac{40}{6} = \frac{100}{m} \qquad \frac{6}{m} = \frac{40}{100} \qquad \frac{m}{6} = \frac{100}{40}$$

Also, it is correct to switch the expressions to the opposite side of the equal sign in each example above.

Have students identify both the horizontal and vertical relationships in each form of the proportion, if appropriate.

Extensions
Focus in on units of measure in proportions. First, have students write each expression as a fraction in lowest terms.

1. 24 : 60
2. $\frac{3 \text{ inches}}{1 \text{ foot}}$
3. $\frac{\text{a nickel}}{\text{a quarter}}$
4. 40 minutes to 2 hours
5. 10 : 30
6. 32 to 4
7. 45 : 18
8. $\frac{2 \text{ dollars}}{50 \text{ cents}}$
9. $\frac{5 \text{ months}}{2 \text{ years}}$

10. $\dfrac{12 \text{ minutes}}{2 \text{ hours}}$

11. $\dfrac{2 \text{ quarters}}{2 \text{ dollars}}$

12. 1 yd. : 12 in.

Once they are comfortable with conversions like these, have students write and solve proportions using equivalent ratios for problems similar to the examples below.

> *It takes about 80 sugar maple trees to make 25 gallons of maple syrup. Mr. Mlyniec made syrup from all of his maple trees. He ended up with 64 quarts of syrup. About how many maple trees did he have?*
>
> *Jogging burns off about 100 calories per mile. Evie jogs at a rate of about 4.5 miles per hour. How many minutes will it take her to burn off the 1,200-calorie lunch she ate at Burger Doodle?*

 Unpumped Prices

Related Topics: capacity, proportional reasoning, volume

Overview
Using customary units, students predict the price of a variety of liquid products and rank them from what they think is most expensive to least expensive. Then they convert the actual prices of the products to cost per unit in order to compare them.

Materials
- *Unpumped Prices* recording sheets, 1 per student (see Blackline Masters)
- containers of familiar liquids (see list on recording sheet)
- optional: calculators, 1 per student

Vocabulary: cup, gallon, ounce, pint, proportion, quart, rate, ratio, unit rate

Prerequisite Skills and Concepts
This lesson is appropriate whether or not students have prior experience with finding unit rates. For students with no prior experience, have all the pairs convert to the same unit rate, such as cost per gallon, when doing the activity.

Instructions

1. Before the lesson, check that each container has the amount of liquid it's supposed to contain, according to its label. To each, add an adhesive label with its price. Place the label on the back of the container.

2. To begin, ask who has heard adults complain about the cost of gasoline. Ask whether anyone can think of a liquid used by many households that is more expensive than gasoline. Have the students define "more expensive" and informally explain ways to determine which of several liquids is more expensive.

3. Ask the class what units are used to measure liquids. As they offer ideas, list them on the board. Then ask for equivalent measures, such as how many ounces in a cup, how many cups in a pint, and so on, to elicit the following list:

8 ounces = 1 cup   2 pints = 1 quart

2 cups = 1 pint   4 quarts = 1 gallon

If appropriate, ask for other equivalents, such as how many cups are in a quart or how many ounces are in a gallon. If someone suggests metric units, decide whether it is appropriate at the time of this lesson for the students to deal with both measurement systems simultaneously.

4. Place the containers on display so that everyone can see them. Distribute the recording sheets. Direct the students to work in pairs to predict the cost of the products listed and rank them from most expensive (1) to least (10). When everyone has finished Step 1 on the recording sheet, have the students share their predictions with the class.

5. Ask students to offer definitions for the terms *rate* and *unit rate*. Verify correct answers.

6. Discuss finding the cost per unit or the unit rate of an item. Present the following example:

If gasoline costs $2.15 per gallon, and Arizona tea costs $1.00 for a bottle containing 20 fl. oz./591 mL, which product costs more? How do you know?

Have students work in pairs to solve this problem and share their solutions and how they found them. In this way, you can be sure that everyone knows how to find a cost per unit or a unit rate.

7. Now tell students to pass around the containers on display and record the quantity of liquid listed for each container and its cost. Also, as they work in pairs, instruct them to find the price per unit or unit rate for each liquid in the table on the recording sheet. Circulate to identify and help students with problems.

8. When all pairs have completed the recording sheet, lead a class discussion. Ask students to share their results and the methods they used to find the costs per unit or unit rates.

Notes to the Teacher

Students work in a real-world context to find costs per unit and unit rates. Students strengthen their estimation skills as they judge the amount of liquid contents for various containers and build mental referents for the size of each unit of capacity.

When you use this activity with your students for the first time, you may find the following comments useful:

❧ Providing the actual containers for students to work with helps solidify their concept of the size of each unit of capacity. As they handle the various bottles and jars while focusing on the amount of contents they hold, they add to their mental reservoir of referents.

❧ If it is not possible for you to obtain the price for one or more of the items listed in the table, these are prices found in 2007.

Product	Amount	Price	Product	Amount	Price
Gasoline	1 gal.	$2.95	Snapple	16 oz.	$1.20
Mild Salsa	7 oz.	$1.45	Liquid Paper	0.68 oz.	$1.19
Pepto-Bismol	8 oz.	$3.49	Nautica Cologne	2.5 oz.	$36.99
Evian Water	1.05 qt.	$1.49	Frappuccino	1.5 cups	$2.75
Tabasco Sauce	2 oz.	$1.49	Vanilla Extract	2 oz.	$7.99
Listerine	1.05 pt.	$3.77			

❧ Students are always astounded at the prices they find, for example, for a gallon of Liquid Paper correction fluid and Tabasco sauce.

❧ Instead of providing the prices, you can have students find the best prices for each item, either by going to their local supermarkets or using the Internet. Suggest to students that they go to www.froogle.com and enter the name of an item.

Extension

Have students work in small groups to gather data for the prices of a particular type of item such as soft drinks, pizza, or hamburgers. Then, have each group find the unit rates for each brand, construct a box plot or other graph to display the data, and present the findings to the class, using a poster or other visual.

Could It Be?

Related Topics: algebraic thinking; distance, rate, and time; proportional reasoning; scatter plot

Overview

Students examine the fictional journey of characters in the popular early-adolescent novel *Walk Two Moons* to determine whether the travel itinerary described is reasonable. In so doing, they deepen their understanding of the relationships between distance, rate, and time.

Materials

◈ road maps or an atlas for Ohio, Illinois, Wisconsin, Minnesota, South Dakota, Wyoming, and Idaho, 1 set per small group of students

◈ *Could It Be?* recording sheets, 1 per student (see Blackline Masters)

◈ calculators, 1 per student

◈ grid paper (4 squares per inch), 1 sheet per student, or graphing calculators, 1 per student

◈ *Walk Two Moons*, by Sharon Creech (1994)

Vocabulary: connected scatter plot, distance, mean rate, rate, scale on a map, time

Prerequisite Skills and Concepts

Students need to be familiar with graphing points on a coordinate grid.

Instructions

1. Introduce the activity with a brief discussion about *Walk Two Moons*, a story about a girl named Sal who takes a trip with her grandparents. Either summarize the story or ask a student who has read the book to do so. Then ask a student to read aloud the introductory paragraph on the recording sheet.

2. Ask students to offer definitions for the terms *distance, rate, time,* and *mean rate,* especially as these terms apply to a trip by car. Verify correct answers.

3. Explain to the students that they will go through several steps to decide whether the itinerary described in the book is realistic. Describe the first two steps of the process and provide any needed clarification, for example:

   • *Step 1: Find the distance traveled by Sal and her grandparents on each day of their journey and the total distance they traveled.* Be sure students can use the scale provided on the maps or in the atlas and understand the symbols for each type of road, such as interstate, multilane federal highway, and multilane state highway. Do this by asking each group to find the fastest route and distance between two specific cities and having volunteers share their answer(s) and method(s).

- *Step 2: Construct and interpret a scatter plot of the trip.* Briefly review, if needed, the steps for constructing a connected scatter plot, in which consecutive points are connected by line segments.

4. Explain that, from this point forward in the activity, each group will make choices about the time (number of hours) and the mean rate (average number of miles per hour) traveled each day and then calculate to see how these factors might affect their decision about the reasonableness of the trip's itinerary.

5. Distribute the recording sheets and other materials. While the students work in small groups, circulate to ask and answer questions and identify problems.

6. When all groups have completed the activity, lead a class discussion about the students' findings, analyses, and conclusions. During the discussion, look for opportunities to emphasize the relationship between distance, rate, and time. Ask additional questions to focus on how changing one of these variables affects the others, such as the following:

- What factors might affect the distance, rate, or time a person travels on a given day? Which of these variables (distance, rate, and/or time) is affected by each factor? (Example: Heavy traffic might affect the rate at which one can travel.)
- How does changing distance, rate, or time affect the other two variables? (Example: If you travel more slowly, your distance will decrease unless you increase the time you travel. Likewise, if you travel more slowly, your time will increase unless you decrease the distance you travel.)

Notes to the Teacher

This activity provides students with an experience that goes beyond simply using the distance-rate-time formula ($d = rt$). It engages them in examining the relationships between distance, rate, and time in the context of a fictional multiday car trip.

When you use this activity for the first time with your classes, you may find the following comments useful:

◈ Finding the distances between the places traveled each day provides students with valuable practice in using scale and/or mileage charts on a map. Because they will likely choose slightly different routes, students' calculated distances may vary. To shorten the time required to do the mileage calculations, consider having students use the website www.freetrip.com.

◈ The completed scatter plot should look similar to the one shown below:

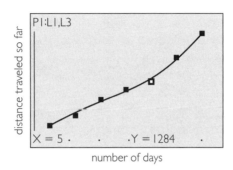

◈ The steeper portions in the scatter plot reflect a longer time or a faster rate. The plot does not, however, indicate which of these variables or combinations of them might be the reason for the longer distance. Ask questions to solicit this understanding (see Instruction 6).

◈ Following is an example of what students will find when they assume Sal and her grandparents traveled the same number of hours each day, that is, 6 hours or 8 hours. The data indicate that the assumption is not reasonable.

Day	Total Distance Traveled on the Day	Mean Number of Miles per Hour if Traveling 6 Hours per Day (rate)	Mean Number of Miles per Hour if Traveling 8 Hours per Day (rate)
1	354	59	44.25
2	196	32.667	24.5
3	378	63	47.25
4	203	33.833	25.375
5	153	25.5	19.125
6	495	82.5	61.875
7	524	87.333	65.5

◈ Following is an example of what students will find when they assume Sal and her grandparents traveled at the same average rate of speed each day, that is, either 50 mph or 65 mph. The data indicate that this assumption, like the previous one, is not reasonable: it is unlikely that the number of hours spent traveling each day would vary as much as the calculated data indicate.

Day	Total Distance Traveled on the Day (distance)	Number of Hours at an Average rate of 50 mph (time)	Number of Hours at an Average rate of 65 mph (time)
1	354	7.08	5.45
2	196	3.92	3.02
3	378	7.56	5.82
4	203	4.06	3.12
5	153	3.06	2.35
6	495	9.9	7.62
7	524	10.48	8.06

Students should realize that the average rates vary because of factors such as the different types of roads, topography, and traffic encountered on different days, as well as events in the book that are not provided. These factors should come up in the class discussion (see Instruction 6).

Extension

Instruct the students to design a travel schedule for Sal and her grandparents, using the following guidelines:

1. Use the distances for each day that you found in Part 1 of the *Could It Be?* activity.
2. Choose reasonable values for the hours traveled and the average speed for each day. Consider such factors as the likely amount of traffic and the kind of topography they would encounter on each day.
3. Show your plan in the following table. Be prepared to explain the factors you considered in making the plan.

Day	Starting Point for the Day; Other Places Visited Along the Way	End Point	Number of Miles Traveled for the Day (distance)	Number of Hours Traveled for the Day (time)	Mean Number of Miles per Hour for the Day (rate)
1	Euclid, OH; Elkhart, IN, and South Bend, IN	Chicago, IL			
2	Chicago, IL; Madison, WI	Wisconsin Dells, WI			
3	Wisconsin Dells, WI	Pipestone, MN			
4	Pipestone, MN; Sioux Falls, SD, and Mitchell, SD	Chamberlain, SD (add 20 miles for side trip to the Missouri River)			
5	Chamberlain, SD	Wall, SD			
6	Wall, SD; Mount Rushmore and Yellowstone National Park	Old Faithful Inn; Yellowstone National Park, WY			
7	Old Faithful Inn; Yellowstone National Park, WY	Coeur D'Alene, ID			

❖ Doing this extension activity will reinforce the relationships between distance, rate, and time and provide extra practice in "juggling" the data. Middle school students enjoy defending their proposals as "most reasonable" or "most ideal."

❖ Allow students who have read the book to offer additional information that would be useful for students when working on the extension. Give students a few days to complete the extension with their partners. Then have the class present, compare, and discuss their plans. Again, ask questions to assess whether the students understand and can manipulate the results so that they are reasonable for situations involving distance, rate, and time.

Students who have read the book or talked with other students who have done so can include details from the story to support the reasoning behind their proposal. For example:

Event	Possible Impact on Itinerary
slower traffic in cities	slower rate on Day 2
Gram gets bitten by a snake late on Day 4	late start (and fewer traveling hours) on Day 5
visit to Mt. Rushmore and eagerness to see Old Faithful	long hours on Day 6

Go for the Golden 1

Related Topics: Fibonacci sequence, geometric constructions

Overview
Students construct a series of rectangles and analyze the ratios involved.

Materials
❖ *Go for the Golden 1* recording sheets, 1 per student (see Blackline Masters)
❖ compasses, 1 per student
❖ straightedges, 1 per student
❖ optional: grid paper with small squares (less than 5 square lengths per inch), 2 sheets per student

Vocabulary: congruent, construct, Fibonacci sequence, golden rectangle, parallel, perpendicular, ratio, similar figures

Prerequisite Skills and Concepts
Using only a straightedge and a compass, students need to be able to construct:

❖ two congruent segments,

◈ the midpoint of a segment, and

◈ perpendicular lines.

One website with good directions for such constructions is http://regentsprep.org/
Regents/math/math-topic.cfm?TopicCode=construc. It also includes online videos.

Instructions

1. Explain to the students that they will be constructing rectangles in a special way and that the final one will be very close to a golden rectangle. Tell the class that this rectangle will be used later in a survey to determine whether people actually seem to prefer its shape to that of other rectangles.

2. Distribute the recording sheets and other materials.

3. Tell students that at specific points during the exploration, as noted on the recording sheet, they will work with a partner.

4. Circulate among the students while they work to answer questions and monitor their progress.

5. When all students have completed their constructions, display them where everyone can see them. Lead a class discussion to help students process the mathematics of this exploration.

Notes to the Teacher

This activity provides students with practice in doing basic geometric constructions and working with ratios. Students analyze the ratios between consecutive Fibonacci numbers and construct a near-golden rectangle. At the end of the exploration, you can informally introduce students to the golden ratio and to the concept of similar rectangles.

When you use this activity with your students for the first time, you may find the following comments useful:

◈ If students are not familiar with the Fibonacci sequence (1, 1, 2, 3, 5, 8, 13, . . .) and the golden rectangle, for which the ratio of its length to its width is about 1.61803, or $\frac{\text{length}}{\text{width}} = \frac{\text{length} + \text{width}}{\text{length}}$, introduce these topics as the lesson progresses.

◈ Following are some of the patterns students find:
  • The lengths of the sides of the rectangles are consecutive Fibonacci numbers.
  • The length-to-width ratio for rectangles with consecutive Fibonacci numbers gets closer to the ratio required for a golden rectangle as the side lengths increase.

- As the rank of the consecutive Fibonacci numbers gets higher, their ratio is closer to that required for a golden rectangle. For example, $13:8 = 1.625$, whereas $21:13 \approx 1.61538\ldots$, which is closer to the golden ratio, $\approx 1.61803\ldots$.
- The final rectangle created by each student has the same length-to-width ratio, regardless of the size of the chosen unit length.
- All the final rectangles created by the students are similar figures, that is, they have the same proportions, or length-to-width ratio; only the size of the rectangles varies, depending upon the size of the initial square each student draws.

If students do not find these patterns, ask questions to elicit them.

❖ The following table displays the correct values for the Table of Ratios for Rectangles on the recording sheet.

Rectangle	Longest Side of New Rectangle (Written as Sum of Parts)	Length (Longer Side)	Width (Shorter Side)	Ratio L : W
A	1	1	1	1:1
B	1 + 1	2	1	2:1
C	2 + 1	3	2	3:2
D	3 + 2	5	3	5:3
E	5 + 3	8	5	8:5
F	8 + 5	13	8	13:8
G	13 + 8	21	13	21:13
H	21 + 13	34	21	34:21
I	34 + 21	55	34	55:31

Extensions

The Fibonacci sequence and the golden ratio are topics that provide a myriad of opportunities for students to work with ratios. Three are suggested below.

❖ Give students the following instructions:

1. Draw a diagonal in the largest rectangle in your drawing, starting at the top left vertex.
2. Starting at any point on the left side of the same rectangle, draw a segment parallel to its length until it intersects with the diagonal.
3. Starting at the intersection you just made, draw a segment parallel to the width of the large rectangle until it intersects the top side of the rectangle.
4. Make a conjecture about the length-to-width ratio of the new rectangle you constructed. Check your conjecture and explain your thinking.

◈ Direct students to construct a true golden rectangle by using the Pythagorean theorem. (See *Go for the Golden 2*, on page 19.)

◈ Have students construct, administer, and analyze the findings of a golden rectangle survey to test the conjecture that people prefer the golden rectangle to all others. (See *Golden Rectangle Survey*, on page 149).

◈ What's with the Factor?

Related Topics: algebraic thinking, similar figures, surface area, volume

Overview
Students investigate rectangular prisms to find out what happens to ratios of side lengths to surface areas and side lengths to volumes as the dimensions of a prism change.

Materials
◈ *What's with the Factor?* recording sheets, 1 per student (see Blackline Masters)
◈ Snap Cubes or wooden cubes, 36 per pair of students
◈ newsprint, 4 or more sheets

Vocabulary: dimensions, ratio, rectangular prism, surface area, volume

Prerequisite Skills and Concepts
Students should have some familiarity with finding the surface area and the volume of rectangular prisms.

Instructions

1. Tell the students they will work in pairs to build and gather data about certain rectangular prisms. Explain that each pair will then study its data and make generalizations about the ratios between the side lengths, the surface areas, and the volumes of related prisms.

2. Ask students to give definitions for the terms *dimensions*, *surface area*, and *volume*, especially as they apply to rectangular prisms. Verify correct answers. Review *rectangular prism*, *ratio*, and *factor*, if needed.

3. Distribute the cubes. Have a student demonstrate building a rectangular prism. Discuss its dimensions. Have another student build a second rectangular prism by doubling the dimensions of the first prism. Discuss its dimensions.

4. Ask for volunteers to explain how to find the surface area and the volume for the two prisms. Do not have the students actually find these measurements.

5. Distribute the recording sheets and review the directions to be sure that they are clear to everyone.

6. Direct students to complete the activity. As the students work, circulate to spot problems and answer questions.

7. When all students have completed the investigation, lead a class discussion based on their findings, observations, and conclusions. Have students write the generalizations on newsprint and post them in the classroom.

8. If appropriate, help students connect their findings to similar figures in general. Help them recall that corresponding sides of similar figures are proportional (have the same scale factor). Help them see that this relationship exists for corresponding edges of two similar prisms. Then, if appropriate, you can also help them see the relationship between the areas of corresponding faces and the relative volumes of the two prisms in the context of similar figures.

Notes to the Teacher

During this activity, students discover what happens to the ratios of length to surface area and length to volume as the dimensions for any rectangular prism are multiplied by the same factor.

When you use this activity with your students for the first time, you may find the following comments useful:

◈ The first prism that students build should contain very few cubes, such as four cubes for a 1-by-2-by-2 prism or six cubes for a 1-by-2-by-3 prism. This will leave students with enough cubes to build the remaining prisms.

◈ Although some students may want to skip building the prisms and work from a drawing or only from numbers, encourage them not to do so. Explain that models make it easier for others to understand their thinking and provide a reliable check for their generalizations.

◈ When the students are comparing their findings, have several pairs report the actual dimensions, surface areas, and volumes of their prisms and record this information on the board or on an overhead transparency. Without this information, it may not be clear to some students that the original dimensions do not affect the ratios that result.

◈ Having the class record on newsprint, and then post, the big generalizations that they discover fosters students' retention and encourages more thinking. It also serves as a valuable reference when studying other solids, such as spheres. For example, you might ask: "What is the ratio of the surface areas of a sphere whose radius is three centimeters and a sphere whose radius is nine centimeters? Explain your reasoning."

Extension

Using a procedure similar to the one described for this lesson, have students investigate the ratios in similar pyramids and cones to see whether the generalizations they found for rectangular prisms are true for similar pyramids and cones. With these figures, your students will need to design nets to build their models or do this investigation numerically by changing the values of the dimensions in the surface area and volume formulas.

Swinging Rates

Related Topics: angles; circumference; distance, rate, and time; proportional reasoning

Overview

Students gather data about pendulums. They then apply their knowledge of circles and the relationships among distance, rate, and time to their data to find the approximate rate of a bob of the pendulum at different amplitudes.

Materials

- stopwatches or other timing devices, 1 per group of four students (**Note:** It is best if the devices can time to at least the nearest tenth of a second.)
- *Swinging Rates* recording sheets, 1 per student (see Blackline Masters)
- calculators, 1 per group of four students
- heavy string, 120–30 centimeters per group of four students
- weight or bob, heavy enough to keep line taut, 1 per group of four students
- protractors, 1 per group of four students
- large chalkboard protractor

Vocabulary: amplitude, angle, arc, circumference, distance, mass, oscillation, period of a pendulum, radius, rate, ratio

Prerequisite Skills and Concepts

Students need to know how to solve simple distance-rate-time problems, find the circumference of a circle, find arcs for given central angles of a circle, and measure angles with a protractor.

Instructions

1. To begin, ask students what a pendulum is and what they know about it. Replicate the following drawing (see page 135) on the board. Explain or review the following definitions, illustrating each on the diagram.

- oscillation: one back-and-forth swing of a pendulum
- period: the time required for one oscillation
- arc: part of a circle that is named by its end points; for a pendulum, the portion of a complete circle that is traveled by the bob in one oscillation
- length: the distance from the point of attachment to the hanging weight
- mass: the mass of the hanging weight (bob)
- amplitude: the largest angle that the pendulum cord makes with the vertical (as shown below)

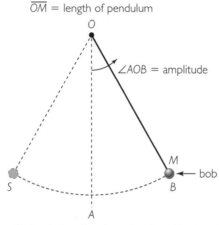

$\overline{OM}$ = length of pendulum

$\angle AOB$ = amplitude

M

bob

S

B

A

oscillation: bob swings from S to B and back to S
period: time required for one oscillation

2. Ask students to give and explain the formulas for *circumference* (C = πd or C = 2πr, where C = circumference, d = diameter, and r = radius) and for *distance* (d = rt, where d = distance, r = rate, and t = time). Verify correct answers and instruct the students to use 3.14 for pi.

3. Demonstrate setup for this investigation. Tie a weight to a piece of heavy string and suspend it from a ceiling tile support or other place so that the pendulum can swing back and forth freely, not touching anything.

4. Explain the first task. Tell students that they are going to make their own pendulums. Then they are going to carefully time five complete swings of two different-length pendulums for different arcs and compare the time it takes to complete these swings with the distance the pendulum travels during that time.

5. Go over the instructions on the recording sheet with the class. Then ask a small group of students to set up a pendulum and demonstrate the steps of the procedure for the class. Use a large chalkboard protractor so everyone can see the angle as you measure it. Pull the bob until the amplitude is 10 degrees. Record the time on the board.

6. Next, ask each group to write down the data required in the table for the example they have just watched. If needed, use any of the following questions to help the students understand what they are to do.

- Ask students for a definition of an *arc*. Students should know that it is part of the circumference of the circle.
- Remind students that there are two versions of the formula for circumference of a circle, one using the diameter and one using the radius (see Instruction 2). Ask them which one is more useful in the current context to encourage them to relate the length of the pendulum to the radius of the full circle.
- Ask students how to find the length of an arc on the circle. The length of the arc that the pendulum travels can be determined by writing a ratio that compares the angle of amplitude with the full circle and setting that equivalent to the ratio of the length of the arc described by the pendulum to the theoretical full circle it would create. Students then need to use the formula for circumference and their knowledge of proportions to find the arc length.

  For example, pulling the bob back to create a 10-degree angle between the original ray made by the pendulum at rest ($\overline{OA}$ in the previous diagram) and the new ray created by the line of the pendulum just before it is released ($\overline{OB}$) causes the pendulum to swing in a 20-degree arc (10 degrees on either side of the original ray). This 20-degree arc represents one-eighteenth of the circle. If the length of the pendulum, for example, is 24 inches, the circumference of the circle is 48π inches, using the formula $C = 2\pi r$. The proportion to find the exact length of one sweep of the arc is $\frac{20}{360} = \frac{x}{2\pi r}$ or $\frac{20}{360} = \frac{x}{48\pi}$, where x is the length of the arc. Therefore, in this example, the length of the pendulums arc is $2.\overline{6}\pi$, or approximately 8.38 inches.
- Ask the students how to use the distance formula to find the rate for each trial. Using the previous example, the students would substitute values in the formula $d = rt$ to get something like $\sim 8.38 = r \cdot 1.4$ seconds (time for one oscillation) and then $r = \sim 6$ cm/sec.

7. Pass out the materials. Explain that before groups start gathering data, they should practice synchronizing the person who is the timer with the student who is starting the pendulum in motion, calling out when each oscillation ends, and signaling the exact moment when the timing should stop. (While the students work to complete their tables, circulate to be sure each group is completing the steps correctly.)

8. When all students have completed the activity, lead a discussion about the patterns groups found and the three questions they answered.

Notes to the Teacher

This activity provides a novel context in which students explore the relationship among distance, rate, and time. Students also strengthen their understanding of the relationships in circles as they apply formulas to the data they collect when they swing pendulums with different amplitudes.

When you use this activity with your students for the first time, you may find the following comments useful:

◈ Be sure that students keep these tips in mind when setting up and working with a pendulum:

- Choose the place of attachment for each pendulum carefully. The pendulum must swing freely with minimal friction and interference.
- The string needs to remain taut or the data will be adversely affected.
- The weight must be released smoothly with as little additional influence on its motion as possible.

◈ Following are some of the patterns often found by students:

- The distance the pendulum travels increases as the amplitude increases.
- For each length of pendulum tested, the time for one oscillation remains constant (or very close to it). The time for one oscillation remains nearly constant even as the amplitude increases, although with larger angles, there is a slight change in frequency. Students often find slight increases in the period of the pendulum at larger angles. This is due to increased air resistance to the bob and friction at the pivot point.
- The speed at which the weight travels over a greater distance must be increasing to keep the total time of each oscillation constant.

Extension
At http://pbskids.org/zoom/games/pendulum/swing.html there is a nice simulation of a pendulum. You will need to download the plug-in Shockwave for it to work. Students can explore further with pendulums doing animated activities and games.

Similarity

Introduction

Perhaps no other single topic in middle school mathematics offers more opportunities to make connections among the content strands of the curriculum than similar figures. When working with similar figures, students usually encounter each of the following:

◈ from the number strand, ratios and proportions involving various forms of rational numbers

◈ from the algebra strand, variables and equations

◈ from the geometry strand, a variety of triangles and other polygons

◈ from the data and probability strand, conjecturing, gathering sets of data, and making generalizations

It often takes many experiences for students to develop facility with ratios and rates, to use equivalent ratios, to understand scale factors, and to create and solve proportions.

Rather than give students the definition of similar figures, the lesson *What Are Similar Polygons?* (page 139) allows students to discover the properties of similar figures for themselves. As they experiment, students learn that similar figures must satisfy two conditions. Students also need explicit experiences to become convinced that neither condition alone is sufficient to guarantee similarity.

The remaining lessons in this chapter provide explorations with similar figures in a variety of different mathematical and real-world contexts.

◈ In *Golden Rectangle Survey* (page 149), students plan and execute a survey about golden rectangles, then analyze their results.

◈ In *Scaling Up and Down* (page 145), students construct and analyze scale drawings.

◈ In *Pythagoras Plus* (page 158), students construct regular polygons other than squares on the sides of right triangles to find out whether the Pythagorean theorem still applies.

◈ In *A Different Look* (page 153), students use pattern blocks to build larger and larger similar figures, record data, and compare the ratios of side lengths to the ratios of their perimeters and areas.

❖ In *Using Indirect Measurement* (page 161), students use several methods to apply their knowledge of similar figures in order to find the height of objects too tall to measure directly.

 ## What Are Similar Polygons?

Related Topics: finding and simplifying ratios, measuring angles, measuring line segments

Overview
Students work with sets of pentagons to find the essential characteristics of similar polygons.

Materials
❖ *What Are Similar Polygons?* shapes, 1 per student (see Blackline Masters)
❖ metric rulers, 1 per student
❖ protractors, 1 per student
❖ large paper quadrilaterals that are similar, 2
❖ optional: additional examples of similar figures
❖ optional: transparency of illustration on page 143

Vocabulary: congruent angles, corresponding angles, corresponding sides, pentagon, polygon, quadrilateral, ratio, regular polygons, similar

Prerequisite Skills and Concepts
Students should know how to measure angles and line segments and how to find and simplify ratios.

Instructions

1. Show the class the two large paper quadrilaterals that you have prepared. Tell them that the two polygons are similar. Ask students how they would define *similar polygons* based on this example. They will most likely offer something like "two polygons that have shapes that look alike." Confirm this informal definition. If needed, draw additional samples, as shown below, on the board to elicit a reasonable informal definition.

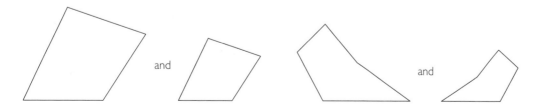

2. Explain to the students that they will investigate the properties of similar pentagons in order to come up with a formal mathematical definition for *similarity*. Ask the students what the terms *corresponding angles* and *corresponding sides* mean. After they offer informal definitions, have students use the two paper quadrilaterals to identify these features. If students are unable to identify these features, demonstrate them and then ask the students to come up with definitions for the terms.

3. Distribute copies of the *What Are Similar Polygons?* shapes. Instruct students to *carefully* cut out the pentagons and then group them into sets of shapes they think are similar. Direct them to compare their sets with a partner. Have them list on a sheet of paper the sets they agree upon, using the letters that are written on the pentagons. Students should find four sets of similar pentagons, one of which contains regular pentagons: A, D, and K; B, E, and J; C, F, and L; and G, H, and I. Lead a short discussion to help students find any errors, but do not announce the correct groupings at this time. Explain that stating that polygons "look alike" is not enough to prove mathematically that they are similar. Tell students that they will be gathering and analyzing data about these pentagons in order to discover the mathematical properties that cause them to look alike.

4. Ask what features the pentagons have that might be important to investigate. After the discussion, during which students will most likely conclude that angles and sides are the two obvious features, tell the students to investigate the angles first. (This investigation is easier and success builds student confidence.) Hand out the protractors.

5. Ask students to define *regular polygon*. Then direct each pair of students to choose one set of look-alike pentagons that are *not* regular polygons. Tell them to label the corresponding angles, using the notation n, n′ (pronounced "n prime"), and n″ (pronounced "n double prime"); o, o′, and o″, and so on, going clockwise inside each pentagon. Next, instruct them to make a chart like the following one and to list the pentagons they've chosen in alphabetical order. This ordering significantly simplifies comparison of findings during the class discussion.

Pentagon	Angle Measure (to the Nearest Degree)				
	$m(\angle n)$	$m(\angle o)$	$m(\angle p)$	$m(\angle q)$	$m(\angle r)$
B	$m(\angle n) =$	$m(\angle o) =$	$m(\angle p) =$	$m(\angle q) =$	$m(\angle r) =$
E	$m(\angle n') =$	$m(\angle o') =$	$m(\angle p') =$	$m(\angle q') =$	$m(\angle r') =$
J	$m(\angle n'') =$	$m(\angle o'') =$	$m(\angle p'') =$	$m(\angle q'') =$	$m(\angle r'') =$

Explain that each student is to measure the angles of the chosen pentagons, and then, in pairs they are to (1) compare data and make any needed changes, (2) make a conjecture about the measures of corresponding angles in similar pentagons, and (3) write the conjecture on their paper.

6. Have students choose a second set of irregular pentagons with which to test their conjecture. Have them record their results as described in Instruction 5. If your students need additional practice measuring angles and time is available, have them find the measures of all pairs of corresponding angles in the remaining sets of pentagons.

7. Lead a brief class discussion about their findings and verify the following conjecture: All pairs of corresponding angles in similar pentagons are congruent. Ask whether this would be true for the regular pentagons as well.

8. Have the class discuss the following: Is having congruent corresponding angles sufficient to define similar pentagons? If everyone in the class thinks that this condition is sufficient, ask students to try to disprove it by thinking of two figures that have congruent corresponding angles but do not look alike. Someone will most likely suggest a square and a nonsquare rectangle. If not, draw the two pentagons shown below on the board.

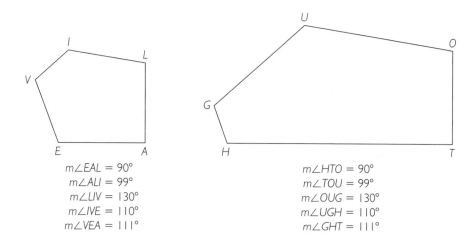

$m\angle EAL = 90°$
$m\angle ALI = 99°$
$m\angle LIV = 130°$
$m\angle IVE = 110°$
$m\angle VEA = 111°$

$m\angle HTO = 90°$
$m\angle TOU = 99°$
$m\angle OUG = 130°$
$m\angle UGH = 110°$
$m\angle GHT = 111°$

9. Hand out the rulers. Tell students they will now investigate corresponding sides in the pentagons they think are similar. As with the corresponding angles, have students label each set of corresponding sides in a group of look-alike pentagons, using the notation a, a′, and a″; b, b′, and b″; and so on, going clockwise inside

each pentagon. Notice side *a* has been labeled to help students label pentagons in a consistent way. Next ask them to make a table like this:

Pentagon	Side Lengths (to the Nearest Tenth of a Centimeter)				
	a	b	c	d	e
A	a =	b =	c =	d =	e =
D	a′ =	b′ =	c′ =	d′ =	e′ =
K	a″ =	b″ =	c″ =	d″ =	e″ =

Explain that each student is to measure the sides of the chosen pentagons to the nearest tenth of a centimeter; then, in pairs, (1) compare their data and make any needed changes, (2) make a conjecture about the lengths of corresponding sides in similar pentagons, and (3) write the conjecture on their paper.

10. Circulate among the students, observing their conjectures. If students are having difficulty, suggest that they investigate the ratios of corresponding sides or follow the alternative suggestion given in the "Notes to the Teacher" section.

11. When all pairs have written a conjecture, lead a discussion and verify the following conjecture: Each of the pairs of corresponding sides in similar pentagons has the same ratio.

12. Ask the students whether the two properties they have found are sufficient to define similar polygons. If all do not agree that they are sufficient, ask whether anyone can draw a pair of polygons that have these two properties but do not have the same shape. Before continuing the discussion, you may want to have students think about this as a homework task. At some point, confirm that these are the properties required for similar pentagons.

13. On another day, have students work in pairs to test the properties on polygons other than pentagons in order to generalize their findings to all sets of similar polygons.

Notes to the Teacher

In this activity students investigate look-alike pentagons in order to formally define *similarity*. Later they see whether their definition can be extended to all similar polygons.

When you use this activity for the first time with your students, you may find the following comments useful:

◈ Emphasize that careful cutting and measuring are essential for the data to be accurate enough to ensure valid conclusions. For best results, tell students to cut along the outside of each edge.

◈ Although many middle school students can quickly point out *corresponding angles* and *corresponding sides*, a demonstration is essential for students who are attempting to identify corresponding angles and sides for the first time and is an excellent review for others.

◈ Suggest to students who are having difficulty measuring angles accurately that they compare the size of two angles by placing an angle from one pentagon on top of the corresponding angle in the other pentagon.

◈ Before considering the conjectures the students make about corresponding angles, note which pairs have made false conjectures. Then have the class consider these conjectures first. Point out to students that one counterexample is usually enough to discard a conjecture and that all mathematicians make false conjectures as a part of doing mathematics.

◈ If students are having difficulty finding ratios of corresponding sides, remind them that order matters; for example, the ratio of a:b must be compared with the ratio a':b', *not* to the ratio b':a'.

◈ If students do not think of finding the *ratios* of corresponding sides, you may want to ask them (or the entire class) to stop working and consider the work of an imaginary student. Then project the following illustration from an overhead transparency.

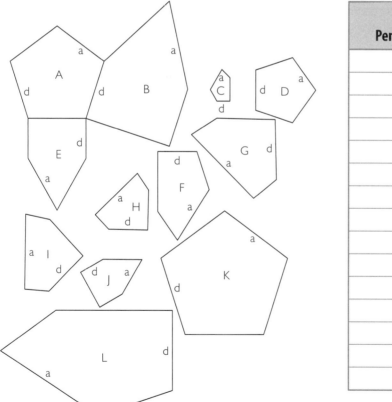

Pentagon	Ratio of Side Lengths a:d
A	
D	
K	
B	
E	
J	
C	
F	
L	
G	
H	
I	

Quickly designate four groups in the class and assign each group one of the four sets of pentagons in the table. Tell them to use their data to determine the ratio a:d using the sides as labeled in the illustration.

Except for the group assigned A, D, and K, who will find a:d = 1:1 in each pentagon, all other groups should find that the ratio a:d = 3:2 in each pentagon. Ask the class to study the table for a minute to make observations that might be helpful in their search for a property in similar polygons related to the lengths of corresponding sides.

The class should conclude the following:

• The ratios of corresponding side lengths within each group of look-alike pentagons could be an important characteristic to examine.

• Finding the ratio of only one pair of corresponding sides is not enough to determine similar pentagons.

If they do not reach both of these conclusions, ask questions to elicit them. (**Note:** Instead of interrupting the investigation, you could do this as a follow-up when everyone is finished with the investigation.)

❖ Sometimes students conjecture that only regular pentagons (or polygons) are similar because they are the only ones for which all their corresponding side lengths are congruent. Use the large paper pentagons to show that, though not regular, they are similar. If appropriate, discuss why all regular pentagons are similar to each other.

❖ Following are the correct measurement data for the students tables:

Pentagon	Side Lengths for Each Pentagon (in cm)					a:d
	a	b	c	d	e	
A	a = 3	b = 3	c = 3	d = 3	e = 3	1:1
D	a′ = 2	b′ = 2	c′ = 2	d′ = 2	e′ = 2	1:1
K	a″ = 4	b″ = 4	c″ = 4	d″ = 4	e″ = 4	1:1
B	a = 4.5	b = 3	c = 4.5	d = 3	e = 4.5	3:2
E	a′ = 3	b′ = 2	c′ = 3	d′ = 2	e′ = 3	3:2
J	a″ = 2	b″ = 1.33	c″ = 2	d″ = 1.33	e″ = 2	3:2
C	a = 1.2	b = 0.7	c = 1.2	d = 0.8	e = 0.8	3:2
F	a′ = 3	b′ = 1.75	c′ = 3	d′ = 2	e′ = 2	3:2
L	a″ = 6	b″ = 3.5	c″ = 6	d″ = 4	e″ = 4	3:2
G	a = 4.5	b = 1.5	c = 3	d = 3	e = 1.5	3:2
H	a′ = 3	b′ = 1	c′ = 2	d′ = 2	e′ = 1	3:2
I	a″ = 3.75	b″ = 1.25	c″ = 2.5	d″ = 2.5	e″ = 1.25	3:2

Extensions

❖ Have students do an activity similar to this one except that each group of students investigates polygons with a different number of side lengths (triangles, hexagons, and so on) to see whether the properties they discovered about similar pentagons are true for other polygons.

❖ Have each group of students make a set of similar polygons. Assign a different polygon (isosceles triangles, trapezoids with two congruent sides, and so on) to each group. This activity is most successful when the students are restricted to whole number lengths for the sides of their polygons. Have groups swap sets of polygons to verify that they are actually similar, using the mathematical definition for similar figures.

 ## Scaling Up and Down

Related Topics: area, measuring length, scale drawings

Overview

Students make scale drawings that reduce large items or enlarge small items and then analyze how they are similar to the real-world objects they depict. Students practice the skills of measuring lengths, choosing a sensible scale, and applying a scale to create an accurate drawing.

Materials

❖ rulers, 1 per student

❖ grid paper, 1 sheet per student

❖ measuring tapes, 1 per pair of students

❖ *Cut Down to Size at High Noon*, by Scott Sundby (2000)

❖ sample scale drawing (see Instruction 4)

Vocabulary: dilate, scale, scale factor, similar figures

Instructions

1. Before class, prepare a sample scale drawing. (See Instruction 4.)

2. To begin the lesson, ask students what they know about scale drawings. Ask them to give examples of scale pictures in real life (blueprints, maps, photographs, and so on).

3. Read the book *Cut Down to Size at High Noon* to the class. Ask the students how mathematics is involved in the story. Lead a short discussion focusing on the mathematics of scale drawings.

Review the meaning of *similar figures*. Then ask students to explain how a scale drawing is related to the object it depicts. Elicit that a scale drawing can dilate the original object (make a smaller or larger similar figure with a different scale than the original object) or replicate the original object (make a figure having the same scale as the original object).

4. Explain to the class that each student will choose an object and make a scale drawing of it, using the following guidelines:

   a. Choose one of your favorite things. Be sure it is either larger than an adult or smaller than your hand.

   b. Measure at least five parts of the original object and record the measures, including the unit.

   c. Use these measurements to choose an appropriate scale for your scale drawing. Your drawing must take up at least half the area of the grid paper you use.

   d. Your work must include the following: a title, your name, the scale drawing (having at least five parts of the object labeled with both the actual and scale measures), and the scale you used.

5. Show students a sample scale drawing you have made. Use it to illustrate each of the guidelines. Discuss how to choose an appropriate scale and how to place the drawing on the grid paper. Describe your evaluation guidelines or the rubric you will be using to evaluate their work. (See Figure 6–1 for examples of student work.)

6. Distribute the materials and set students to work. When all students have completed their scale drawings (which usually takes part of one day in class and several days outside of class), have partners exchange papers to check each other's drawings. Instruct students to confirm that the indicated scale was appropriately applied to each measurement.

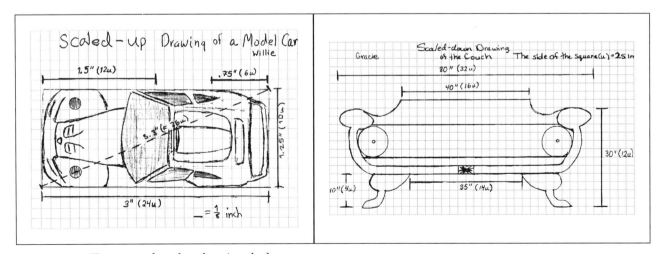

Figure 6–1 *Two examples of students' scale drawings*

7. Have students share with the class the decision-making processes they used in choosing their scale factors and any problems they encountered in constructing the actual scale drawings. Then lead a discussion about the connection between scale drawings and similar figures, including the relationship of angles in the original objects to those in their drawings and the relationship of linear measures in the original objects to those in the drawings.

8. Display the student papers on a bulletin board or other prominent place in the classroom.

Notes to the Teacher

This activity gives students practice in making scale drawings and connecting scale drawings to the original objects they depict. Students measure the lengths of objects, choose an appropriate scale to use, and use that scale to make their drawings. Finally, they practice using a scale as they check a classmate's drawing for accuracy.

When you use this activity with your students for the first time, you may find the following comments useful:

◈ This activity can be done using either customary or metric units of measure. However, because they have more familiarity with the customary units, students usually find that system easier to work with when doing the activity for the first time.

◈ Although students usually find that they need to measure more than five parts of their original object in order to make their scale drawing accurate, have them record only five measures on their actual scale drawing to avoid cluttering the page.

◈ Show students page 27 of *Cut Down to Size at High Noon*. Write the key, as shown there, on the board: $\frac{1}{16}'' = 1$ *square*. Ask students what it means. Then elicit that it is incorrect because a square measures area whereas the side of a square measures length. Point out that they will be measuring lengths and need to indicate this correctly when they record their scales.

◈ To help students who are having difficulty choosing an appropriate scale for their drawing, have one or more volunteers explain to the class how they determined their scale and how they knew it was appropriate.

◈ Some students fail to take enough measurements of their objects. If you encounter this situation, show former students' work or your sample, pointing out all the measurements that were not written on the final drawing but were necessary to make an accurate depiction. This also provides an opportunity to elicit that angles in the original object will be represented by congruent angles in the scale drawing.

◈ During the final discussion, help students connect their scale drawings to similar figures by doing the following:

- Elicit once again the properties of similar figures: All corresponding angles are congruent and all corresponding lengths are proportional (have the same scale factor).
- Ask whether the face of the original object and the scale drawing of that object are similar figures. Occasionally, students will think they are not similar because the original object is three-dimensional; in this case, remind them that the scale drawing depicts only a two-dimensional view of the object.
- Emphasize that corresponding angles in similar figures are congruent by showing student work (such as the first example in Figure 6–1). Students quickly conclude that any angles in the original figure remain the same in the scale drawing.
- Ask volunteers to explain how the corresponding lengths between the original object and the scale drawing are proportional. Look for two kinds of explanations:

  Using proportions: The student in the first example in Figure 6–1 could show the following proportion for a scale of "side length of a square $= \frac{1}{8}$ inch":

$$\frac{1 \ [\textit{side length of one square on graph paper}]}{\textit{length of car on graph paper}}$$

$$= \frac{0.125'' \ [\textit{actual side length of one square}]}{3'' \ [\textit{actual length of car}]}$$

$$0.125n = 3$$

$$n = 24 \ \text{side lengths to represent length of model car}$$

For each measure on the model car, the same basic proportion could be used, substituting the length of a part of the car for 3 in the previous proportion to find the number of side lengths needed to represent that part of the car in the scale drawing.

Using a scale factor: Again referring to the first example in Figure 6–1, since the side length of a square equals $\frac{1}{8}$ inch on the grid paper, every inch is represented by eight side lengths of squares in the drawing. That means the scale factor between the model car and the scale drawing is eight. Since the model car is 3 inches long, multiply three by eight to find the number of side lengths needed in the scale drawing to represent the total length of the model car. Multiply every measure of the model car by eight, the scale factor, to find the number of side lengths needed to represent that measure in the scale drawing.

Extensions

◈ Ask the students to do a second scale drawing, changing either (1) the units they must use (customary or metric) or (2) the scale of their drawing (if they did an enlargement the first time, they must do a reduction for the second drawing, and vice versa).

◈ Ask the students to find the area of their scale drawing and use the result to estimate the approximate area of that face of the actual object. They should take into account the contours of the real object. If appropriate, have them also measure the corresponding face of the actual object to find its approximate surface area. Then lead a discussion about the relationship between the scale factor of corresponding linear parts and the scale factor that connects the areas of the actual object and that of the scale drawing.

Golden Rectangle Survey

Related Topics: angles, percent, probability, ratio

Overview
Students create and conduct a survey, then analyze the results, to test a claim that is centuries old. The claim: People have a preference for a golden rectangle.

Materials
◈ golden rectangles, 1 per student (see *Go for the Golden 2,* on page 19)
◈ compasses, 1 per pair of students
◈ straightedges, 1 per pair of students
◈ protractors, 1 per pair of students
◈ 3-by-5-inch index cards, 1 per student

Vocabulary: golden ratio, golden rectangle, precision, proportion, ratio

Prerequisite Skills and Concepts
Students should have some familiarity with the Fibonacci sequence and the golden ratio.

Instructions

1. Before class, prepare a survey sheet as directed in Instruction 4.

2. Ask students to define a *golden rectangle*. Remind students, if necessary, that the ratio of the sides of a golden rectangle is about 1.62 to 1. Tell the class that for centuries there have been claims that most people seem to subconsciously favor such rectangles. Ask how many of the students believe this is true. Explain that they will test this claim using surveys they design.

3. Tell students that each of them will create a survey sheet containing a golden rectangle and three other rectangles that are *not* golden. If necessary, review the appropriate constructions. You might do this by asking a volunteer to give the instructions for constructing a rectangle using only a compass and a straightedge while another volunteer follows those instructions at the board or on an overhead transparency.

   Distribute the golden rectangles that the students constructed during the *Go for the Golden 2* lesson (page 19) or provide each student with the instructions to construct one (see Blackline Masters).

4. Post and go over the following guidelines:

   a. Construct four rectangles on a blank sheet of paper.
   b. The rectangles can be placed anywhere on the survey sheet and oriented in any direction.
   c. The rectangles should fill most of the paper, and each rectangle should be clearly labeled *A*, *B*, *C*, or *D* at random.
   d. One of the rectangles must be a golden rectangle. The other three rectangles should have a length-to-width ratio that is not close to the golden ratio.
   e. Write your name on the back of the survey sheet.

   Show a sample survey to the class, so the students can see the general format desired. You may also do a quick survey of the class to see which rectangle the students prefer as a launch for the activity. This addition raises the interest level of most classes.

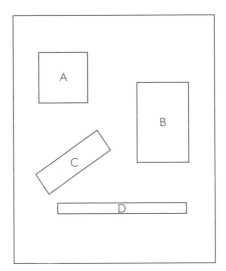

5. Hand out the materials. Circulate as students work, checking that they are constructing only one golden rectangle and three nongolden rectangles.

6. As students complete their survey sheets, ask them to exchange surveys with a partner. Have partners check each other's surveys, using the following guidelines:

   a. Does each rectangle have four right angles?

   b. Is one of the rectangles a golden rectangle? Measure and find the ratio of length to width to verify your answer. On the back of the survey, write down the measures and the ratio you find.

   c. Do any of the other three rectangles look a lot like a golden rectangle? If so, indicate on the back of the survey which one has to be redrawn.

   d. Are the rectangles labeled A, B, C, and D?

   e. When you are done, write the following on the back of the survey sheet: *Survey sheet checked by* _____ and fill your name in the blank.

   f. Return the survey to the owner.

7. After all surveys have been checked, have the students discuss the wording they are going to use when conducting the survey. First, explain the following:

   a. Uniformity is an important part of a valid survey, and the wording the class agrees upon should be used by everyone in the class.

   b. Comments and questions should not, in any way, give the impression that the surveyor is looking for a particular answer.

   c. The same person should not participate in more than one student's survey.

   Next, have students work in pairs or small groups to suggest appropriate wording for their interviews and then share their ideas with the entire class. When the class has agreed upon the exact phrasing it wants to use, have each student write the script on an index card for handy reference when conducting the survey.

8. Allow time for each student to administer the survey to twenty people. Discuss the importance of asking people of different ages, different occupations, and so on. Suggest that the students record the results on the back of the survey, using tally marks:

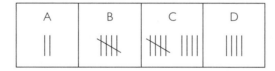

9. After all students have brought their results to class, compile them. Record the number of respondents out of twenty that chose the golden rectangle from each student's survey sheet.

10. Lead a class discussion about the validity of the following statement: People prefer the golden rectangle more than any other rectangle. Have the class calculate the percent of respondents that chose the golden rectangle as well as each of the others. Then, have them analyze the results by comparing their percentages with the results theoretical probability would predict (25 percent for each rectangle).

Notes to the Teacher

In this lesson, students create and conduct a survey and then analyze the results. This lesson reinforces what students have learned about the golden rectangle and its special property.

When you use this activity with your students for the first time, you may find the following comments useful:

❖ Take time to discuss the ratios of length to width that students find for their classmates' golden rectangles. Emphasize that the ratio for each golden rectangle in the survey should round to 1.62 or 1.6. If appropriate, discuss error in measurement and the degree of precision that is appropriate in different situations.

❖ The wording the students use with the respondents to the survey should be similar to the following:

- *"Students in my class are conducting a survey. Has anyone shown you a survey like this today?"*

  If the answer is yes, thank the person and move on. If the answer is no, continue:

- *"Please choose which one of the rectangles on this page you like the best."*

  If the person asks for clarification, add:

- *"Tell me which rectangle seems to have the most pleasing shape to you."*

❖ If one student's results are very unusual (for example, a rectangle other than the golden one is chosen by most participants), have the students discuss why they think this happened. Look back at the rectangles on that individual's survey. Usually when this happens, the survey has another rectangle with proportions close to a golden rectangle. Also have the class decide whether the results of that survey should be omitted from the class results.

❖ Help the class understand that theoretically, the probability for a participant choosing the golden rectangle on any particular survey like theirs is $\frac{1}{4}$ or 25 percent because each rectangle has the same chance of being picked. The theoretical probability that one particular rectangle out of four (in this case, the golden rectangle) would be chosen most often on *every* student's survey is extremely low, $(\frac{1}{4})^x$ when x equals the number of surveys conducted. For example, if twenty students conducted a survey, this probability would be $(\frac{1}{4})^{20}$, or about 0.0000000000009. This leads into a discussion about the validity of the claim that people prefer the proportions of the golden rectangle to others, which almost always intrigues students.

Extension

If your students are proficient in drawing and measuring the lengths of segments or if you want this activity to focus mainly on ratio, let the students use *The Geometer's*

Sketchpad or similar software to do their constructions and measurements. This leaves more time for them to compare ratios, not just for the golden rectangles, but for other groups of rectangles as well. Each small group of students could make a conjecture and use the rectangles and responses from the class's surveys to see whether the conjecture is supported. For example, they might check to see whether the respondents preferred squares to rectangles for which the length-to-width ratio is greater than 1.5. Of course, these additional investigations can be also done without computer technology, time permitting.

 ## A Different Look

Related Topics: area, linear functions, perimeter, visual patterns

Overview
In this lesson students build larger and larger similar shapes using pattern blocks. Students work with the shapes to see how the scale factor between similar figures is related to their areas and perimeters.

Materials
◈ pattern blocks: 14 each of triangles, squares, rhombi, and trapezoids per student and 9 hexagons per student
◈ *A Different Look* recording sheets, 1 per student (see Blackline Masters)
◈ rulers, 1 per student

Vocabulary: area, base unit, congruent, coordinate graph, corresponding angles, linear function, perimeter, regular polygons, scale factor, similar figures

Prerequisite Skills and Concepts
Students should understand and be able to find the perimeter and area of polygons. They should know that the corresponding angles of similar figures are congruent and their corresponding sides are proportional.

Instructions

1. Explain to the students that they will be exploring perimeter, area, and similar figures using pattern blocks. Take a few minutes to introduce, or review, the different pattern block pieces.

2. Ask students to offer definitions for the terms *perimeter*, *area*, *regular polygon*, *similar figures*, and *scale factor*. Verify correct answers.

3. Tell students that they will be building sets of larger and larger similar shapes. Draw an equilateral triangle (in green, if possible) on the board. Next to it draw four more equilateral triangles, as illustrated below.

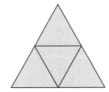

Explain that in a set of similar triangles, the single green triangle is identified as Stage 1. Write *Stage 1* beneath the single green triangle. Explain that the figure containing four triangles is Stage 2. Label it. Point out that the base unit for this set of figures is a green triangle and therefore only green triangles can be used to build each successive stage. Have students find the perimeter and the area of Stage 1 ($P = 3$, $A = 1$) and then Stage 2 ($P = 6$, $A = 4$). Ask what the scale factor between the two stages is. Students should respond that the length of the sides of the Stage 2 triangle is twice that of the Stage 1 triangle or the perimeter of Stage 2 is twice that of Stage 1.

4. Distribute the materials. Tell the students that they will work in pairs to build larger and larger similar triangles using only green pattern blocks. Instruct them to find the perimeter and area of each stage and to record all their findings on their recording sheet, being careful to put the information in the appropriate columns. Explain that they are to look for patterns in their data and make predictions. Further explain that they will do the same steps for other pattern block shapes. For each set of figures, the shape used for Stage 1 will be the base unit of area for that set.

5. Give students the following guidelines:
   a. As you do each part of the investigation, compare and discuss findings with your partner. Be prepared to explain your predictions and thinking with other members of the class.
   b. After you complete the last section of the investigation, write a summary of the investigation.

6. When all students have completed the activity, lead a class discussion. Have students share their findings and summaries. Discuss any differences and help students resolve them.

Notes to the Teacher

In this activity students use different pattern blocks for the base unit as they build sets of similar figures. Through this experience, students reinforce what they know about perimeter, area, and similar figures and connect these concepts to functions. In addition, the opportunity to connect the scale factor between similar figures to their perimeters and areas is embedded in the lesson.

When you use this activity for the first time with your students, you may find the following comments useful:

◈ It is easy to find the perimeter at each stage by counting because all sides of all the shapes measure 1 inch, with the exception of the trapezoid, whose longest side is 2 inches. Students can also confirm their answers using a ruler.

◈ Students can also count to find the area, but point out to them that they are measuring with a base unit other than the standard square unit. For example, when exploring with the green triangles, the area for each stage is the number of green triangles it contains. When exploring with the yellow hexagon, the area for each stage is the number of yellow hexagons it contains, and so on.

◈ As they work with the triangles, some students may need to trace the original shape and then spin the pattern block to see how the corresponding interior angles compare with each other. This is a good way to verify that the angles are congruent, an essential step in verifying that larger stages of the triangle pattern are similar.

◈ The students' drawings for the triangles should look like these:

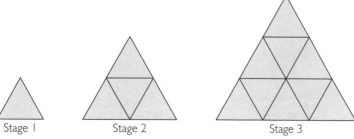

Stage 1   Stage 2   Stage 3

◈ As you circulate among the students, encourage them to look for visual patterns in the early stages of the triangles. Then ask them to connect these visual patterns to the data in the table or the symbolic rule they find for Stage n. Students usually see the 3n pattern for perimeter as it represents three copies of the length of a side, which comes easily from the definition of an equilateral triangle. The area pattern does not always come so easily, and many students will describe it as $n \times n$ before they recognize that this is n^2.

Correct data for the triangles are shown in the following table.

Stage	Number of Inches on Each Side	Perimeter in Inches	Area in Base Units (Number of Equilateral Triangles)
1	1	3	1
2	2	6	4
3	3	9	9
4	4	12	16
5	5	15	25
10	10	30	100
100	100	300	10,000
n	n	$3n$	n^2 or $n \times n$

❖ With some classes, you may want to stop for a class discussion after all pairs of students have completed Part 1 of the investigation. Similarly, you may decide to break for discussion after each section of the investigation. If so, prepare an assignment for students who finish early to do while they wait or allow them to do an assignment of their choice.

❖ A common error students make when doing Part 2 is to make a quadrilateral that has congruent angles but not four equal sides. Correct figures for Stages 1, 2, and 3 are shown below.

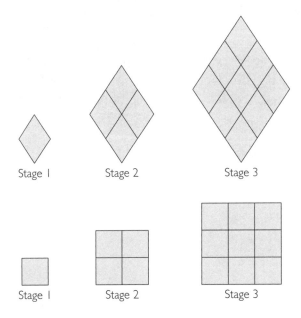

Stage 1   Stage 2   Stage 3

Stage 1   Stage 2   Stage 3

❖ The arrangements for isosceles trapezoids and regular hexagons can be quite frustrating for some students. Looking at the data patterns from the first two stages of the isosceles trapezoid can be helpful. Once they have a good guess for the total number of trapezoids needed to build Stage 3 or 4, they usually are able to construct the figure.

One arrangement for stages using trapezoids:

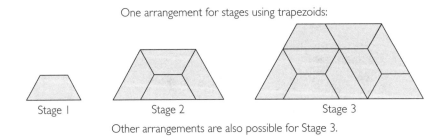

Stage 1   Stage 2   Stage 3

Other arrangements are also possible for Stage 3.

❖ Most students notice that they cannot build the higher stages of the regular hexagon by using only hexagons. An appropriate assignment is to ask students to explain in writing why this can't be done. Otherwise, you can allow the students to break a rule of the activity and use other pieces from the pattern block set. Although students may use many different combinations of shapes to build the larger stages, they should notice (and it should be brought up in the class discussion) that all successful combinations will be made using pattern blocks equal to the same number of regular hexagons. Some students will discern this from the chart while others may need to stack their pieces into a column of blocks arranged into regular hexagons to prove that the total number is the same.

Here is one possible arrangement for the pattern of similar hexagons:

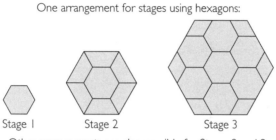

One arrangement for stages using hexagons:

Stage 1   Stage 2   Stage 3

Other arrangements are also possible for Stages 2 and 3.

Note that in the Stage 2 drawing above, the six isosceles trapezoids could be traded for three regular hexagons, making a total of four base units. Similarly, the six rhombi around the corners of the design in Stage 3 could be traded in for two regular hexagons, making a total of nine base units.

❖ This lesson's emphasis on measuring area in a nonstandard base unit forces students to think of area in a different way and is good preparation for the lesson that takes a new look at the Pythagorean theorem (page 158).

Extension

Have the students plot the points determined by the data they found in this lesson on a coordinate graph. Tell them to use the stage number as the *x*-coordinate and the perimeter as the *y*-coordinate for each set of shapes. Have students use a different color for each series of points so they can see the different perimeter relationships for each shape. Ask students the following questions:

❖ Why are some of the lines that represent the perimeter data steeper than others?

❖ If you plot the areas (*x* equals stage number, *y* equals area) for each set of figures, what will the graphs look like?

❖ How could you add another column to your data to make the area graphs reflect the area of all the figures using the same base unit? (Omit the set of orange squares and use the green triangle as the base unit of area for all the shapes.)

◈ After adjusting the area data, predict what the graphs would look like. (The graphs would be curves, with the distance between each pair of coordinates increasing.)

In a class discussion, contrast the linear functions represented by the perimeter graph with the curve produced by the growth in the area function. If appropriate, ask students what patterns they might predict if it were possible to construct a regular polygon with a side length of –2.

If appropriate, help students draw the connection between the ratio of the perimeters and the ratio of the areas of each pair of similar shapes: the ratio of the areas is the square of the ratio of the perimeters.

 Pythagoras Plus

Related Topics: area, Pythagorean theorem, regular polygons, right triangles

Overview
Students construct regular polygons on the sides of right triangles to see whether the Pythagorean theorem is true for shapes other than squares.

Materials
◈ rulers or straightedges, 1 per student
◈ protractors, 1 per student
◈ compasses, 1 per student
◈ 11-by-14-inch or larger blank paper, 1 sheet per student
◈ *What's Your Angle Pythagoras?* by Julie Ellis (2004)

Vocabulary: apothem, hypotenuse, leg (in triangles), Pythagorean theorem, regular polygon

Prerequisite Skills and Concepts
Students should

◈ be familiar with the Pythagorean theorem and how to use it to find the side lengths of right triangles;

◈ know how to do basic constructions with a compass and a straightedge or with a ruler and a protractor (the following website has good instructions, including online videos, for such constructions; http://regentsprep.org/Regents/math/math-topic.cfm? TopicCode=construc.); and

◈ know how to find the measure of each interior angle in a regular polygon.

Instructions

1. Introduce this exploration by reading *What's Your Angle Pythagoras?* to the class. In this book, young Pythagoras uses square tiles to discover the theorem named after him and uses it to solve problems. Explain that you have a question related to the Pythagorean theorem for the class to investigate.

2. Ask for a volunteer to explain the Pythagorean theorem in his own words. Then pose this question to the students: "Suppose that *What's Your Angle Pythagoras?* is a true story. What do you think would have happened if the spilled tiles were not square, but another shape that had congruent sides and congruent angles?"

   After what most likely will be a lively discussion, elicit from the students that squares are regular polygons and that regular polygons always have congruent sides and congruent angles. Pose another question: "What do you think would happen if each side of a right triangle was an edge of a regular triangle, regular hexagon, regular octagon, or other regular polygon? Would the sum of the areas of the polygons on the two legs equal the area of the polygon on the hypotenuse?"

3. Distribute the materials. Tell each student to construct a right triangle in the center of the large sheet of paper and have a partner check for accuracy. If appropriate, you may want to suggest that they use a Pythagorean triple, such as 3-4-5, as measures of the triangle's side lengths.

4. Give the following instructions:
   a. Select a regular polygon.
   b. Construct it on each side of your right triangle.
   c. Find the area of each polygon you have constructed.
   d. Compare the sum of the areas of the polygons on the legs with the area of the polygon on the hypotenuse.

5. Have students share their work with their partners, and then lead a class discussion. As students share their findings, have them list the following information in a table on the board: the lengths of the sides of their right triangle; the shape they built on the sides of their right triangle; and whether the Pythagorean theorem held true.

Notes to the Teacher

This activity provides practice in constructing a right triangle and regular polygons, finding the areas of regular polygons, and using the Pythagorean theorem.

When you use this activity with your students for the first time, you may find the following comments useful:

◈ Emphasize that accuracy in doing constructions and calculations is essential for drawing valid conclusions.

◈ Starting with right triangles that have whole number lengths (for example, 3, 4, and 5; 5, 12, and 13; 6, 8, and 10; 8, 15, and 17, and so on) will make finding the areas of the regular polygons and seeing the relationships among those areas easier for students.

◈ Alternatively, you can let students use pattern blocks for a more concrete experience. For example, if a student draws an equilateral triangle along each side of a 3-, 4-, and 5-inch right triangle, she can fill the triangles in with the green triangular pattern blocks and then count them. The student would find nine triangles on one leg, sixteen on the other, and twenty-five triangles on the hypotenuse, thus confirming the Pythagorean theorem.

◈ If students are struggling to find the areas of their regular polygons, suggest breaking the polygons into shapes for which they know how to find the area. At this point, most students will divide their polygons into triangles, as shown below.

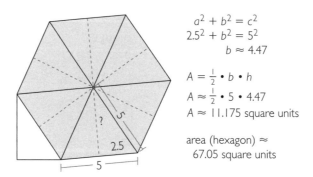

$$a^2 + b^2 = c^2$$
$$2.5^2 + b^2 = 5^2$$
$$b \approx 4.47$$

$$A = \frac{1}{2} \cdot b \cdot h$$
$$A \approx \frac{1}{2} \cdot 5 \cdot 4.47$$
$$A \approx 11.175 \text{ square units}$$

area (hexagon) $\approx$
67.05 square units

◈ Sometimes one or more students discovers a shortcut for finding the area of any regular polygon, that is, area = $\frac{1}{2}$ • side length • altitude of each congruent triangle (apothem) • number of sides, or area = $\frac{1}{2}$ • perimeter of polygon • apothem. Be sure to have the student(s) share these findings with the class, and name the method after the student(s) who discovered it.

❖ If some students finish early, ask them to choose a different regular polygon or a different right triangle, repeat the steps, and see whether the results support their conclusion from their first exploration.

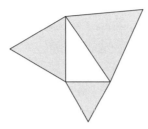

Extensions

❖ Have students investigate whether the Pythagorean theorem is true for polygons that are similar but not regular.

❖ With dynamic software such as *The Geometer's Sketchpad*, it is relatively easy for students to check out whether the Pythagorean theorem holds for any similar figures with corresponding parts having the same ratios as the sides of the triangle.

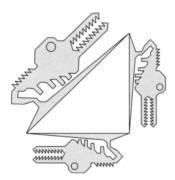

 Using Indirect Measurement

Related Topics: angles and angles of reflection, ratio, right triangles

Overview

Students use various indirect measurement methods to find the height of tall objects. Each pair carries out two different methods and then the class shares and compares all four methods.

Materials

❖ *Using Indirect Measurement* method cards, 2 different cards per pair of students (see Blackline Masters)

❖ metric measuring tapes (as long as possible) or meter sticks, 1 per pair of students

❖ objects located outdoors such as a tall tree or a flagpole, especially ones that will interest students, such as humorous or whimsical statues, gigantic playground equipment, or unusual objects of art (**Note:** Several pairs may measure the same object.)

❖ clinometers, up to 6 for a class of twenty-four students (see "Notes to the Teacher" section)

❖ mirrors (at least 3-by-4 inches) with a small dot in the center, up to 6 for a class of twenty-four students

❖ grid paper for Method 4

Vocabulary: corresponding parts, parallel, perpendicular, plumb bob, proportion, ratio, scale drawing, sighting an object, similar figures

Prerequisite Skills and Concepts

Students should know how to set up and solve proportions. They should also be familiar with the following concepts:

❖ In similar triangles, corresponding angles are congruent and pairs of corresponding sides have the same ratio.

❖ Two "nested" similar triangles are formed when a line is drawn parallel to one side of a triangle and intersects the other two sides.

❖ If two angles in a pair of triangles are congruent, the third angles are also congruent and the triangles are similar.

❖ The sides opposite congruent angles in a triangle are congruent.

❖ When a light ray hits a mirror at an angle, it is reflected at the same angle.

Instructions

1. Before this lesson, obtain, make, or have the students make clinometers (see "Notes to the Teacher" section for instructions). Also make or copy and enlarge the drawings shown below (see page 163) to help students understand each method of indirect measurement they will be using.

2. To begin, ask students how they would measure the height of a tall tree or a building. Unless they suggest it, explain that they can use what they have learned about similar figures to get a very good estimate for the height of such objects. To explain each method, display the drawings you enlarged and go through the steps as described on the corresponding method cards.

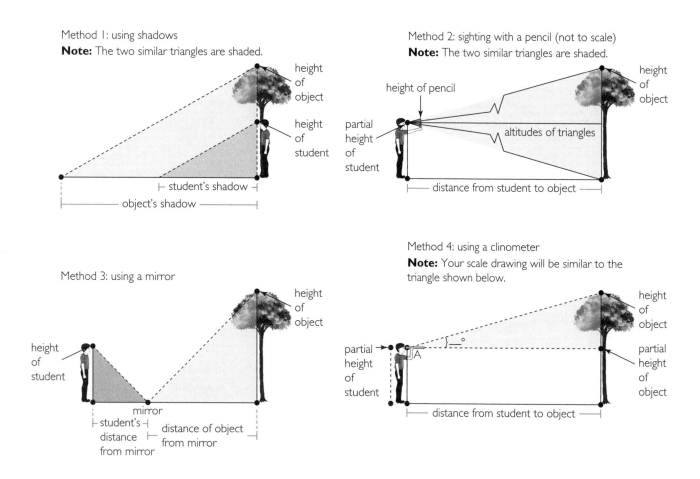

Method 1: using shadows
Note: The two similar triangles are shaded.

height of object

height of student

├ student's shadow ┤

├───────── object's shadow ─────────┤

Method 2: sighting with a pencil (not to scale)
Note: The two similar triangles are shaded.

height of pencil

height of object

partial height of student

altitudes of triangles

├───── distance from student to object ─────┤

Method 3: using a mirror

height of student

height of object

mirror

├ student's ┤
distance from mirror

├── distance of object from mirror ──┤

Method 4: using a clinometer
Note: Your scale drawing will be similar to the triangle shown below.

height of object

partial height of student

°

A

partial height of object

├───── distance from student to object ─────┤

3. Demonstrate how to use a clinometer for the class. The angle they measure will be read as the number of degrees between 90 degrees and the degree measure through which the string falls. For example, in the illustration below, the student would record *20°*.

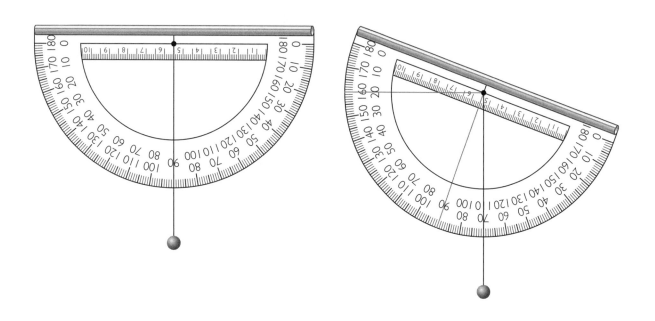

4. Give two different method cards and the appropriate materials to each pair of students. They will measure the same object, using two different methods for each object. Remind the students that the measures they calculate will always be estimates of the actual heights, but that careful measuring will give them more accurate results.

5. When all students have completed their measurements and calculations, have pairs of students who measured the same object compare results. Then lead a whole-class discussion about their findings, any challenges they faced, the mathematics they used, and situations in which these methods would be useful, such as finding how high a tree is before cutting it down or how high the face of a cliff is before rappelling or bungee jumping.

Notes to the Teacher

This activity provides students with hands-on experiences with several different methods of indirect measurement, all of which involve similar figures. It can both solidify students' understanding of similar figures and strengthen their view of mathematics as a practical, worthwhile endeavor.

When you use this activity with your students for the first time, you may find the following comments useful:

◈ To construct a clinometer, you will need glue, a drinking straw, a semicircular protractor, string, and a weight (washers work well) to serve as a plumb bob.

  1. Glue a straw to the straight edge of the protractor.
  2. Attach the weight to the string.
  3. Tape the weighted string to the center of the edge of the protractor, as shown below.

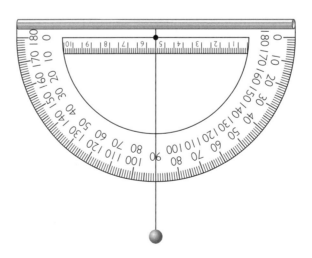

◈ It is important for students to realize that the accuracy of the clinometer method depends on both the reading of the angle using the clinometer and the reproduction

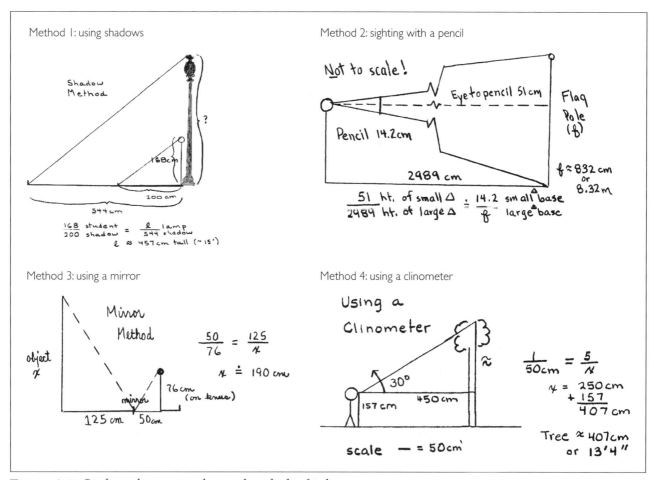

Figure 6–2 *Students demonstrated several methods of indirect measurement.*

of this angle on grid paper. Since the scale drawing must be a triangle that is similar to the actual scene depicted, it is important to double-check the angle formed by sighting with the clinometer and to use a protractor carefully when constructing the angle. Students can use the perpendicular lines on the graph paper to help construct the third side of the triangle.

◈ Drawings and work from your students will vary (see Figure 6–2 for some examples).

Extension

Identify a tall object for which the height can be found (a flagpole or building) through research, blueprints, or city records. Have students work with the same partner for this lesson. Have partners estimate the height of the object using one of the methods for indirect measurement that they did not use before. Have the class compile its data and do statistical analysis (finding the range, mean, mode, and median and creating box plots). Have students examine the spread of the data and determine whether one method produced more consistent results than the others. They can also discuss whether one method produced estimates that were significantly closer to the actual height of the object than the estimates obtained through the other methods.

CHAPTER 7

Mass/Weight, Temperature, and Density

Introduction

There is no area of mathematics that offers more opportunities to engage students in explorations that connect to the real world than measurement. Topics related to the environment (pollution, waste management, population challenges, and climate change), health (nutrition, fitness, and health risks), and technology (data storage, processing speeds, and easy access to enormous amounts of data) offer exciting opportunities to do measurement and reason about the results.

This chapter contains three lessons that both target topics in the measurement strand and also offer powerful and important connections to real-world phenomena. We believe the ultimate goal of teaching measurement in middle school is to provide such investigations. In the lesson *Wise Up* (below), which focuses on mass and weight, students study popular cereals to determine the cost per gram and the percent of each cereal box that is "wasted." Focusing on temperature, the lesson *Cool Dogs* (page 170) requires students to record, graph, and analyze the cooling rates of different types of hot dogs. Using both old and new pennies, students work in pairs to find the coins' weight and volume in the lesson *Exploring Density* (page 175). Once they have gathered the data, students interpret their findings and compare their two sets of results to foster an understanding of density.

We have included the three lessons in this book because of the importance of the topics and also as a reminder that there is a plethora of measurement topics that provide appropriate contexts in which to introduce, reinforce, or extend the big ideas of the measurement strand. From angstroms to light-years, and from Apgar scores to body mass indices, we encourage you to explore such topics with your students to foster an understanding of real-world applications of measurement while strengthening their appreciation of the power and utility of mathematics.

 **Wise Up**

Related Topics: mass/weight, metric measurement, percent, rates, surface area

Overview

Students work with several popular cereals to determine the cost per gram and the percent of each cereal box that is wasted.

Materials

- ◈ cereal, 1 box each of five different kinds
- ◈ zip-top bags, large enough to hold the contents of one cereal box, at least 5
- ◈ balances, 5
- ◈ metric rulers, 5
- ◈ *Wise Up* recording sheets, 1 per student (see Blackline Masters)
- ◈ clear sandwich bag containing 100 regular-size paper clips and labeled "50 grams"
- ◈ permanent marker
- ◈ optional: calculators, 1 per group

Vocabulary: centimeter, gram, percent of error, referent, square centimeter, surface area, unit cost

Instructions

Note: This lesson will take at least two classes to complete.

Day 1

1. Prior to the lesson, do the following:

   a. Remove the cereal from each cereal box, put it into a zip-top bag, label the bag with the name of the cereal, and return the bag to the box.

   b. On each cereal box, write the price using a permanent marker.

   c. On each cereal box, cover up the information about its weight.

   d. Determine the weight of one empty zip-top bag.

   e. Set up a table with the cereal boxes and the balances.

2. To begin the lesson, pose this question to the class: "How would you decide which cereal to buy if you did the shopping for your family?" Have a short discussion about factors that might contribute to the decision. Explain to the students that they will be investigating five different kinds of cereal for information that might influence their decisions as "wise consumers" (people who use the factors that are the most important to make shopping choices).

3. Ask students to define *gram* and *unit cost*. Verify correct answers and ask for any referents the students have for 50 grams. Pass around 50 grams (about one hundred regular-size paper clips in a sandwich bag) to provide an immediate referent for mass.

4. Help the class determine the method to be used for finding the *actual* weight of cereal in a box. Show them that the cereal from each box has been put into a zip-top bag. Most likely, they will suggest weighing the bag with the cereal inside and then subtracting the weight of the bag. If not, ask questions to elicit this method. Then tell the class the weight of the zip-top bag.

5. Explain that they will work in pairs to gather data for all five cereals, and when they are done, they are to return to their seats to do calculations and write their conclusions. Caution the class that every pair must complete these steps before the class ends, so everyone needs to be especially mindful of gathering data in a timely manner.

6. Discuss and, if needed, work through an example of determining cost per gram and/or percent of error.

7. Distribute the recording sheets. Let students know that they will do only Parts 1 and 2 today. Monitor the students as they gather data for accuracy and time efficiency.

8. When all students have completed their work, provide the weight listed on each cereal box to the class. Then lead a discussion about their findings and conclusions.

Day 2

1. Before class, do the following:
   a. Remove the cereal from each zip-top bag and pour it back into its original box.
   b. Remove the balances.
   c. Put out the rulers.

2. Have students locate their recording sheets. Ask students to define *dimensions*, *surface area, centimeter, square centimeter* (cm^2), and *percent of error*. Verify correct answers and solicit what *percent of waste* means in this situation (percent of the cereal box's cardboard not needed to hold the cereal).

3. Tell the students that in pairs they are to do the following for each type of cereal:
   a. Estimate the surface area of the box.
   b. Measure the dimensions of the cereal box and find its surface area.
   c. Measure the dimensions of that part of the box not taken up by the cereal and find the amount of wasted surface area (cardboard).
   d. Find the percent of waste.
   e. Make conjectures about why the cereal companies might choose to make the boxes larger than necessary.

4. When all students have completed their work, lead a discussion about their findings and conclusions.

Notes to the Teacher

This activity provides hands-on experience with metric weight in grams and surface area in square centimeters. It improves students' skills in estimating metric weights, surface area, and percents.

When you use this activity with your students for the first time, you may find the following comments useful:

❖ As a prelesson activity, poll your classes to find their favorite cereals (a real-world use for mode!) and use those for the lesson. Or check www.lavasurfer.com/cereal-stats.html for the best-selling cereals.

❖ To facilitate classroom management, write a letter on each cereal box and have pairs of students rotate in alphabetical order. That is, if they start with Box A, they then work with boxes B, C, D, and E, in that order. If they start with Box B, they work in the order B, C, D, E, and A, and so on. This system helps avoid two or more pairs needing to work with the same box to finish gathering data.

❖ Give the students an assignment to work on while they are not doing measurements or calculations for this investigation.

❖ If you have large classes and only one or two balances, you may want to use six cereals and have each pair gather complete data for three of the boxes and then share the actual weights once they have returned to their seats.

❖ In calculating the amount of cardboard wasted for each cereal box, some students may need help to realize that the top of the cereal box should not be included as waste.

❖ Students often correctly point out that cereals settle after the boxes are packaged during shipping and handling. Such comments offer the opportunity to discuss the inevitability of inaccuracies in measurement and the value of using percents as a way to compare values in a relative, rather than absolute, way.

Extension

Have the class do a comparison of the nutritional values of different cereals. Ask students to bring in the panels from their cereal boxes at home that contain nutrition facts. Have them compare both the amount and the percent of the recommended daily amount for the ingredients among the cereals.

 **Cool Dogs**

Related Topics: algebraic thinking, functions, rates, temperature

Overview

This lesson provides a real-world context for students to perform an experiment that engages them in measuring, observing, and making conjectures. Students record and graph the cooling rates of different types of hot dogs and then analyze the data.

Materials

◈ hot dogs of different kinds, such as beef, chicken, regular, and nonmeat, that all weigh the same, 1 per student

◈ package labels, 1 from each type of hot dog used

◈ cooking device capable of heating the hot dogs for 50 seconds

◈ small paper plates, 1 per student

◈ paper towels, 1 per student

◈ food thermometers with a Celsius scale, preferably digital, at least 1 per pair of students

◈ scales calibrated in grams, at least 4

◈ timers or watches with a second hand, 1 per pair of students

◈ grid paper with a unit length $\leq \frac{1}{5}$ inch, 1 sheet per student

◈ colored pencils, one color for each type of hot dog, 1 per student

◈ overhead transparencies with a grid that matches the students' grid paper, 1 for each type of hot dog

◈ overhead marking pens, one color for each type of hot dog, at least 1 of each color

◈ newsprint or blank overhead transparencies, at least 2 sheets (see Instruction 1)

◈ optional: calculators, 1 per student

Vocabulary: cooling rate, linear function, nonlinear function, unit rate

Prerequisite Skills and Concepts

It would be helpful if students had some experience with cooling rates and their graphs.

Instructions

Note: Depending on the amount of equipment, such as the number of thermometers, and the cooking device available, this activity can take several class periods to complete.

1. Before class, do the following:

   a. Using a permanent marker, place a mark on each thermometer about three and half inches from its tip.

   b. Write the steps to be used by each pair of students on a sheet of newsprint or an overhead transparency. (See Instruction 5.)

c. On an overhead transparency, prepare a class chart on which each student will list the highest and lowest temperature readings he made while heating his hot dog. Use the following headings: Student, Lowest Temperature Recorded, and Highest Temperature Recorded.

2. Tell the students that they will do an investigation to decide the answer to the question, "What kind of hot dogs would you recommend people buy and why?" Ask the class what factors are important to people who eat hot dogs. Students will probably mention taste and possibly nutritional value. If they do not mention temperature, ask whether this might be a factor for some people (After all, who likes to eat a cold hot dog?). Explain to the students that they will be determining, then comparing, the cooling rates of different kinds of hot dogs. (Each pair will investigate two kinds of hot dogs.)

3. Ask students to offer definitions for the terms *rate* and *unit rate*. Verify correct answers.

4. Have students suggest categories of information that they think people would consider when purchasing hot dogs and/or would affect the rate at which a hot dog cools. Make a list of their suggestions. Then create a table like the one shown below. Using the labels from the hot dog packages, have students fill in the appropriate columns in the table. Leave the headings for temperature readings (the last four columns) blank until after the students have gathered data.

Hot Dog Data												
Brand	Type	Weight (g)	Total Fat (g)	Saturated Fat (g)	Protein (g)	Number of Calories	Price of Package	Unit Price	Temp at 80 Seconds	Temp at 260 Seconds	Mid-range Cooling Rate	Mean Unit Cooling Rate
	regular	56g										
	chicken	56g										
	beef	56g										
	nonmeat	56g										

5. Display the list of instructions you have prepared and explain the procedure that each pair will follow to gather its data.

a. Prepare a data sheet numbered from 5 to 300 seconds in intervals of 5 on a sheet of lined paper. Record the kind of hot dog at the top of the sheet.

b. Weigh the hot dog, trim off excess if needed, and record the weight on your data sheet. (See "Notes to the Teacher" section.)

c. Have your timer, thermometer, and data sheet close at hand.

d. Place one hot dog on a small paper plate and cover it with a paper towel.

e. Heat the hot dog for 50 seconds in the cooking device. Quickly insert the thermometer (up to the mark on the thermometer) into the hot dog and start timing.

f. One student in the pair reads aloud the temperature every 5 seconds and the other student records the data.

g. Record the temperatures at 5-second intervals for 5 minutes (300 seconds).

h. Repeat the steps for your second hot dog.

i. Enter the lowest and highest temperatures you recorded for each hot dog on the class chart.

6. Demonstrate inserting the thermometer into a hot dog.

7. After all students have gathered data, display the transparency containing the lowest and highest temperature readings obtained by each student. Have students discuss what they notice about the overall range of temperatures for the hot dogs.

8. Next, tell students that each of them will graph the data for the pair's two hot dogs. Explain that both sets of data will be graphed on the same sheet of grid paper with two different-colored pencils. Have the class discuss and agree upon what label will be used for each axis, the scale to use, and any breaks in the axes.

9. While the students are working, circulate to choose at least one student to graph the data for each kind of hot dog on an overhead transparency. Also, be sure that the students you select have used the same labels, scale, and breaks in the axes so that the transparencies can be laid atop one another for direct comparison.

10. When everyone is ready, have the selected students place their transparencies on the projector so that the axes align. If there are two very different graphs for a particular type of hot dog, display each one separately along with graphs of the other types of hot dogs to let the class make conjectures about what factors might have caused the different results. Eventually, have the class decide which graph seems to be "typical" for each type of hot dog.

11. Next, ask each pair to discuss the class data and graphs and list its observations on lined paper. Ask each pair to look for overall patterns and to consider any patterns in the data for the interval from 80 to 260 seconds.

12. When everyone is ready, have students share their observations with the class. Encourage students to add observations of others with which they agree to their original list.

13. Next decide on a reasonable method that the class should use to compare the cooling rates for the hot dogs. You have many choices ranging from simply drawing conclusions based upon the visual patterns observed in the graphs to using regression formulas with graphing calculators.

    One option is to ask students to calculate the total rate of change for the 3-minute interval from 80 seconds (after all types of hot dogs have begun to cool) to 260 seconds for each type of hot dog. Then ask them to find the *mean unit rate* during that interval. For example, the total rate of change for a 3-minute interval might be 13 degrees and the mean unit rate would be $\frac{13}{3}$ or about 4.3 degrees. Strictly speaking, these are not mathematically valid measures of cooling since the rates of cooling are not constant, but they can be used for comparisons among the different kinds of hot dogs; this method provides extra practice with finding rates and unit rates. You can decide whether you are comfortable with using this idea with your class.

14. Have each pair of students consider the nutritional value and other information in the class table to make and record a conjecture(s) about the factor(s) that cause the different cooling rates among the kinds of hot dogs. Then have students share their conjectures. Most often students speculate that the total amount of fat causes the difference in the cooling rates: the more fat grams a hot dog has, the slower it cools. This conclusion is consistent with the data, but it remains a conjecture since the students have proof only for correlation, not for a causal relationship.

15. Finally, return to the original question, What kind of hot dogs would you recommend people buy and why? Ask students to put their thoughts in writing and then share them in a class discussion.

Notes to the Teacher

This activity provides a real-world context (cooling rates for different kinds of hot dogs) for gathering data, graphing nonlinear functions, and making conjectures based on data. It also provides practice with the concepts of rate and unit rate as students use their findings to derive these measures for the temperature of the hot dogs as they cool.

When you use this activity for the first time with your students, you may find the following comments useful:

◈ If you have time constraints, you can weigh the hot dogs before class and trim off any excess to be sure they all weigh the same number of grams. Many single hot dogs weigh 56 or 57 grams.

◈ It is easier and safer to use a small microwave than to cook the hot dogs in water. To make sure all hot dogs are heated the same amount, consistently have either one or two hot dogs (from two different pairs) in the microwave at the same time. Be sure the same procedure is used for the whole class.

◈ Be sure the hot dogs you use have as wide a range of total fat content as you can locate. Notice that the values listed in the following table provide clear contrasts between the different kinds of hot dogs.

	Hot Dog Data: Michael and Lian
Brand	Type	Weight (g)	Total Fat (g)	Saturated Fat (g)	Protein (g)	Number of Calories	Price of Package	Unit Price	Temperature at 80 Seconds	Temperature at 260 Seconds	Mid-range Cooling Rate	Mean Unit Cooling Rate
	regular	56g	14g								$\frac{6.6°}{3 \text{ min.}}$	$\approx\frac{2.2°}{\text{min.}}$
	chicken	56g	9g								$\frac{9.6°}{3 \text{ min.}}$	$\approx\frac{3.2°}{\text{min.}}$
	beef	56g	6g								$\frac{12.5°}{3 \text{ min.}}$	$\approx\frac{4.2°}{\text{min.}}$
	nonmeat	56g	0g								$\frac{17.6°}{3 \text{ min.}}$	$\approx\frac{5.8°}{\text{min.}}$

◈ Ideally, you want to have several pairs of students doing the experimenting at the same time. Your ability to do this, however, will depend upon the number of thermometers and the method of cooking the hot dogs that are available. While not heating their hot dogs, the rest of the students can be recording the nutritional value of all the types of hot dogs being used by the class and working on another assignment until their turn comes to heat their hot dogs.

◈ Remind the class that the more accurate the data gathered are, the easier it is to find patterns. In this case, the student reading and calling out the temperature must try to focus on doing each reading in the same way, that is, saying the temperature that is displayed *exactly* as each five-second interval ends.

◈ Following are some observations student pairs often make about the class data and graphs:

- The data and graphs do not look quite like the cooling graphs they have seen before. Of course, this will come up only if students have prior experience with cooling graphs.
- The temperature readings for each kind of hot dog increase before they start to decrease.
- The amount of time the temperature continues to rise varies among the different kinds of hot dogs.
- The hot dogs do not cool at a constant rate. Once cooling begins, the rate of cooling slows down over time for every kind of hot dog.

- During the first 80 seconds of cooling time, the data and graphs are quite different for the different kinds of hot dogs.
- The graphs for the interval from 80 to 220 seconds are almost linear for each kind of hot dog, but the rates of change are not the same among the different kinds of hot dogs.

Extension

In order to be safe to eat, hot foods need to remain at least 60 degrees Celsius to prevent the growth of bacteria. Have your students do an activity similar to this one in which they compare the cooling rates for different foods to find out how long they remain safe to eat after being removed from the oven.

It is easiest to do this investigation with a small microwave oven. Have students cook various foods (for example, corn, macaroni and cheese, chicken noodle soup) according to the recommendations from the manufacturer or the automatic features of the microwave oven. Then have them students use a food thermometer with a Celsius scale, preferably digital, to take a temperature reading every 20 seconds for the first 5 minutes and then once a minute until the temperature falls below 60 degrees Celsius. End by having them graph the cooling rates of different types of foods and analyze the data. A nice follow-up is to have the students write up the results for their parents.

Be sure that the containers students use are microwave safe and do not heat up in the microwave.

 ## Exploring Density

Related Topics: algebraic thinking, coordinate graphing, slope

Overview
Students work in pairs to find the weight and volume of old and new pennies. They interpret and compare their results to foster an understanding of density.

Materials
- U.S. pennies dated before 1982, 25 pennies per pair of students (pairs can share)
- U.S. pennies dated after 1984, 25 pennies per pair of students (pairs can share)
- graduated cylinders, 1 per pair of students
- water, at least 20 milliliters per pair of students
- balances, 1 per pair of students (pairs can share)
- *Exploring Density* recording sheets (see Blackline Masters)
- grid paper, 1 sheet per student
- colored pencils, 1 each of two colors per student

Vocabulary: cubic centimeter, density, intercept, mass, meniscus, milliliter, slope, volume, weight

Prerequisite Skills and Concepts

Students should have prior experience finding a line of best fit and an equation for a set of data that approximates a linear function.

Instructions

1. Explain to the students that they will explore the property of *density*. Do not provide a definition. Instead emphasize two facts: (1) density is a derived measure that relates the *mass* and *volume* of an object, and (2) the density of a wooden cube is greater than the density of a foam cube of the same size. Tell them to search for both informal and mathematical ways to define *density* as they proceed through this exploration.

2. Show the class two sets of pennies. Tell them that in 1982, the U.S. government changed the materials used to make pennies. Up until that time, the alloy used to make pennies was primarily copper, but since then pennies have been made from a zinc alloy with a thin copper coating. As a result of this change, the older pennies, those minted before 1982, and the newer pennies, those minted after 1984, have distinctly different densities.

3. Pass out the recording sheets and other materials and briefly outline the procedure to be used. While students work, circulate to spot problems and answer questions.

4. When all students have completed the questions on the recording sheet, lead a discussion. Include the following topics:
   - comparison of graphs for older pennies and newer pennies
   - comparison of the slopes of the two graphs
   - meaning of slope in this context
   - comparison of the density of older pennies and newer pennies
   - definitions of *density*—informal and formal
   - student answers and explanations for Questions 5 and 6

Notes to the Teacher

This activity allows students to explore the concept of density through a hands-on experience. It involves gathering and analyzing data, graphing sets of data, and finding both the line of best fit and the corresponding symbolic rules for the sets of data.

When you use this activity for the first time with your students, you may find the following comments useful:

◈ Pennies for the years 1982 through 1984 are not included because the change in the composition of pennies took place over a two-year period at the various sites where they are minted. Excluding pennies made during those years helps ensure that the data are as reliable as possible.

◈ In going over the steps the students should follow, be sure they understand that for each new stage of the exploration, they must record only the total volume of all the pennies in the graduated cylinder and the total mass of all pennies in the graduated cylinder so far (*not* including the initial volume or mass of the water or the graduated cylinder). Watch for errors related to this part of the procedure as you circulate while the students are working.

◈ Talk with students about the meniscus (the curved upper surface of the water in the graduated cylinder) that they must consider when measuring the volume of the water and pennies for each stage of the exploration. Be sure they understand that it doesn't matter whether they measure from the top, middle, or bottom of the meniscus as long as they are consistent in the way they make this measurement from stage to stage. (See Figure 7–1 for an example of student data.)

◈ If a pair of students is having trouble deciding what the slope in the graphs represents, remind them that slope can be thought of as $\frac{\text{the change in } y}{\text{the change in } x}$ and ask them to substitute the name for the quantities that are changing in this exploration rather using y and x. When they suggest, $\frac{\text{the change in mass}}{\text{the change in volume}}$, remind them that, for a linear model, the slope remains the same between any two points. Since $(0, 0)$ can be considered as the first point in this situation (pennies can't have negative mass or volume), then slope $= \frac{\text{mass}}{\text{volume}}$. If they still have doubts, ask them to divide mass by volume for any number of older pennies in the data chart (except for zero pennies, of course) to see that the quotient is close to nine.

Data Table				
Number of Pennies	Pennies minted before 1982		Pennies minted after 1984	
	Volume of Pennies (ml)	Mass of Pennies (g)	Volume of Pennies (ml)	Mass of Pennies (g)
0	0	0	0	0
5	1.5	14.0	1.7	12.5
10	3.0	28.1	3.5	24.1
15	5.0	44.5	5.7	37.0
20	6.5	61.5	7.4	50.8
25	8.5	77.0	9.1	63.4

Figure 7–1 *One student's data table showed weight and volume of pennies.*

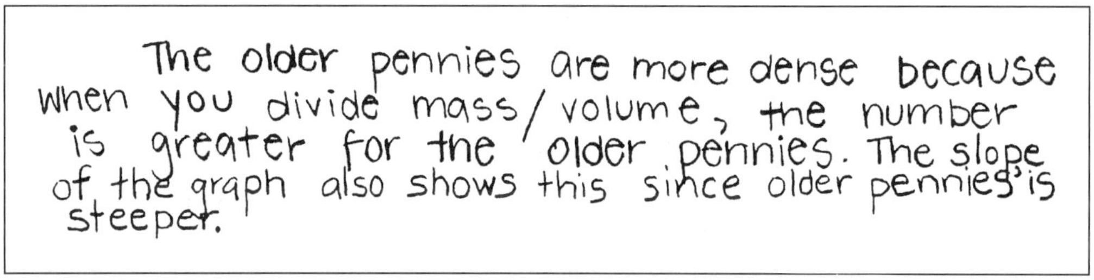

The older pennies are more dense because when you divide mass/volume, the number is greater for the older pennies. The slope of the graph also shows this since older pennies is steeper.

Figure 7–2 *One student's answer to Question 4 on the recording sheet.*

◈ See Figure 7–2 for one student's answer to Question 4 on the recording sheet.

◈ For question 5, since density $= \frac{\text{mass}}{\text{volume}}$, and the density for the pre-1982 pennies is about 9 grams per cubic centimeter, the students should be able to use the formula to find that the volume of fifty older pennies would be approximately 17 cubic centimeters or 17 milliliters.

◈ For Question 6, students can again use the density formula and the density for newer pennies (about 6.85 grams per cubic centimeter) to find that their mass would be approximately 119 grams.

Extension

Have students use the same procedure they used in this lesson to find the density for other U.S. or foreign coins. They can also use the Internet to find out which metals are used in making those coins and make hypotheses about which metals have greater density. One website that has information about the composition of U.S. coins is www.usmint.gov/about_the_mint/index.cfm?action=coin_specifications.

Blackline Masters

Bigger and Bigger

Cylinder Mystery

The Difference an Angle Makes 2

If I Were a . . .

Exploring Rates: Reading Rates

Exploring Rates: Shooting Hoops

Exploring Rates: Tracing Stars

Rows of Stars

Hello, Proportions

Unpumped Prices

Could It Be?

Go for the Golden 1

What's with the Factor?

Swinging Rates

What Are Similar Polygons?

A Different Look

Using Indirect Measurement Method Cards

Wise Up

Exploring Density

Decimeter Strips

Glue ten decimeter strips end to end to form one meter-long stick.

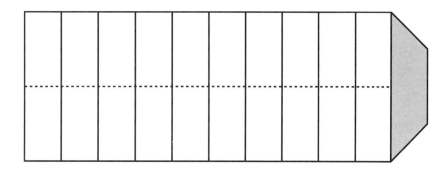

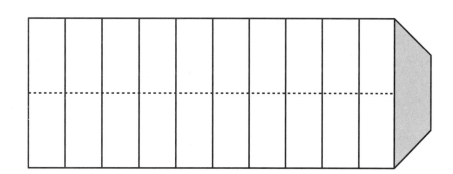

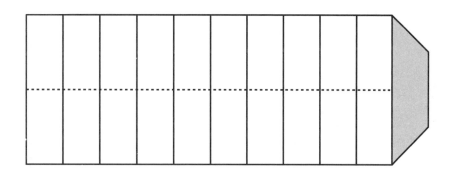

Procedures for Mini Metric Field Meet Events

Standing Broad Jump

Stand behind the starting line. From a standing position, jump as far as you can. Estimate in centimeters the distance from the starting point to the point closest to the starting line that any part of your body touched. Have your partner record your estimate. Then, with the help of your partner, find and record the actual measurement.

Plate Discus Throw

Stand behind the starting line. Toss a styrofoam plate as far as possible without leaning across the line. The distance of the throw will be measured from the starting line to the part of the plate that is closest to the starting line. Estimate how many meters long the throw was. Have your partner record the estimate. Then, with the help of your partner, find and record the actual measurement.

Straw Javelin Toss

Stand behind the starting line. Throw a drinking straw as far as possible without leaning across the line. Estimate in centimeters the distance from the starting point to the closest part of the straw. Have your partner record your estimate. Then, with the help of your partner, find and record the actual measurement.

Cotton Ball Shot Put

Stand behind the starting line. Toss a cotton ball as far as possible without leaning across the line. Estimate in millimeters the distance from the starting point to the closest part of the cotton ball. Have your partner record your estimate. Then, with the help of your partner, find and record the actual measurement.

Standing Triple Jump

Stand behind the starting line and start from a standing position. The triple jump starts with a *hop*—take off with and land on the same foot (e.g., right). Then comes the *step,* which begins with the *same foot as the hop* (right) and ends on the other foot (left). Finally, move the back foot (right) even with the front foot (left) and then jump with both feet together. Thus, the foot-strike pattern is R, R, L, together (or L, L, R, together). Estimate in centimeters the distance from the starting point to the point closest to the starting line that any part of your body touched at the end of the jump. Ask your partner to record your estimate. Then, with the help of your partner, find and record the actual measurement.

From *Sizing Up Measurement: Activities for Grades 6–8 Classrooms* by Ann Lawrence and Charlie Hennessy.
© 2007 by Math Solutions Publications.

Mini Metric Field Meet

Event	Estimated Distance	Actual Distance	Difference Between Estimate and Actual Distance	Percent of Error
Standing Broad Jump	_____ cm	_____ cm	_____ cm	_____
Plate Discus Throw	_____ m	_____ m	_____ m	_____
Straw Javelin Toss	_____ cm	_____ cm	_____ cm	_____
Cotton Ball Shot Put	_____ mm	_____ mm	_____ mm	_____
Standing Triple Jump	_____ m	_____ m	_____ m	_____

Constant Perimeter

Do all work on grid paper.

1. Work with a partner to list all rectangles that have a perimeter of 24 units, using whole number side lengths only. After completing each of the following steps individually, compare your results with your partner's and make any needed changes or additions.

2. Use a straightedge to help you draw each of the rectangles in your list on a coordinate graph. Use the origin as the bottom left vertex of each rectangle.

3. Organize the measures of the bases and altitudes of the rectangles into a three-column T-chart with the following headings: Length of Base; What I See/Think; and Length of Altitude.

4. In writing, summarize any patterns you notice in your table or in the rectangles you have drawn.

5. Using a different-colored pencil than the one you used to draw the rectangles, mark a point at the top right vertex of each rectangle you graphed.

6. Describe in writing what the graph looks like and the pattern made by the points you have just marked. Explain why your answer makes sense when compared with your table.

7. Write a function rule in words and/or symbols for the points you marked. Explain why this rule makes sense for all rectangles with a perimeter of 24 units. Be prepared to explain your findings and your function rule to the class. Be sure your explanation shows that you understand what the perimeter of a rectangle is.

From *Sizing Up Measurement: Activities for Grades 6–8 Classrooms* by Ann Lawrence and Charlie Hennessy.
© 2007 by Math Solutions Publications.

That's Irrational!

Follow the steps below to create a number line that will accurately display irrational numbers as well as whole numbers.

1. Using a straightedge, draw a horizontal line, as shown below.

2. Place a point on the line close to its left end. Open your compass to a length you want for the unit length (the distance between 0 and 1) on your number line. It is fine if your unit length is different than that of other students. Using your compass, mark on your number line the positions for the whole numbers 1 through 5, as shown below. When you have finished making the arcs, do not change the setting of your compass.

3. Graph a point at each intersection of your number line and an arc. Label each point with its coordinate.

4. Construct a line perpendicular to your number line that passes through the origin.

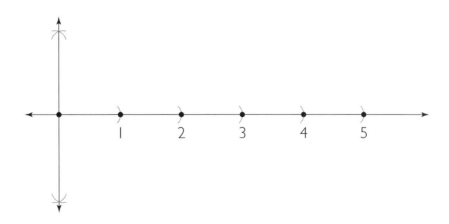

From *Sizing Up Measurement: Activities for Grades 6–8 Classrooms* by Ann Lawrence and Charlie Hennessy.
© 2007 by Math Solutions Publications.

5. Place the point of your compass (set at the unit length you chose) at the origin and mark the unit length above 0 on your new line. Label the point A.

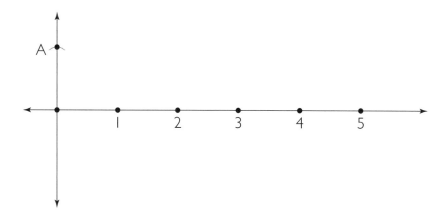

6. Connect point A to the graph of 1 to form a right triangle.

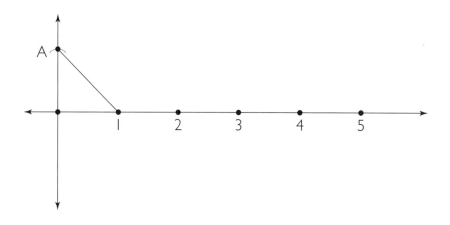

7. Set your compass length to match the hypotenuse of the right triangle. Place the point of your compass at the origin and draw a circle.

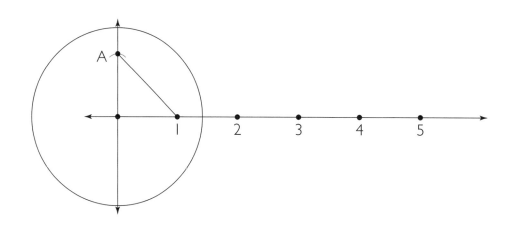

8. Graph a point at the intersection of the circle and your number line (to the right of the origin). Determine the coordinate of the new point. What kind of a number is it? Show your work and explain your thinking on your paper.

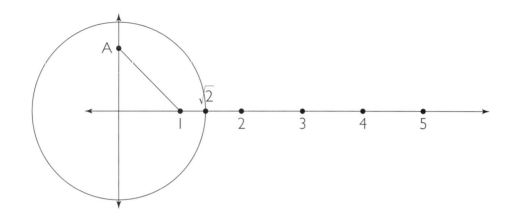

9. Now that you have one irrational number displayed on your number line, use a similar method to find and display the location of these irrational numbers: $\sqrt{3}$, $\sqrt{5}$, and $\sqrt{7}$. Show your work and explain your thinking on your paper.

10. Compare your completed number line with those of some of your classmates. How are they similar? How are they different? Explain the mathematical reasons for those similarities and differences.

Go for the Golden 2

Use the following steps to construct a golden rectangle. It has a special length-to-width ratio, which is approximately 1.61803. It is a shape that people through the centuries have claimed is the most pleasing of all possible rectangles.

Part I

Use your straightedge and compass for the following instructions.

1. Construct a square whose side measures 2 units. Be sure that all sides are congruent and all angles measure 90 degrees. Pick any length for your unit. It is not important that your unit be the same size as that of any other student.

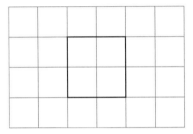

2. Construct a segment that connects the top left vertex of the square with the midpoint of its right side. Using mathematics you know, find the exact length of this segment without using a measuring tool and record it here: _____

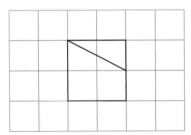

3. Use a compass to construct a circle. Use the segment you constructed in Step 2 as its radius and the midpoint of the square's side as its center.

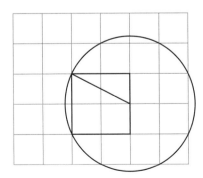

4. Extend the right side of the square upward until it intersects with the circle. Using mathematics you know, find the exact length of the segment between the bottom right corner of the square and the new intersection on the circle and record it here: _____

This segment is the length of your golden rectangle.

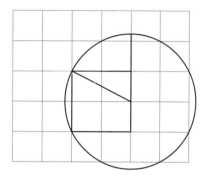

5. Construct a line perpendicular to the length of your golden rectangle that passes through the point where the vertical segment intersects with the circle.

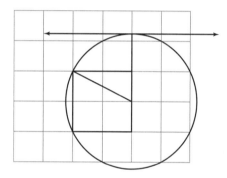

6. Extend the left side of the original square to intersect the perpendicular line you constructed in Step 5. The shaded rectangle shown at the right is your golden rectangle. Write an expression for the exact length-to-width ratio of your golden rectangle: _____

Use a calculator to find the decimal approximation for this expression and record it here: _____

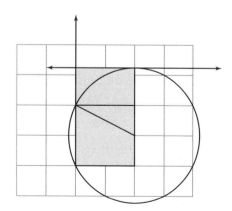

From *Sizing Up Measurement: Activities for Grades 6–8 Classrooms* by Ann Lawrence and Charlie Hennessy.
© 2007 by Math Solutions Publications.

Part 2

Work with your partner to answer the questions below.

1. Compare your rectangle with those of other students. How are they alike? How are they different?

_____

_____

_____

_____

_____

2. One definition for a golden rectangle is that the following must be true: $\frac{\text{length}}{\text{width}} = \frac{\text{length} + \text{width}}{\text{length}}$. Use your findings to see whether this equation is true for your golden rectangle. Show your work and conclusion below.

3. Could the mathematical statement $\frac{\text{length}}{\text{width}} = \frac{\text{length} + \text{width}}{\text{length}}$ be true for a rectangle that is not a golden rectangle? Why?

_____

_____

_____

_____

_____

4. Do you find the appearance of your golden rectangle pleasing? Explain your thinking.

_____

_____

_____

_____

_____

From *Sizing Up Measurement: Activities for Grades 6–8 Classrooms* by Ann Lawrence and Charlie Hennessy.
© 2007 by Math Solutions Publications.

What's My Angle?

Part 1: Interior Angles of Polygons

1. Use a straightedge to draw a large triangle on a blank sheet of paper. Label the vertices *A*, *B*, and *C*. Measure each interior angle of the triangle with a protractor. Record the measure of each angle on the sheet of paper with your drawing.

2. Have your partner check your measures. Make any needed corrections and find the sum of the angles. Record the sum in your drawing.

3. In the table below, record the number of sides and angles, the measures of each individual interior angle, and the sum of the interior angles in your triangle.

Personal Polygon Data			
Type of Polygon	**Number of Sides and Angles**	**Measures of Each Interior Angle**	**Sum of Interior Angles**
triangle			
quadrilateral			

4. On the back side of the paper with your triangle, draw a large quadrilateral using the straightedge. Label the vertices *A*, *B*, *C*, and *D*. Measure each interior angle and have your partner check your measures. Make any needed corrections and then find the sum of the angles. Record the data for your quadrilateral on your drawing and in the table above.

5. Repeat the same procedure for a pentagon and then for a hexagon, using another sheet of paper. Be sure to record the measure of each angle in the drawing. Compare your results with your partner's. If your sums are the same, enter the data into the appropriate columns of the following table (Number of Sides and Angles and Total of All Interior Angles). If not, compare with another pair of students, resolve any differences, and then record the data. Then transfer the appropriate data for triangles and quadrilaterals from your first table to the following one.

From *Sizing Up Measurement: Activities for Grades 6–8 Classrooms* by Ann Lawrence and Charlie Hennessy. © 2007 by Math Solutions Publications.

Polygon Data				
Type of Polygon	Number of Sides and Angles	Total of All Interior Angles	Total Number of Interior Triangles	Total of All Exterior Angles
triangles				
quadrilaterals				
pentagons				
hexagons				
octagons				
decagons				
dodecagons				
36-gons				
n-gons				

6. List any patterns you find in the data so far.

_____

_____

_____

7. Compare patterns with your partner and make any needed changes or additions.

Part 2: Interior Triangles of Polygons

1. If you draw one diagonal in your quadrilateral (going from any vertex to a nonadjacent vertex), how many triangles are formed? Compare your results with your partner's. Record the information in your table.

2. Choose any vertex in your pentagon and draw a diagonal to each nonadjacent vertex. How many triangles are formed? Compare your results with your partner's. Record the information in your table.

3. Repeat the process with the hexagon.

From _Sizing Up Measurement: Activities for Grades 6–8 Classrooms_ by Ann Lawrence and Charlie Hennessy.
© 2007 by Math Solutions Publications.

4. Be prepared to explain why you cannot do this process with your triangle.

5. List any new patterns you see in the table. Be prepared to explain why they make sense to you.

_____

_____

_____

6. Write a rule in words for finding the total of the interior angle measures for any polygon.

_____

_____

_____

Compare your rule with that of your partner. Be prepared to explain during class discussion why your rule makes sense.

Part 3: Exterior Angles of Polygons

1. Construct and measure each exterior angle of your original triangle. Record the measures on your drawing. Have your partner check your measures.

2. Find the sum of the exterior angles of your triangle. Compare your results with your partner's. Make any needed changes and record the sum in your table.

3. Find the sum of each interior angle in your triangle with the exterior angle adjacent to it. What do you notice?

_____

_____

_____

4. Repeat Steps 1 through 3 for at least two more of the polygons that you have drawn.

5. List the patterns you found when exploring exterior angles in various polygons.

_____

_____

_____

Compare and discuss the patterns you found with your partner. Be prepared to explain why these patterns make sense.

From _Sizing Up Measurement: Activities for Grades 6–8 Classrooms_ by Ann Lawrence and Charlie Hennessy.
© 2007 by Math Solutions Publications.

Angles in the Round

1. List the measure of each marked angle. Then compare and discuss your answers with your partner.

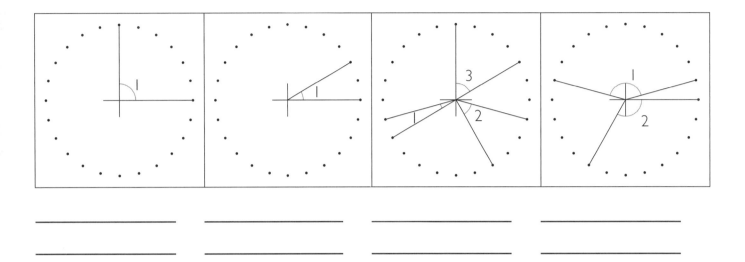

_____   _____   _____   _____

_____   _____   _____   _____

_____   _____   _____   _____

What information did you use to find the measures of the marked angles?

_____

_____

_____

2. Construct and mark each listed central angle. Then compare and discuss your answers with your partner.

m(angle 1) = 45°	m(angle 1) = 135°	m(angle 1) = 180°	m(angle 1) = 210°
m(angle 2) = 120°	m(angle 2) = 60°	m(angle 2) = 30°	m(angle 2) = 90°

What did you notice as you constructed the angles?

_____

_____

_____

3. List the measure of each marked angle. Then compare and discuss your answers with your partner.

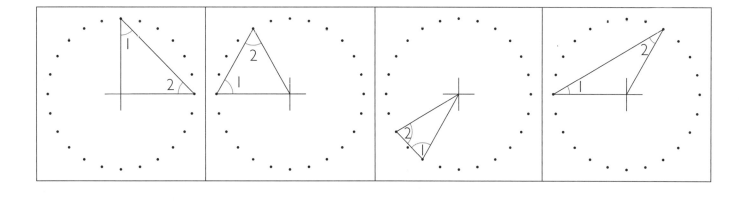

_____   _____   _____   _____

_____   _____   _____   _____

_____   _____   _____   _____

What information did you use to find the measures of the marked angles?

_____

_____

_____

4. Discuss with your partner ways to find the measure of Angle 1 in the illustration below. Then find the measure of each angle in the triangle.

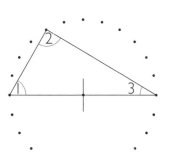

m(angle 1) = _____

m(angle 2) = _____

m(angle 2) = _____

Explain how you found the measures of the angles in the triangle shown in Step 4.

_____

_____

_____

5. Move the vertex of Angle 2 in the triangle above from F to I as shown below. What happens to the measures of each angle in the triangle? Compare and discuss your answers with your partner.

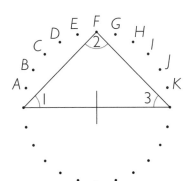
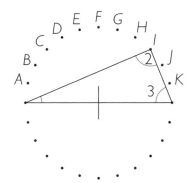

m(angle 1) = _____

m(angle 2) = _____

m(angle 3) = _____

Now move the vertex of Angle 2 to other points (one example is shown on the right above). Use the following table to record your results.

	A	B	C	D	E	F	G	H	I	J	K
m(angle 1)											
m(angle 2)											
m(angle 3)											

Compare and discuss your answers with your partner. What patterns did you find? What conclusions can you draw? Explain your thinking.

_____

_____

_____

_____

_____

_____

From *Sizing Up Measurement: Activities for Grades 6–8 Classrooms* by Ann Lawrence and Charlie Hennessy.
© 2007 by Math Solutions Publications.

About the Area of a Circle Method Cards

Method 1: Counting Squares

You need: a sheet of centimeter grid paper and a compass

1. Draw a circle with a radius of 10 centimeters on the centimeter grid paper.
2. Count all the whole square centimeters that lie completely inside the circle. This underestimates the area of the circle.
3. Count the number of squares that lie partly inside and partly outside the circle. Add this number to the number you counted in Step 2. This total overestimates the area of the circle.
4. Average the two estimates. This is the approximate area of the circle.

Method 2: Inscribing and Circumscribing Squares

You need: a copy of a circle with a radius of 10 centimeters, a compass, a protractor, and a ruler

1. Circumscribe a square around the circle with a radius of 10 centimeters. Find its area.
2. Inscribe a square inside the circle. Find its area.
3. Average the areas of the two squares. This is the approximate area of the circle.

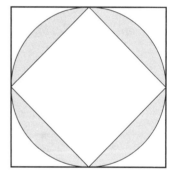

Method 3: Using the Octagonal (Egyptian) Method

You need: a copy of a circle with a radius of 10 centimeters, a compass, a protractor, and a ruler

1. Circumscribe a square around the circle with a radius of 10 centimeters. Find its area.
2. Divide the square into nine congruent squares.
3. Construct an octagon by drawing a diagonal in each corner square as shown at the right.
4. Find the area of the octagon. This is an approximation of the area of the circle.

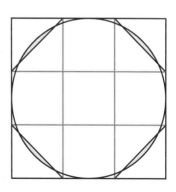

From *Sizing Up Measurement: Activities for Grades 6–8 Classrooms* by Ann Lawrence and Charlie Hennessy.
© 2007 by Math Solutions Publications.

Method 4: Weighing the Circle

You need: a linoleum circle with a radius of 10 centimeters, a supply of 1-by-10-centimeter linoleum rectangles, 9 1-by-1-centimeter linoleum squares, and a pan balance

1. Place the linoleum circle on one side of the pan balance.
2. Balance the circle with linoleum rectangular and square pieces placed on the opposite side of the pan balance.
3. Count the number of rectangular and square pieces you used. The total area of all the pieces approximates the area of the circular region.

Method 5: Using a Curvy Parallelogram

You need: a copy of a circle with a radius of 10 centimeters, a compass, a protractor, and a ruler

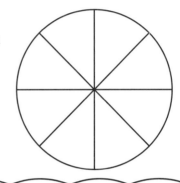

1. Divide the circle with radius of 10 centimeters into eight congruent sectors.
2. Cut out the sectors and arrange them to form a curvy parallelogram. Find the approximate area of the curvy parallelogram. This approximates the area of the circle.

Method 6: Using Beans

You need: a copy of a circle with a radius of 10 centimeters; a compass; a protractor; a ruler; 3 pieces of tape, each approximately 10 centimeters long; and a bag of beans

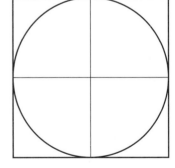

1. Cover the circle with one layer of beans. (Use a cardboard collar to "corral" the beans.)
2. Circumscribe a square around the circle. Cut it into four congruent squares as shown at the right.
3. Rearrange the four squares to form a rectangle. Tape the pieces together.
4. Place the beans from Step 1 on the rectangle, pushing them to one end of it.
5. Find the area of the part of the large rectangle covered by the beans. This area approximates the area of the circle.

From *Sizing Up Measurement: Activities for Grades 6–8 Classrooms* by Ann Lawrence and Charlie Hennessy.
© 2007 by Math Solutions Publications.

About the Area of a Circle Instructions

This investigation uses six different methods to approximate the area of a circle. Follow the steps below to complete the activity.

1. Paired Investigations

Work with your partner to use the three methods you are assigned to approximate the area of a circle having a radius of 10 centimeters. Make sure you agree on your results and that each of you can explain what you did for each method.

2. Recording Results

Using the format given below, record your results and thinking about each method you used on a separate sheet of paper.

Method Number ___: Include its title.

Description: List the steps you did.

Result: Record your results.

Analysis: Describe why the method makes sense mathematically. Explain what you think about the accuracy of this method. Add any thoughts you have after doing or hearing about other methods.

3. Class Discussion

As your classmates report their methods and findings, use the format in Step 2 to make notes about their methods and findings.

4. Reflecting on This Investigation

After all the methods have been discussed, individually answer the following questions on your paper: *Which method do you think is the best for approximating the area of a circular region? Why?*

Extra

If you and your partner finish early, invent another method to approximate the area of a circle. Try it and then describe your method in writing, including your results.

From *Sizing Up Measurement: Activities for Grades 6–8 Classrooms* by Ann Lawrence and Charlie Hennessy.
© 2007 by Math Solutions Publications.

Centimeter Grid Paper

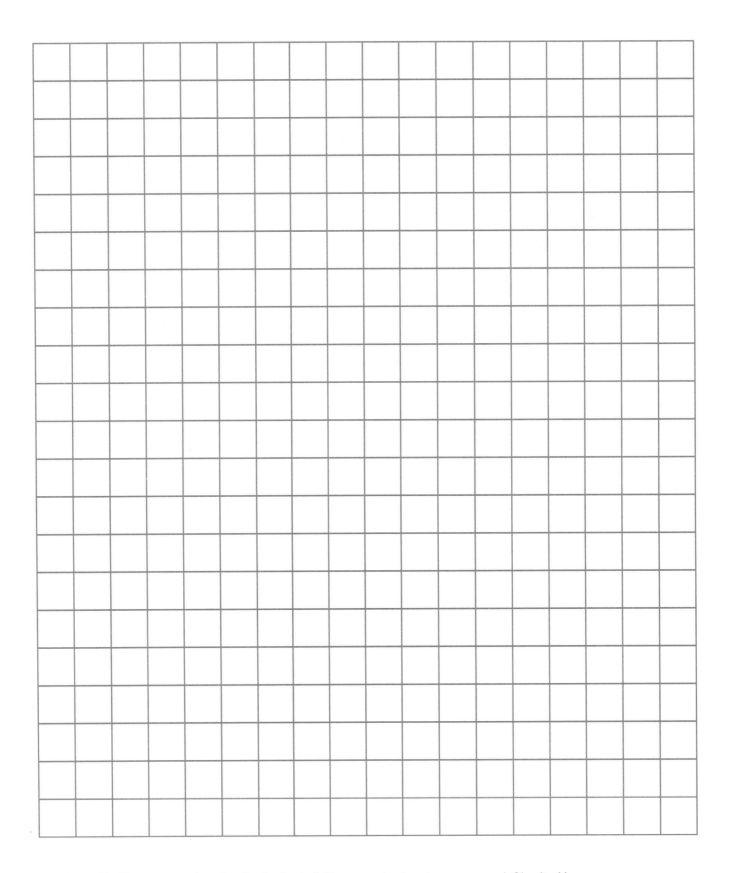

Circle with 10-Centimeter Radius

Orange You Glad . . . ?

Group Members: _____

_____

_____

Part 1

Follow the steps below to make a conjecture about how to find the surface area of a sphere.

1. Squeeze and mold your orange to make it model a sphere as closely as possible.

2. Cut your orange in half to expose a great circle of the orange.

3. Trace a great circle of your orange on a paper towel.

4. Estimate how many of these great circles you think you can cover with pieces of your orange's peel.

Record: _____

5. Trace a few more great circles than you think you will need on your paper towels.

6. Tear off pieces of the orange peel, each about $\frac{3}{4}$ to 1 square inch.

7. Use the pieces of peel to cover as many circles as possible. Each circle must be covered entirely without any gaps or overlaps.

Part 2

Use your results to answer the following questions in complete sentences. Work together to develop your answers. Then create a transparency summarizing your findings and conclusions. Each of you needs to be prepared to explain your group's thinking to the whole class.

1. Write a mathematical expression that tells the amount of area you covered for each circle. What does r in your expression stand for?

_____

_____

2. How many circles did you cover in all, using the entire peel of the orange? Based on your results, write an equation that tells the surface area of your orange.

_____

_____

3. Do you think your equation (formula) will work to find the surface area of any sphere? Explain your reasoning.

_____

_____

_____

From *Sizing Up Measurement: Activities for Grades 6–8 Classrooms* by Ann Lawrence and Charlie Hennessy.
© 2007 by Math Solutions Publications.

How Do You Grow?

Part 1

1. With color tiles, build the rectangles for the first three stages as shown below. Then build and draw the rectangles for Stage 4 and Stage 5. Finally, draw the outline for the rectangles and label the side lengths for Stages 10, 100, and *n*.
2. Use a three-column T-chart to find the perimeter for each stage. Show your work.
3. Use a three-column T-chart to find the area for each stage. Show your work.
4. Use the information in your T-charts to complete the table below.

Stage	Drawing	Base	Height	Perimeter	Area
1		2	1		
2		4	2		
3					
4					
5					
10	Draw and label side lengths only.				
100	Draw and label side lengths only.				
n	Draw and label side lengths, using variable expressions.				

From *Sizing Up Measurement: Activities for Grades 6–8 Classrooms* by Ann Lawrence and Charlie Hennessy.
© 2007 by Math Solutions Publications.

Part 2

Answer each of the following questions on lined paper. Then discuss your answers with your partner and make any changes or additions you would like. Be prepared to explain each of your answers to the class.

1. What patterns do you notice in your table? In writing, describe each pattern and why it make sense.

2. Compare patterns that relate to perimeter with those that relate to area. How are they alike? How are they different? How do these similarities or differences make sense with what you know about perimeter and area?

3. Construct two graphs on the same sheet of grid paper. Graph the base-versus-perimeter data using one color and the base-versus-area data using a different color. Explain how the appearance of the graphs makes sense with what you know about perimeter and area.

4. Will the rules (expressions for Stage *n*) you found work for any set of rectangles in a predictable way? Explain.

5. The values given below are for rectangles that belong to the set of rectangles you have explored in this investigation. Use your rules to find the value for each unknown measure:

   a. base = 40 inches; height = _____

   b. height = 200 feet; perimeter = _____

   c. perimeter = 72 centimeters; base = _____; height = _____

   d. area = 128 square feet; base = _____; height = _____

From *Sizing Up Measurement: Activities for Grades 6–8 Classrooms* by Ann Lawrence and Charlie Hennessy.
© 2007 by Math Solutions Publications.

Liquid Capacity

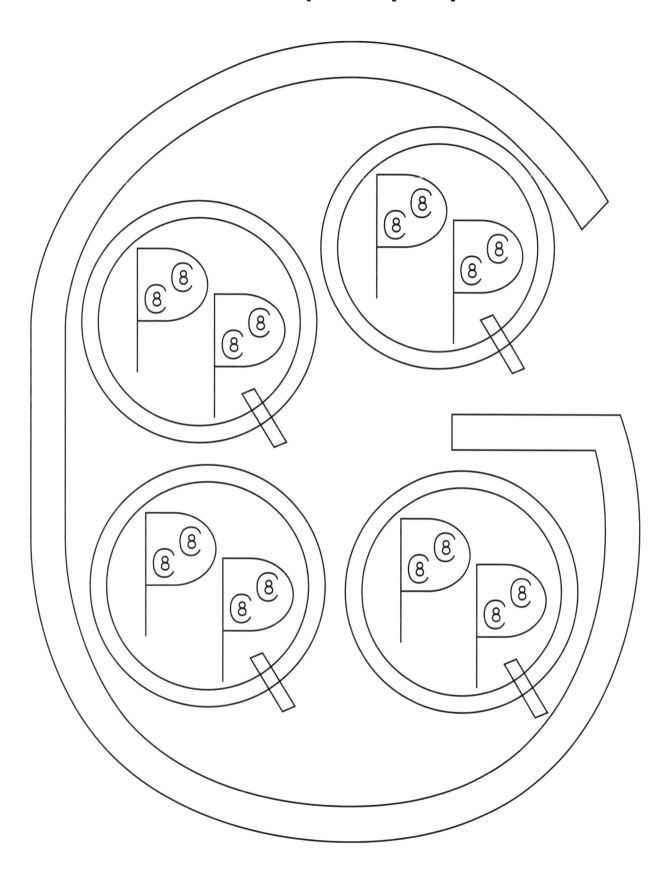

Fishing for Formulas

Cube or Other Rectangular Prism

1. Use a sheet of thick paper with a grid of 1-centimeter squares printed on it to make a net for a cube or another rectangular prism with an open top.
2. Predict the volume of your prism. Write your prediction on your paper.
3. Have the teacher check your net before you cut it out.
4. Cut out your net and tape the edges tightly so it will hold rice.
5. Use the gridlines and squares to help you verify the volume of your prism. Record your findings, and explain any differences between them and your prediction.

Pyramid

1. Use another sheet of thick paper to make a net for a pyramid, using the following rules:
   a. The base (bottom face) of the pyramid must be congruent to the base of your rectangular prism.
   b. The height of the pyramid must be the same as the height of your rectangular prism. Hint: Use the Pythagorean theorem to find the measure of the hypotenuse (the slant height) you must use for your net.
2. Have the teacher check the new net before you cut it out.
3. Cut out your net and tape the edges tightly together, except the edges of the base. The base should be a "trap door," as shown below.

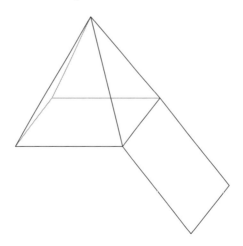

From *Sizing Up Measurement: Activities for Grades 6–8 Classrooms* by Ann Lawrence and Charlie Hennessy.
© 2007 by Math Solutions Publications.

4. Predict the volume of the pyramid. Write your prediction on your paper.

5. Predict how many times you will have to fill the pyramid with rice to completely fill the rectangular prism. Write your prediction on your paper.

6. Hold the pyramid upside down (with the point facing downward). Fill it carefully with rice. Be sure the sides do not bulge outward.

7. Pour the rice from the pyramid into the prism. If needed, revise your predictions for the volume of the pyramid and the number of times you will have to fill it with rice to completely fill the prism. Record.

8. Verify your prediction by continuing to fill the pyramid with rice and pouring it into the prism until the prism is completely filled.

9. Write a statement about your findings.

10. Use your findings to write a formula for calculating the volume of your pyramid. Substitute numbers into your formula and compare the results with the volume you found for your rectangular prism.

11. Explain in writing how the comparison of the volumes of the prism and the pyramid fits with what you found when pouring rice from the pyramid into the prism.

12. Write your results in the class data table.

From *Sizing Up Measurement: Activities for Grades 6–8 Classrooms* by Ann Lawrence and Charlie Hennessy.
© 2007 by Math Solutions Publications.

The Difference an Angle Makes I

Part 1: Getting Ready

1. **a.** In the circle you were given, what is the length in centimeters of the diameter? _____
   b. Write an expression containing π for the circumference of the circle.

   _____

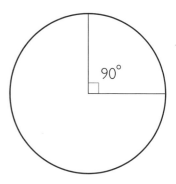

2. Using the center of the circle as its vertex, and two radii as its sides, construct a central angle of 90°, 120°, 150°, 180°, 210°, or 240°, as assigned by your teacher.

3. Your angle intersects with the circle to form a sector. What fraction of the circle's circumference is the curved edge of this sector? (Be prepared to explain your thinking.) _____

Part 2: Making Cones and Cylinders and Gathering Data

1. Carefully cut out the sector you constructed.
2. Take the rest of the circle and tape the radii together to form a cone.
3. Measure and record the diameter of the cone in centimeters. _____
4. Find and record the height of the cone by using both direct measurement and the Pythagorean theorem. Show your work.
5. Use rice to find the volume of the cone in milliliters.
6. Using the remaining paper from the sheet that you used to make your circle, make a net for a cylinder so that the base of the cylinder is congruent to the base of the cone and the heights of the cone and cylinder are the same.
7. Construct a cylinder from your net. Use rice to find its volume in milliliters.
8. Complete the following table, using data from your classmates who worked with a circle having the same diameter as yours.

Data for Circles with Diameter = _____ Centimeters					
Size of Sector Removed *m*(central angle)	Diameter of Cone (in cm)	Area of Base of Cone and Cylinder (in square cm)	Height of Cone and Cylinder (in cm)	Volume of Cone (in ml)	Volume of Cylinder (in ml)
90°					
120°					
150°					
180°					
210°					
240°					

From *Sizing Up Measurement: Activities for Grades 6–8 Classrooms* by Ann Lawrence and Charlie Hennessy.
© 2007 by Math Solutions Publications.

9. Graph the data from the table on grid paper. Use the volume of the cone as the *x*-coordinate and the volume of the cylinder as the *y*-coordinate for the point representing each pair of figures.

Part 3: Analyzing Your Findings

Answer the following questions on your own paper. Then compare and discuss your answers with your partner. Be sure you can explain your thinking.

1. Describe the pattern in the data for the diameter of the cones. Explain why this pattern makes sense.

2. Describe the pattern in the data for the height of the cones. Explain why this pattern makes sense.

3. Describe the pattern in the data for the volume of the cones. Explain why this pattern makes sense.

4. What do the data and graph tell you about the rate of change in the volumes of the cones when compared with the volumes of the related cylinders?

5. Starting with the circles your group used, if you know the volume of a cylinder, what do you know about the volume of a cone having the same area of the base and the same height as the cylinder? Do you think this pattern would work if you started with a circle of a different size? Explain your reasoning.

6. Now look at the data and graph of the students who started with a circle having a different diameter. What do you notice? Based on this data, review your response to Question 5. If you revise your thinking, explain why you did so.

From *Sizing Up Measurement: Activities for Grades 6–8 Classrooms* by Ann Lawrence and Charlie Hennessy.
© 2007 by Math Solutions Publications.

On the Ball

Part 1: Thinking About the Volume of Rectangular Prisms

1. Using cubes, build a rectangular prism that has a base that is 3 cubes by 6 cubes and a height of 2 cubes.

   a. What is the area of the base of the prism? _____ square units

   b. What is the volume of the prism? _____ cubic units

2. Break the prism into three smaller prisms, each having a base of 2 cubes by 3 cubes and a height of 2 cubes.

   a. What is the area of the base of each small prism? _____ square units

   b. What is the sum of the areas of the bases of all three small prisms? _____ square units

   c. What is the total volume of the three prisms? _____ cubic units

   d. Fill in the statements below with the correct value or word:
   For this problem, the sum of the areas of the bases of all three small
   prisms × _____ = the volume of all three prisms.

   For any number of rectangular prisms having the same _____, the sum of the areas of the
   bases × the height = the total volume of all the prisms.

Part 2: Thinking About the Volume of a Sphere

1. Cut the ball you were given into hemispheres.

2. From one of the hemispheres, cut a piece that is shaped as much as possible like a square pyramid with a "bulging base." Make sure that the base of each "pyramid" is part of the surface area of the sphere and that the apex of the pyramid is at the center of the sphere. Each member of your group needs to cut out one "pyramid."

From *Sizing Up Measurement: Activities for Grades 6–8 Classrooms* by Ann Lawrence and Charlie Hennessy.
© 2007 by Math Solutions Publications.

3. Imagine that the entire sphere has been cut into "pyramids" like the ones you have made. Now answer the following questions:

   a. Write a mathematical expression for the surface area of the entire sphere.

   _____

   b. Look at the drawing below.

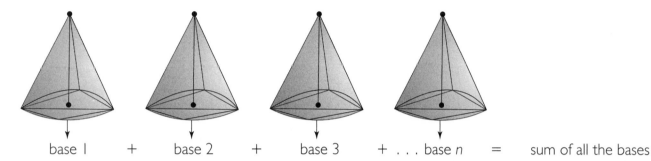

   base 1   +   base 2   +   base 3   + . . . base *n*   =   sum of all the bases

   c. What do you know about the sum of all the bases of the "pyramids"? Relate this sum to a measure of the sphere.

   _____

   _____

4. Use what you know about rectangular pyramids and spheres to answer each question below.

   a. Write the formula for the volume of a rectangular pyramid. _____

   b. What do you know about the height of each "pyramid"? Relate this height to a measure of the sphere.

   _____

   c. Complete the formula for the volume of each small "pyramid" by filling the blank. The missing word is a part of the sphere.

$$\text{volume} = \frac{B\text{(symbol for the area of base of the pyramid)} \bullet \underline{\qquad}\text{(word or symbol for the appropriate measure of the pyramid)}}{3}$$

5. Complete the formula for the total volume of a sphere by filling in the blanks with symbols that represent what you have concluded in Questions 3 and 4.

$$\text{volume of a sphere} = \frac{\underline{\qquad}\text{(sum of bases of all "pyramids")} \bullet \underline{\qquad}\text{(height of "pyramids")}}{3}$$

Or, using only symbols,

$$V = \frac{\underline{\qquad} \bullet \underline{\qquad}}{3}$$

Or, in simplest form,

$$V = \frac{\underline{\qquad}}{3}$$

From *Sizing Up Measurement: Activities for Grades 6–8 Classrooms* by Ann Lawrence and Charlie Hennessy.
© 2007 by Math Solutions Publications.

Bigger and Bigger

Part I

1. Use your cubes to build the rectangular prisms for the first three stages.
2. Use an expanded T-chart to show how to find the surface area for each stage.
3. Use a T-chart to show how to find the volume for each stage.
4. Transfer the information from your T-charts to the table below and complete the table.

Stage	Drawing/Sketch	Length	Width	Height	Surface Area	Volume
1		1	2	1		
2		2	4	2		
3						
4	Label side lengths only.					

From *Sizing Up Measurement: Activities for Grades 6–8 Classrooms* by Ann Lawrence and Charlie Hennessy. © 2007 by Math Solutions Publications.

Stage	Drawing/Sketch	Length	Width	Height	Surface Area	Volume
5	Label side lengths only.					
10	Label side lengths only.					
100	Label side lengths only.					
n	Label side lengths only, using variable expression.					

Part 2

Answer each of the following questions on your own paper. Then discuss your answers with your partner and make any changes or additions you would like. Be prepared to explain each of your answers to the class.

1. What patterns do you notice in your table? Describe each pattern you find in words. Explain how the pattern fits with what you know about surface area, volume, or both.

2. Compare the patterns you found for surface area with the patterns you found for volume. How are they alike? How are they different? Explain how these similarities or differences fit with what you know about surface area and volume.

3. Construct two graphs on the same sheet of grid paper. Graph the coordinates of the length and surface area data using one mark or color and the coordinates of the length and volume data using a different mark or color. Explain how the appearance of the graphs fits with what you know about surface area and volume.

4. Will the patterns you found in this set of prisms be the same for any set of rectangular prisms? Explain why or why not.

5. The values given below are for rectangular prisms that belong to the set you have explored in this investigation. Use the patterns you noticed to find the value for each unknown measure:

   a. length = 10 inches; height =_____

   b. width = 200 feet; surface area = _____

   c. surface area = 160 square centimeters; length = _____; width =_____;
      height = _____

   d. volume = 1,024 cubic feet; height = _____

Cylinder Mystery

Part I

Compare the volumes of three cylinders, all having the same circumference but different heights.

1. Use two pieces of 8.5-by-9-inch tagboard to make three cylinders: one 9 inches high, one 6 inches high, and one 3 inches high. The circumference of each cylinder must be 8 inches.

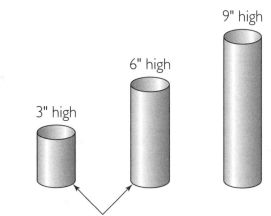

These two cylinders are constructed from the same piece of tagboard.

2. Place one 8-by-8-inch piece of tagboard under the 3-inch-high cylinder. Place the other 8-by-8-inch piece under the 6-inch-high cylinder. Imagine filling the smaller cylinder with popcorn and pouring it into the larger cylinder until the larger cylinder is filled. Predict how many times you would have to fill the 3-inch-high cylinder to do this. Write your prediction in the following data table.

3. Now fill the 3-inch-high cylinder with popcorn and pour it into the 6-inch-high cylinder. Continue filling and pouring until the taller cylinder is completely filled. Keep a count of how many times you fill the shorter cylinder. Write your results in the data table.

4. Compare the volumes of the two cylinders. The volume of the 6-inch-high cylinder with a circumference of 8 inches is how many times larger than the volume of the 3-inch-high cylinder with the same circumference? Write your answer in the data table.

5. Put the popcorn back in the original popcorn container. Now do Steps 2, 3, and 4 using the 3- and 9-inch-high cylinders. Be sure to record both your predictions and your results in the data table.

From *Sizing Up Measurement: Activities for Grades 6–8 Classrooms* by Ann Lawrence and Charlie Hennessy.
© 2007 by Math Solutions Publications.

Cylinder Mystery Data Table					
Cylinder	Height	Circumference	Radius	Prediction: Number of Original Cylinders Needed to Fill This Cylinder	Actual: Number of Original Cylinders Needed to Fill This Cylinder
Set 1 Original Cylinder	3"	8"		███████	███████
Steps 2–4	6"	8"			
Step 5	9"	8"			
Set 2 Original Cylinder	3"	8"		███████	███████
Steps 2–4	3"	16"			
Step 5	3"	24"			

Part 2

Compare the volumes of three cylinders with different circumferences but the same height.

1. Use the 16.5-by-3-inch piece of tagboard to make a cylinder 3 inches high with a circumference of 16 inches. Use the 24.5-by-3-inch piece of tagboard to make a cylinder 3 inches high with a circumference of 24 inches.

2. Place one 8-by-8-inch piece of tagboard under the 3-inch-high cylinder with the circumference of 8 inches from Part 1. Place the other 8-by-8-inch piece under the 3-inch-high cylinder with a circumference of 16 inches. Imagine filling the narrower cylinder with popcorn and pouring it into the wider cylinder until the wider cylinder is filled. Predict how many times you would have to fill the original cylinder to do this. Write your prediction in the data table.

3. Now fill the original 3-inch-high cylinder with a circumference of 8 inches with popcorn and pour it into the cylinder with a circumference of 16 inches. Continue filling and pouring until the wider cylinder is completely filled. Keep a count of how many times you fill the narrower cylinder. Write your results in the data table.

4. Compare the volumes of the two cylinders. The volume of the 3-inch-high cylinder with a circumference of 16 inches is how many times larger than the volume of the cylinder with the same height and a circumference of 8 inches? Write your answer in the data table.

5. Put the popcorn back in the original popcorn container. Now repeat steps 2, 3, and 4 using the 3-inch-high cylinder with a circumference of 8 inches and the cylinder with a circumference of 24 inches. Be sure to record both your predictions and your results in the data table.

From *Sizing Up Measurement: Activities for Grades 6–8 Classrooms* by Ann Lawrence and Charlie Hennessy. © 2007 by Math Solutions Publications.

Part 3

Analyze the patterns in your results. Write your answers for the following questions on a separate sheet of paper.

1. Work together to list patterns you see in your table.

2. Discuss the following questions with your partner. Then write your own answers for each.

   a. How does the volume of a cylinder grow when its height is doubled or tripled? How does this make sense to you mathematically?

   b. How does the volume of a cylinder grow when its circumference is doubled or tripled? How does this make sense to you mathematically?

   c. Do you think these same patterns would be found for any set of cylinders (ones with different dimensions for the original cylinder)? Why does your answer make sense mathematically?

3. Show your understanding of the results of this investigation by doing the following:

   a. Without doing any calculations, compare the volumes of the following: Cylinder 1—circumference = 8 inches, height = 12 inches; Cylinder 2—circumference = 32 inches, height = 3 inches.

   b. Substitute values in the formula for volume of a cylinder to verify your comparison.

   c. Write an explanation that you think is mathematically sound about why these results occurred.

From *Sizing Up Measurement: Activities for Grades 6–8 Classrooms* by Ann Lawrence and Charlie Hennessy.
© 2007 by Math Solutions Publications.

The Difference an Angle Makes 2

Part 1: Getting Ready

1. a. What is the length, in centimeters, of the diameter of the circle you were given? _____

    b. Write an expression containing π for the circumference of the circle. _____

2. Using the center of the circle as its vertex and half the diameter as one of its sides, construct a central angle of 30 degrees.

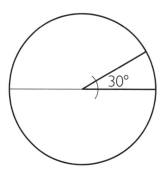

3. Your angle intersects with the circle to form a sector less than 180°. What fraction of the circle's circumference is the curved edge of this sector? (Be prepared to explain your thinking.) _____

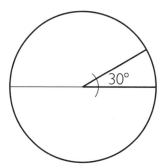

4. Extend the new radius you constructed to form a pair of vertical angles. What is the measure of the new angle you formed? _____

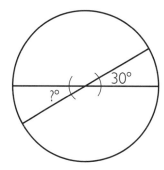

From *Sizing Up Measurement: Activities for Grades 6–8 Classrooms* by Ann Lawrence and Charlie Hennessy. © 2007 by Math Solutions Publications.

5. Construct another central angle of 30 degrees adjacent to the first angle. Extend the new radius to form another pair of vertical angles. Repeat these steps until your circle looks like the one shown below.

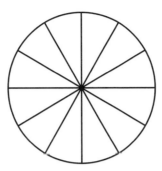

6. What is the measure of each central angle? _____

7. What fraction of the circumference of the circle does each of these sectors contain? _____

Part 2: Making Cones and Gathering Data

1. Carefully cut out one of the 30-degree sectors of your circle. Discard this sector.

2. Take the rest of the circle and tape the radii together edge-to-edge to form a cone.

3. Without measuring, predict the diameter of the cone. (Be prepared to explain your thinking.) Write your prediction in centimeters in the following table.

4. Measure and record the slant height and diameter of the cone to the nearest tenth of a centimeter.

5. Predict the volume of the cone in milliliters. The total volume of the rice you were given is about 350 milliliters. Record your prediction in the table.

6. Fill the cone with rice. Use a paper funnel to pour the rice from the cone into the graduated cylinder. Record the actual volume of the cone in the table.

7. Repeat the steps above, removing one additional sector of the circle each time to make a new cone. For each new cone, you will need to untape the old cone, flatten it, and cut away another sector. Then tape what is left of the circle into a cone and repeat Steps 3 through 6. Observe carefully to find patterns in the table that occur as the number of sectors removed increases.

8. When you have completed the table, graph your data. Use the size of the sector removed (in degrees) as the x-coordinate and the volume of the cone as the y-coordinate for each point. The coordinates for the first cone you made will be (30, volume of cone in ml).

Size of Sector Removed, or m(Central Angle)	Prediction for Diameter of Cone (in cm)	Actual Diameter of Cone (in cm)	Slant Height of Cone (in cm)	Prediction for Volume of Cone (in ml)	Actual Volume of Cone (in ml)
30°					
60°					
90°					
120°					
150°					
180°					
210°					
240°					
270°					

Part 3: Analyzing Your Findings

Answer the following questions on your own paper. Then compare and discuss your answers with your partner. Be sure you can explain your thinking.

1. Describe the pattern in the data for the diameter of the cones. Explain why this pattern makes sense.

2. Describe the pattern in the data for the slant height of the cones. Explain why this pattern makes sense.

3. Describe the pattern in the data for the volume of the cones. Explain why this pattern makes sense.

4. What do the data and graph tell you about the rate of change in the volumes of the cones? Make a conjecture about why this happens.

5. Describe at least one thing about this investigation that surprised you. Make a conjecture about why this happened.

From *Sizing Up Measurement: Activities for Grades 6–8 Classrooms* by Ann Lawrence and Charlie Hennessy.
© 2007 by Math Solutions Publications.

If I Were a . . .

Choose an animal that has an attribute or ability that you find interesting. Do the following steps to compare yourself to that animal.

1. Set up a ratio about the animal you chose and one of its attributes or abilities, using the information given.

2. Set up a parallel ratio about yourself, using a variable and an appropriate measuring tool.

3. Find the answer (value of the variable), using an appropriate method.

4. Use numerical information about an object with which most people are familiar to express your answer in another way. (**Note:** You may have to do some research to find an appropriate object to use.)

5. Make a poster to show your mathematical thinking and procedures. Be sure you include the following on your poster:
- a title (for example, "If I Could Hop Like a Frog . . .")
- a mathematical statement of your findings, including the measurement you found and your comparison to a common object
- your mathematical reasoning, including the following: (1) how you set up the ratios; (2) how you solved for the missing measure, in both words and numbers; (3) your comparison to an everyday object, in both words and numbers; and (4) an illustration of the solution

6. Be prepared to explain your work to your classmates.

From *Sizing Up Measurement: Activities for Grades 6–8 Classrooms* by Ann Lawrence and Charlie Hennessy. © 2007 by Math Solutions Publications.

Exploring Rates

		Reading Rates	
Kind of Reading	**Number of Words in 140 Seconds**	**Rates**	
		Number of Words/Second	*Number of Seconds/Word*
Silent			
Aloud			

Explain what each of your rates means in one or more sentences (include your results).

Number of Words/Second: _____

_____

_____

Number of Seconds/Word: _____

_____

_____

From *Sizing Up Measurement: Activities for Grades 6–8 Classrooms* by Ann Lawrence and Charlie Hennessy.
© 2007 by Math Solutions Publications.

Exploring Rates

Shooting Hoops			
Hand Used	Number of Hoops in 80 Seconds	Rates	
		Number of Hoops/Minute	*Number of Seconds/Hoop*
Dominant			
Nondominant			

Explain what each of your rates means in one or more sentences (include your results).

Number of Hoops/Minute: _____

_____

_____

Number of Seconds/Hoop: _____

_____

_____

From *Sizing Up Measurement: Activities for Grades 6–8 Classrooms* by Ann Lawrence and Charlie Hennessy. © 2007 by Math Solutions Publications.

Exploring Rates

		Tracing Stars	
		Rates	
Hand Used	**Number of Stars in 80 Seconds**	*Number of Stars/Minute*	*Number of Seconds/Star*
Dominant			
Nondominant			

Explain what each of your rates means in one or more sentences (include your results).

Number of Stars/Minute: _____

_____

_____

Number of Seconds/Star: _____

_____

_____

From *Sizing Up Measurement: Activities for Grades 6–8 Classrooms* by Ann Lawrence and Charlie Hennessy.
© 2007 by Math Solutions Publications.

Rows of Stars

From *Sizing Up Measurement: Activities for Grades 6–8 Classrooms* by Ann Lawrence and Charlie Hennessy.
© 2007 by Math Solutions Publications.

Hello, Proportions

Write a proportion using equivalent ratios for each problem below. Then solve the proportion for the unknown value. Show your work and thinking.

1. 6 miles : 40 minutes : : _____ miles : 100 minutes

2. 10-minute phone call : $1.80 cost : : 25-minute phone call : _____ cost

3. 200 miles : 40 hours : : _____ miles : 36 hours

4. 8 weeks : $7.20 : : 3 weeks : _____

5. _____ students : 18 parents : : 25 students : 150 parents

From *Sizing Up Measurement: Activities for Grades 6–8 Classrooms* by Ann Lawrence and Charlie Hennessy.
© 2007 by Math Solutions Publications.

Unpumped Prices

1. Predict the cost of liquids in the chart below and rank them from most expensive (1) to least expensive (10).

Predicted Rank	Liquid Product	Amount Given	Price Given	Price/_____
	Gasoline	1 gallon		
	Mild Salsa			
	Pepto-Bismol			
	Evian Water			
	Tabasco Sauce			
	Listerine			
	Snapple			
	Liquid Paper			
	Nautica Cologne			
	Frappuccino			
	Vanilla Extract			

2. Choose a unit rate (for example, price/ounce or price/gallon) and complete the table above.

3. Show your work and explain your thinking below for any *two* items in the table.

From *Sizing Up Measurement: Activities for Grades 6–8 Classrooms* by Ann Lawrence and Charlie Hennessy. © 2007 by Math Solutions Publications.

Could It Be?

In the book *Walk Two Moons*, by Sharon Creech, Sal and her grandparents drive from Ohio to Idaho. Many details are given in the book about each day's journey.

Was the itinerary of this imaginary trip realistic? Could it have really happened the way it is described in the book?

Follow the directions below to help you answer these questions.

Part 1: Calculating Mileage

Use road maps to determine the number of miles traveled each day of the trip. Find the fastest route, traveling on interstate highways whenever possible. Use your findings to complete the table.

Day	Starting Point for the Day; Other Places Visited Along the Way	End Point	Number of Miles Traveled for the Day	Total Number of Miles So Far
1	Euclid, OH; Elkhart, IN, and South Bend, IN	Chicago, IL		
2	Chicago, IL; Madison, WI	Wisconsin Dells, WI		
3	Wisconsin Dells, WI	Pipestone, MN		
4	Pipestone, MN; Sioux Falls, SD, and Mitchell, SD	Chamberlain, SD (add 20 miles for side trip to the Missouri River)		
5	Chamberlain, SD	Wall, SD		
6	Wall, SD; Mount Rushmore and Yellowstone National Park	Old Faithful Inn; Yellowstone National Park, WY		
7	Old Faithful Inn; Yellowstone National Park, WY	Coeur D'Alene, ID		

Part 2: Constructing a Scatter Plot

Using the information in the last column of your table, construct a connected scatter plot to display the day (*x*-coordinate) and the total distance traveled so far (*y*-coordinate) at the end of each day of the trip. Now use your scatter plot and your table to answer the following questions:

a. During which day of the trip did Sal and her grandparents travel farthest? Explain.

b. Which better helps you think about the daily progress Sal and her grandparents made, the table or the scatter plot? Explain your thinking.

From *Sizing Up Measurement: Activities for Grades 6–8 Classrooms* by Ann Lawrence and Charlie Hennessy. © 2007 by Math Solutions Publications.

Part 3: Using Your Calculator

How many hours did Sal and her grandparents travel each day? How fast did they travel each day? Your scatter plot does not tell you this information, but your calculator can help you find the answers.

Distance and Time

Is it reasonable to assume that Sal and her grandparents traveled the same amount of time (number of hours) each day? Follow the directions below to help you answer this question.

1. In the second column of the following table, record the mileage you calculated in Part 1.
2. Choose a reasonable number of hours that Sal and her grandparents might travel each day. Use your calculator to find their average number of miles per day. (Hint: rate = distance/time). Record your data in the third column.
3. Repeat this process, using a different number of hours that Sal and her grandparents might travel each day. Record your data in the fourth column.

Day	Total Distance Traveled on the Day	Mean Number of Miles per Hour if Traveling _____ Hours per Day	Mean Number of Miles per Hour if Traveling _____ Hours per Day
1			
2			
3			
4			
5			
6			
7			

4. Based on the results you've recorded, is it reasonable to assume that Sal and her grandparents traveled the same length of time (number of hours) each day? Explain your thinking.

Speed and Distance

1. In the second column in the table below, record the mileage you calculated in Part 1.

2. Choose a reasonable rate of speed that Sal and her grandparents might have traveled at each day. Use your calculator to find the average number of hours they traveled each day. (Hint: time = distance/rate). Record your data in the third column.

3. Repeat this process, using a different rate of speed at which Sal and her grandparents might have traveled each day. Record your data in the fourth column.

Day	Total Distance Traveled on the Day	Number of Hours at an Average Rate of _____ mph	Number of Hours at an Average Rate of _____ mph
1			
2			
3			
4			
5			
6			
7			

4. Based on the results you've recorded, is it reasonable to assume that Sal and her grandparents traveled at the same average rate (miles per hour) each day? Explain your thinking.

Part 4: Wrapping Up

Write a short paragraph that reflects what you learned. Answer the following questions:

1. Was the itinerary of Sal and her grandparents reasonable? Why?

2. Could the journey really have happened the way it is described in the book? Explain your reasoning.

Go for the Golden 1

You will construct a set of rectangles that emerge from a spiraling pattern of squares. The largest figure in your pattern will approximate a golden rectangle, which has a special length-to-width ratio of approximately 1.61803. It is a shape that people through the centuries have claimed is the most pleasing of all possible rectangles. (**Note:** The grid shown behind the illustrations are meant to make directions clearer.)

Part 1: Use your ruler and compass

1. Construct a very small square, 1 unit by 1 unit, near the middle of your paper. Be sure that all sides are congruent and all angles measure 90 degrees. Label this square A. It is not important for your square to be the same size as that of any other student. Enter the information for this figure in the table that follows.

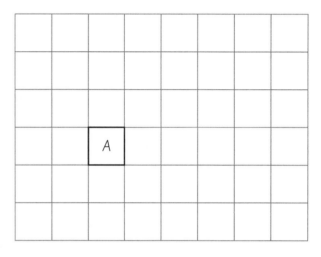

2. Add another 1-by-1-unit square to the left of Square A. Notice that you have created a rectangle that is 2 units by 1 unit. Label this rectangle B. Enter the information for this new figure.

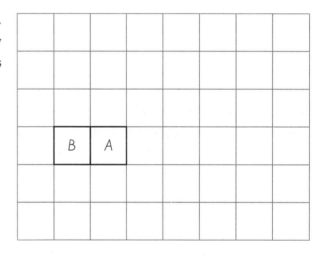

3. Construct a 2-by-2 square above Rectangle B. Notice that you have created a rectangle that is 3 units by 2 units. Label this rectangle C. Enter the information for this new figure.

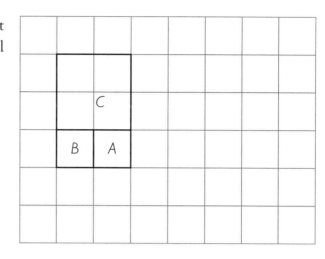

4. Construct a 3-by-3 square to the right of C. Notice that you have created a rectangle that is 5 units by 3 units. Label this rectangle D. Enter the information for this new figure.

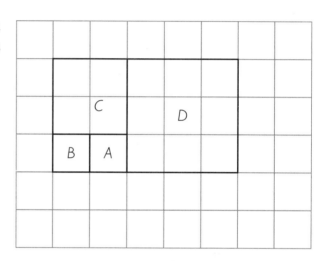

5. Notice the spiraling pattern for the placement of each new square. In what direction do you think the next square will be placed? After checking your answer with your partner, construct a 5-by-5 square. Label the new rectangle E. Enter the information for this new figure.

6. Predict the dimensions of the next square: _____. Discuss your reasoning with your partner. Then continue the spiraling process of adding squares, noting the length and width of the new rectangle formed, and entering the information for each new figure until you complete Rectangle I.

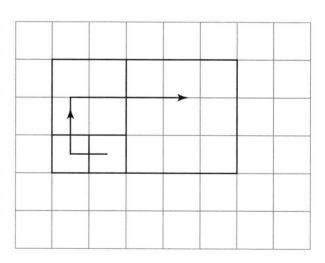

From *Sizing Up Measurement: Activities for Grades 6–8 Classrooms* by Ann Lawrence and Charlie Hennessy.
© 2007 by Math Solutions Publications.

Rectangle	Longest Side of New Rectangle (Written as Sum of Parts)	Length (Longer Side)	Width (Shorter Side)	Ratio L : W
A	1	1	1	
B	1 + 1			
C	2 + 1			
D				
E				
F				
G				
H				

Table of Ratios for Rectangles

Part 2: Work with your partner to answer the questions below

1. What pattern do you find in the lengths of the longest sides of the rectangles?

_____

2. What pattern(s) do you find in the length-to-width ratios of the rectangles?

_____

_____

3. If you continue to construct larger and larger rectangles using the same growth pattern, what can you predict about the length-to-width ratios for larger and larger rectangles?

_____

_____

4. Compare your drawing with those of your classmates. What can you conclude?

_____

_____

5. Do you find the appearance of your largest rectangle pleasing? Explain your thinking.

_____

_____

From *Sizing Up Measurement: Activities for Grades 6–8 Classrooms* by Ann Lawrence and Charlie Hennessy.
© 2007 by Math Solutions Publications.

What's with the Factor?

Part 1

Work with your partner to do the following steps:

1. Prism 1: Use your cubes to build a rectangular prism of your choice. Keep the dimensions small so you will have enough cubes to build the next two prisms, which will be larger than this one. Record all information for this prism in Table 1.

2. Prism 2: Build a rectangular prism having dimensions that are double those of Prism 1. Record all information for this prism in Table 1.

3. Prism 3: Build a rectangular prism having dimensions that are triple those of Prism 1. Record all information for this prism in Table 1.

4. Prism 4: Predict, without building it, the data for a rectangular prism having dimensions that are quadruple (four times as big as) those of Prism 1. Record all information for this prism in Table 1.

Table 1					
Prism	**Base**	**Altitude**	**Height**	**Surface Area**	**Volume**
1					
2					
3					
4 (prediction)					

Part 2

Work with your partner to do the following steps:

1. Using your data from Table 1, find the ratios required in Table 2 for the first three rows. List all ratios in simplest form.

2. Use all your findings to make a conjecture about the surface area and volume of a rectangular prism whose dimensions are multiplied by any factor. Record your ratios in the last row of Table 2. Use the variable f to represent the scale factor.

Table 2						
Description of the Second Prism Compared with the First Prism	**Prism**	**Base Layer of Prism**		**Ratio of Heights of Prisms**	**Ratio of Surface Areas**	**Ratio of Volumes**
		Ratio of Bases	**Ratio of Altitudes**			
all dimensions doubled	old 1	$\frac{1}{2}$				
	new 2					
all dimensions tripled	old 1					
	new 3					
all dimensions quadrupled	old 1					
	new 4					
all dimensions multiplied by any factor, f	old 1					
	new f					

Part 3

Using the data in your tables, talk with your partner about each of the following questions. Then answer each question on lined paper. Be prepared to explain your thinking to the class.

1. When the dimensions of a rectangular prism are doubled, how do the ratios of corresponding dimensions of the two prisms compare with the ratio of their surface areas? Why does this make sense?

2. When the dimensions of a rectangular prism are doubled, how do the ratios of corresponding dimensions of the two prisms compare with the ratio of their volumes? Why does this make sense?

3. What pattern(s) do you find in the data in the third, fourth, and fifth columns of Table 2? Why do they make sense?

4. What pattern(s) do you find in the data in the Ratio of Surface Areas column? Why do they make sense?

5. What pattern(s) do you find in the data in the Ratio of Volumes column? Why do they make sense?

6. Predict, then verify, the ratios of surface areas and volumes for two rectangular prisms if the ratio of their side lengths is 2 : 3.

7. Would the ratios in your table be the same if, for example, you doubled the number of cubes used to make the second prism instead of doubling the measure of each dimension? Explain your thinking.

From *Sizing Up Measurement: Activities for Grades 6–8 Classrooms* by Ann Lawrence and Charlie Hennessy.
© 2007 by Math Solutions Publications.

Swinging Rates

Part 1: Conducting the Experiment

1. Select two lengths for your pendulum.

2. Using one pendulum, do the following steps as accurately as possible:

   a. One person holds a protractor.

   b. The second person pulls the bob of the pendulum until the amplitude is 15 degrees. This person says, "Start," as he releases the bob, announces the number of each of the first four oscillations as it ends, and says, "Stop," at the end of the fifth oscillation.

   c. The third person keeps time and announces the total elapsed time after the fifth oscillation.

   d. The fourth person records the time for five oscillations in the following table. Then she divides the total time by five to find the mean time (period) for each oscillation and records it in the table.

   e. Do a second trial.

   f. If the times are markedly different, do a third trial at the same amplitude to confirm which of the first two trials was more accurate. In this case, use the time of the third trial to replace that of the "oddball" trial.

3. Repeat the steps above for each amplitude listed in the table.

4. Repeat the entire procedure for the other pendulum length.

From *Sizing Up Measurement: Activities for Grades 6–8 Classrooms* by Ann Lawrence and Charlie Hennessy.
© 2007 by Math Solutions Publications.

Part 2: Completing the Table

1. Fill in the third column in the table. Use the length of each pendulum (Column 4) as the radius of the imaginary circle and use that information to complete the next two columns.
2. Finally, use the distance (arc length) and time (period) that you measured to calculate the rate at which the pendulum traveled to complete the oscillation at each amplitude.

Trial	Amplitude (In Degrees from Center)	Ratio of Amplitude to Full Circle	Length of Pendulum (Radius of Circle in cm)	Circumference of Circle	Arc Length	Time (Five Oscillations)	Period (Mean Time/ Oscillation)	Rate (cm/sec)
Pendulum 1								
1	15							
2	15							
1	30							
2	30							
1	45							
2	45							
1	60							
2	60							
Pendulum 2								
1	15							
2	15							
1	30							
2	30							
1	45							
2	45							
1	60							
2	60							

Part 3: Looking for Patterns

With the other members of your group, look for patterns in your table and list them on a sheet of paper. Discuss each of the following questions. Then individually record your answers on your own paper.

1. Did anything surprise you about the time required for five oscillations with different amplitudes? Explain your thinking.
2. How did knowing about central angles, arcs, and circumference of circles help you find the speed of the pendulum for each trial?
3. How did knowing the formula distance = rate • time help you find the speed of the pendulum for each trial?

From *Sizing Up Measurement: Activities for Grades 6–8 Classrooms* by Ann Lawrence and Charlie Hennessy.
© 2007 by Math Solutions Publications.

What Are Similar Polygons?

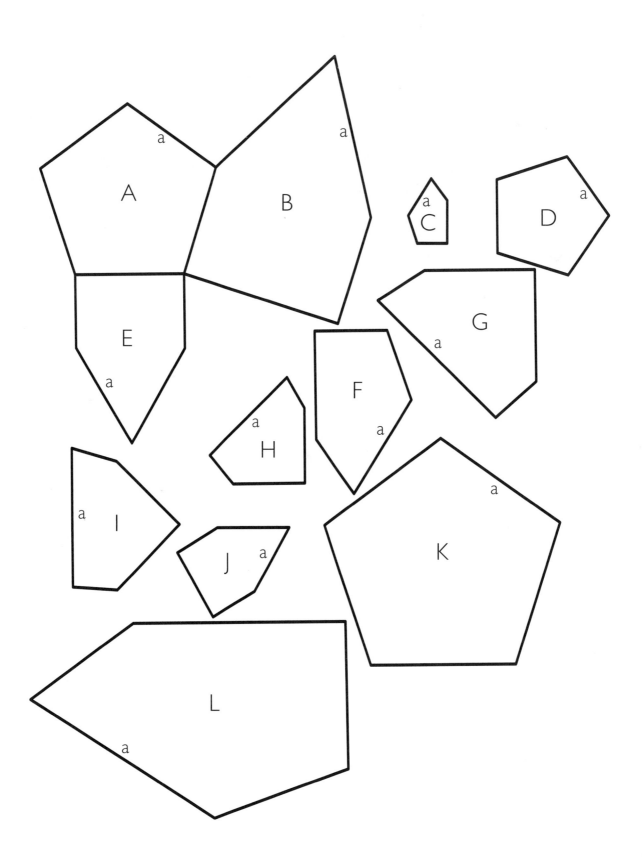

From *Sizing Up Measurement: Activities for Grades 6–8 Classrooms* by Ann Lawrence and Charlie Hennessy.
© 2007 by Math Solutions Publications.

A Different Look

Part 1: Growing Triangles

1. Place a group of green triangles on your desk. The triangles are congruent. What does this mean?

   _____

2. Examine a single equilateral triangle. This triangle is a Stage 1 triangle. Find the length of its sides and compare the three angles. What did you notice?

   _____

3. Build a Stage 2 triangle. *The scale factor between the first two stages must be two.* What does this mean?

   _____

   Neatly sketch your Stage 2 triangle on a sheet of lined paper. What is its perimeter in inches? What is its area in base units? (The base unit is the green triangle you used for Stage 1.)

4. Now build a Stage 3 triangle. It must be built using only Stage 1 triangles, be similar to the first triangle, and have a scale factor of three.

5. Carefully trace your Stage 3 triangle on your lined paper.

6. At this point, stop building to share and talk with your partner about your results. Then record your information in the following chart.

Stage	Number of Inches on Each Side	Perimeter in Inches	Area in Base Units (Number of Equilateral Triangles)
1			
2			
3			
4			
5			
10			
100			
n			

7. Combine triangles with your partner to build Stages 4 and 5 and record the data for those stages. Using the information in your table, find patterns to predict the results for Stages 10, 100, and n. Be sure each of you can explain your results and thinking to other members of the class.

From *Sizing Up Measurement: Activities for Grades 6–8 Classrooms* by Ann Lawrence and Charlie Hennessy. © 2007 by Math Solutions Publications.

Part 2: Growing Quadrilaterals

Repeat Steps 1–7 from Part 1, using an equilateral quadrilateral (either the orange square or the blue rhombus) as the base unit.

Stage	Number of Inches on Each Side	Perimeter in Inches	Area in Base Units (Number of Squares or Rhombi)
1			
2			
3			
4			
5			
10			
100			
n			

Part 3: Growing Trapezoids

Repeat Steps 1–7 from Part 1, using a red isosceles trapezoid as the base unit. Be careful: the larger stages of this pattern are challenging to build.

Stage	Lengths of Sides in Inches	Perimeter in Inches	Area in Base Units (Number of Trapezoids)
1	1, 1, 1, and 2	5	1
2			
3			
4			
5			
10			
100			
n			

From *Sizing Up Measurement: Activities for Grades 6–8 Classrooms* by Ann Lawrence and Charlie Hennessy.
© 2007 by Math Solutions Publications.

Part 4: Growing Hexagons

Repeat Steps 1–7 from Part 1, using a yellow regular hexagon as the base unit. Building even Stage 2 or 3 of this pattern is difficult. You will have to "break a rule" that you have been following in order to build these stages. Record the pieces you use to build Stages 2 and 3 on your lined paper.

Stage	Lengths of Sides in Inches	Perimeter in Inches	Area in Base Units (Number of Stage 1 Regular Hexagons)
1			1
2			
3			
4			
5			
10			
100			
n			

Part 5: Reflection

Write about the mathematical ideas of this investigation. Be sure you answer each of the following questions:

1. How are the definitions of *perimeter, area,* and *similar figures* the same in this investigation as in others you have done? How are they different?

2. What patterns did you find for perimeter and area for all the shapes you used in this investigation? Why do these patterns make sense?

3. What makes all the figures in the patterns for each shape in this investigation similar? Why does this makes sense?

4. What one mathematical idea in this investigation was new for you, or what became clearer?

From *Sizing Up Measurement: Activities for Grades 6–8 Classrooms* by Ann Lawrence and Charlie Hennessy.
© 2007 by Math Solutions Publications.

Using Indirect Measurement Method Cards

Method 1: Using Shadows

You and your partner need a metric tape measure. (**Note:** The sun must be casting shadows to use this method.)

1. Estimate and record the height, in centimeters, of the object you have selected.
2. Stand beside the object. Stand still while your partner measures and records your height and the length of your shadow, both to the nearest centimeter.
3. Together measure and record the length of the object's shadow to the nearest centimeter.
4. Make a drawing. Include the object you measured and the method you used. Show the two similar triangles in this situation. Label the known measures and use a variable for the unknown measure.
5. Using what you know about similar figures, calculate the height of the object. Show and label your work.
6. Now switch roles and repeat Steps 2 through 5.

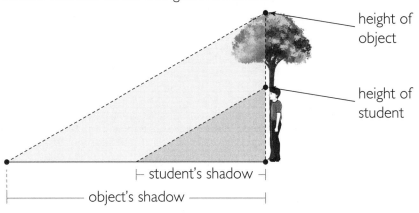

Method 1: using shadows
Note: The two similar triangles are shaded.

height of object

height of student

student's shadow

object's shadow

Method 2: Sighting with a Pencil

You and your partner need a metric tape measure and an extra pencil.

1. Estimate and record the height, in centimeters, of the object you have selected.
2. Measure and record the length of your pencil to the nearest tenth of a centimeter.
3. Standing some distance from the object, hold the pencil at arm's length. Keeping the pencil perpendicular to the ground, move forward or backward until the top of the pencil lines up with the top of the object and the bottom of the pencil lines up with the bottom of the object.

    Stay in this position while your partner measures and records to the nearest tenth of a centimeter (1) the distance (parallel to the ground) from your eye to the pencil and (2) the distance (parallel to the ground) from your feet to the object.
4. Make a drawing. Include the object you measured and the method you used. Show the two similar triangles in this situation. Label the known measures and use a variable for the unknown measure.
5. Using what you know about similar figures, calculate the height of the object. Show and label your work.
6. Now switch roles and repeat Steps 3 through 5.

Method 2: sighting with a pencil (not to scale)
Note: The two similar triangles are shaded.

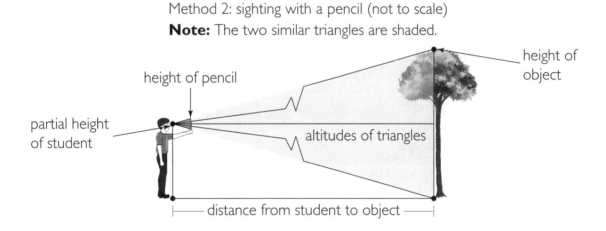

height of pencil

partial height of student

altitudes of triangles

height of object

distance from student to object

From *Sizing Up Measurement: Activities for Grades 6–8 Classrooms* by Ann Lawrence and Charlie Hennessy.
© 2007 by Math Solutions Publications.

Method 3: Using a Mirror

You and your partner need a metric tape measure and a mirror with a small dot in its center.

1. Estimate and record the height, in centimeters, of the object you've selected.
2. Place a small mirror face up on the ground some distance from the object, so that it is at the same level as the bottom of the object.
3. Slowly back away from the mirror until you see the top of the object even with the dot in the center of the mirror.

    Stay in this position while your partner measures and records to the nearest centimeter (1) the distance from you to the dot on the mirror and (2) your height from the ground to the middle of your eye.
4. Together measure and record the distance from the bottom of the object to the dot on the mirror, to the nearest centimeter.
5. Make a drawing. Include the object you measured and the method you used. Show the two similar triangles in this situation. Label the known measures and use a variable for the unknown measure.
6. Using what you know about similar figures, calculate the height of the object. Show and label your work.
7. Now switch roles and repeat Steps 2 through 6.

Method 3: using a mirror

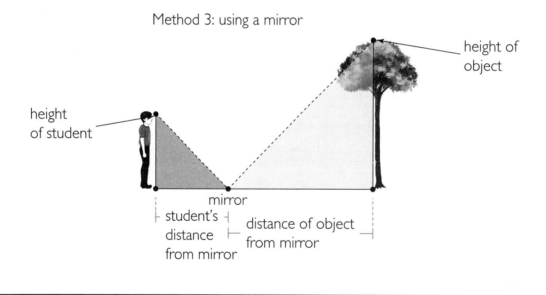

height of object

height of student

mirror

student's distance from mirror

distance of object from mirror

Method 4: Using a Clinometer

You and your partner will need a clinometer to use this method.

1. Estimate and record the height, in centimeters, of the object you've selected.

2. Stand a measured distance (for example, 40 meters) from the object. Look through the straw of the clinometer until you see the top of the object.

3. Hold the clinometer steady, continuing to sight the top of the object while your partner reads the angle shown by the string.

4. Verify the reading from Step 3. If you agree on the angle, go to the next step. If not, take a third reading and determine which angle you will use. (Be prepared to explain the reasoning behind your choice.)

5. Have your partner measure the distance from the ground to the middle of your eye.

6. Make a scale drawing on grid paper. Include the object you measured and the method you used. Label the known measures, including the angle found by using the clinometer, and use a variable for the unknown measure.

7. Using what you know about scale drawings and similar figures, calculate the height of the object. Show and label your work.

8. Now switch roles and repeat Steps 2 through 7.

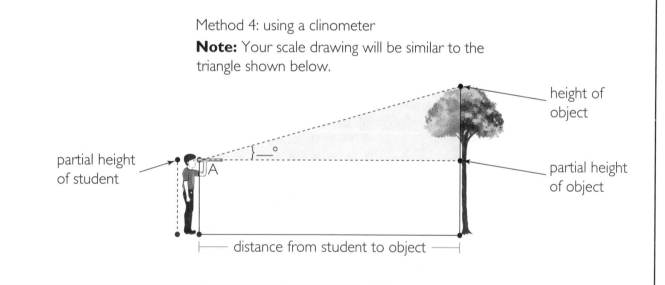

Method 4: using a clinometer

Note: Your scale drawing will be similar to the triangle shown below.

partial height of student

height of object

partial height of object

distance from student to object

From *Sizing Up Measurement: Activities for Grades 6–8 Classrooms* by Ann Lawrence and Charlie Hennessy.
© 2007 by Math Solutions Publications.

Wise Up

Part 1

Work with your partner to complete the following table. Do not include the box in your estimated or actual weights.

Name of Cereal	Estimated Weight (in Grams)	Weight Listed (in Grams)	Actual Weight (in Grams)	Your Percent of Error	Cost/Gram
A					
B					
C					
D					
E					

Part 2

Answer each of the following questions on your own paper. Then compare answers with your partner and make any needed changes. Be prepared to explain your reasoning.

1. How good were your estimates of weight? Explain why you think you were or were not a good estimator.

2. If you compare the costs per gram, which cereal is the best buy? Why?

3. Is the cost per gram a good way for deciding which cereal is the best buy? Explain your thinking.

4. Would you consider yourself a wise consumer if you used cost per gram as the only factor to decide which cereal to buy? Why or why not?

5. What other factors might people use to determine which cereal to buy? Do you think these factors would make a person a wiser consumer? Explain your thinking.

From *Sizing Up Measurement: Activities for Grades 6–8 Classrooms* by Ann Lawrence and Charlie Hennessy.
© 2007 by Math Solutions Publications.

Part 3

Work with your partner to complete the following table.

Name of Cereal and Dimensions of Cereal Box (cm)	Estimated Surface Area of Box (cm²)	Actual Surface Area of Box (cm²)	Percent of Error	Dimensions of Wasted Surface Area (cm²)	Wasted Surface Area (cm²)	Percent of Waste*
A						
B						
C						
D						
E						

* Waste is the amount of unneeded cardboard. It is any cardboard used beyond the amount needed to make each cereal box exactly large enough to hold the cereal. Only the lateral surface area above the height of the cereal is waste, since the top of the box is needed.

Part 4

Answer each of the following questions on your own paper. Then compare answers with your partner and make any needed changes. Show your methods and be prepared to explain your reasoning.

1. How good were your estimates of surface area? Explain why you think you were or were not a good estimator.

2. If you compare the percents of waste, which cereal would be the best buy? Why?

3. Is the percent of waste a wise way to decide which cereal is the best buy? Explain your reasoning.

4. Would you consider yourself a wise consumer if you used percent of waste as the only factor to decide which cereal to buy? Why or why not?

5. For what reasons do you think the cereal companies might include this wasted cardboard in the boxes?

From *Sizing Up Measurement: Activities for Grades 6–8 Classrooms* by Ann Lawrence and Charlie Hennessy.
© 2007 by Math Solutions Publications.

Exploring Density

Part I

1. Check to see that in one set of your pennies, all coins have dates before 1982 (older pennies) and in the other set, all have dates after 1984 (newer pennies).

2. Pour 20 milliliters of water into a graduated cylinder.

3. Use a balance to determine the mass of the graduated cylinder, including the water. Record the mass (in grams) here.

   _____ g _____ g

4. Add five older pennies to the graduated cylinder. Find the volume of the pennies that you have added. Enter it into the data table.

5. Using a balance, find the mass of the five older pennies by subtracting the old mass from the new mass. Enter it into the data table.

6. Add five additional older pennies to the graduated cylinder. Find the volume of all the pennies so far. Enter it into the data table.

7. Using a balance, find the mass of all the pennies so far. Enter it into the data table.

8. Repeat Steps 6 and 7 until you have added and recorded the data for a total of twenty-five older pennies.

9. Repeat Steps 2 through 8 with the set of newer pennies. Enter all data into the data table.

DATA TABLE

Number of Pennies	Pennies Minted Before 1982		Pennies Minted After 1984	
	Volume of Pennies (ml)	Mass of Pennies (g)	Volume of Pennies (ml)	Mass of Pennies (g)
0	0	0	0	0
5				
10				
15				
20				
25				

From *Sizing Up Measurement: Activities for Grades 6–8 Classrooms* by Ann Lawrence and Charlie Hennessy.
© 2007 by Math Solutions Publications.

Part 2

Using volume as the independent (x) variable and mass as the dependent (y) variable, graph both sets of data on the same graph. Use one color for the older pennies and a different one for the newer pennies.

Part 3

Answer the following questions based on your data and graph on a separate sheet of paper.

1. What is the slope of the line that best fits the points for the older pennies?

2. What is the slope of the line that best fits the points for the newer pennies?

3. Explain what slope means and what it represents in this investigation.

4. From this exploration, what can you conclude about the density of older U.S. pennies versus the density of newer U.S. pennies? Explain your reasoning and tell how the graph supports your thinking.

5. If you were given 50 older pennies, and their mass was 150 grams, estimate the volume of the pennies and explain your reasoning.

6. If you were given 50 newer pennies and their volume was 17.4 milliliters, estimate the mass of the pennies and explain your reasoning.

7. Define *density* in your own words (do not give a formula).

From *Sizing Up Measurement: Activities for Grades 6–8 Classrooms* by Ann Lawrence and Charlie Hennessy.
© 2007 by Math Solutions Publications.

Glossary

We have included in this glossary mathematical terms and phrases directly related to measurement that appear in the book and that we think are both mathematically important and likely to be new to your students. We tried to write definitions that are mathematically accurate and also useful to your students, who are trying to make sense of ideas that are new to them. We chose language that is accessible to middle school students, and we have provided examples and illustrations when we felt they were needed.

We hope that you use the definitions in this glossary as guidelines but give your students opportunities to express the ideas in their own words and to listen to how their classmates express those ideas. We don't expect our students to use the language we choose or to memorize our definitions. A reasonable goal is that students recognize the terms and phrases and can use them correctly in the context of the learning activities they experience. Keep in mind that students will have further opportunities to formalize their thinking as they continue to develop their understanding of measurement through subsequent experiences.

adjacent angles: two angles that have a common vertex and a common side

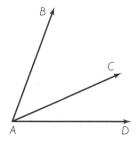

Angle *BAC* is adjacent to angle *CAD*.

alternate exterior angles: a pair of angles on opposite sides of a transversal and outside the two lines cut by the transversal

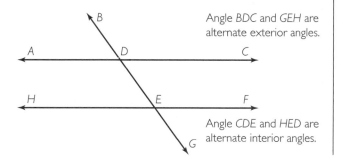

Angle *BDC* and *GEH* are alternate exterior angles.

Angle *CDE* and *HED* are alternate interior angles.

alternate interior angles: a pair of angles on opposite sides of a transversal and inside the two lines cut by the transversal

altitude: a line segment, or the length of a line segment, that gives the height of a polygon, polyhedron, cone, cylinder, or other geometric figure

apex: in a three-dimensional figure, the point at which all faces except the base meet

apothem: for a regular polygon, the perpendicular distance from its center to one of its sides

area: the measure of the amount of surface inside a closed figure; area is measured in square units

base of a polygon: the side on which a polygon "sits"; the side of a polygon that is perpendicular to its height

base layer of a solid figure: the "bottom" face of a three-dimensional figure; the face whose shape is the basis for classifying a prism or pyramid

base unit: a shape or size used to measure length, area, or volume; for example, a base unit for measuring area could equal 1 square inch or 1 triangle of a specific shape and size, such as the green pattern block

capacity: a measure of how much liquid or other pourable substance a container can hold

Celsius scale: a metric scale for measuring temperature that sets the freezing point of water at 0 degrees (0°C) and the boiling point at 100 degrees (100°C)

central angle: in a circle, an angle formed by two radii

circumference: the distance around a circle or sphere

complementary angles: a pair of angles containing a total of 90 degrees

construct: the process of correctly representing a geometric figure, usually done with only a compass and straightedge

cooling rate: the change in temperature divided by the change in time; the pattern of the temperature of a particular substance as it loses heat; such rates do not have a constant rate of change

corresponding angles: a pair of congruent angles in the same position in similar figures; a pair of angles that lie on the same side of a transversal cutting two other lines and also both lie in the same relative position to the two lines

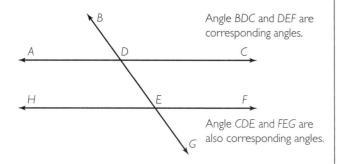

Angle *BDC* and *DEF* are corresponding angles.

Angle *CDE* and *FEG* are also corresponding angles.

corresponding parts: angles or sides of polygons or other two-dimensional figures that are in the same position

corresponding sides: sides of polygons or other two-dimensional figures that are in the same position

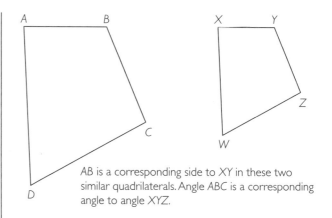

AB is a corresponding side to *XY* in these two similar quadrilaterals. Angle *ABC* is a corresponding angle to angle *XYZ*.

cubic units: units used to measure capacity and volume, for example, cubic centimeter, cubic inch, milliliter

degree: a unit of measure for angles based on dividing a circle into 360 congruent angles with a common vertex at the center of the circle; a unit of measure for temperature

density: the ratio of mass to unit volume of a material or object; density is often expressed in grams per cubic centimeter or kilograms per cubic meter

dilate: to reduce or enlarge a figure so that the corresponding angles remain congruent and the ratio of corresponding lengths remains the same

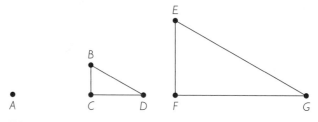

Triangle *BCD* has been dilated from point *A* to form triangle *EFG*. The ratio of corresponding sides is 2:5.

dimensions: the lengths of the sides of a geometric figure or the number of ways a figure can be measured; for example, a line segment is one-dimensional: only its length can be measured

estimate: an approximation of a quantity, such as a measure, based on judgment

exterior angle (in a polygon): an angle, outside a polygon, formed between one side of the polygon and the extension of an adjacent side

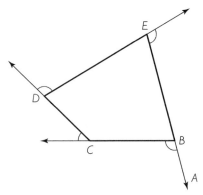

∠ABC is an exterior angle of quadrilateral BCDE.

exterior angles (of intersecting lines): all angles formed above or below the original lines when a transversal intersects two lines

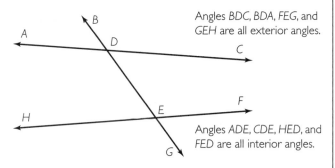

Angles BDC, BDA, FEG, and GEH are all exterior angles.

Angles ADE, CDE, HED, and FED are all interior angles.

Fahrenheit scale: a scale for measuring temperature that sets the freezing point of water at 32 degrees (32°F) and the boiling point at 212 degrees (212°F)

great circle: a circle on a sphere that has its center at the center of the sphere; therefore, the radius of a great circle equals the radius of the sphere

height: a measure of a polygon or solid figure, taken as the perpendicular distance from the base of the figure; in a triangle, the perpendicular distance between the base and the vertex opposite the base

height of a cone or pyramid: the length of a perpendicular line segment from the vertex to the base

height of a cylinder or prism: the length of a perpendicular line segment between the bases

interior angle (in a polygon): an angle lying between two adjacent sides of a polygon

interior angles (of intersecting lines): all angles formed in the area between the original lines when a transversal intersects two lines (see illustration above for **exterior angles**)

irrational number: a number that cannot be written as either a terminating or a repeating decimal; a never-ending, nonrepeating decimal number

mass: the amount of matter in an object; mass is usually measured against an object of known mass, often in pounds or kilograms

mean rate: an average rate; the quotient found by dividing the sum of two or more given rates by the number of rates given

meniscus: the curved top of a liquid in a cylinder with a small radius; the bottom of the meniscus is used to measure the volume of a liquid

net: short for *network*: an arrangement of two-dimensional figures that can be folded to make a polyhedron

percent of error: a measure of how inaccurate a measurement is compared with how large the actual measurement is; found by the formula

$$\frac{\text{difference between measured value and actual value}}{\text{actual value}} \times 100$$

perimeter: the distance around a two-dimensional shape

polyhedron: a solid figure with flat faces that are polygons

precision: degree of accuracy; the smaller the unit used, the more precise the measure

prism: a polyhedron with two parallel, congruent bases; its other faces are always parallelograms, and often rectangles

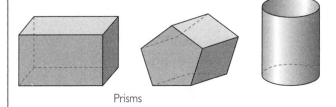

Prisms

proportional: having equivalent ratios; the lengths of corresponding sides in similar figures are proportional

pyramid: a solid figure with a polygon as its base and triangles with a common vertex (the apex) as its other faces

rate: a ratio that compares two quantities having different units of measure

rate of change: a measure of how fast change is occurring; for example, if the output of a function increases by three for every consecutive increase of one in the input, the rate of change is three; a rate of change may be constant, as in the example, or not

ratio: a comparison of two quantities by division

ray: part of a line, with one end point, that extends infinitely in one direction

real number: a rational or irrational number; {real numbers} = {rational numbers} ∪ {irrational numbers}

rectangular prism: a prism whose faces are all rectangles

rectangular pyramid: a pyramid with a rectangle as its base

referent: a familiar length or object that is used as a point of reference for comparison in estimation

reflex angle: an angle having a measure between 180 degrees and 360 degrees

scale: an indicator of length or distance having a graduated sequence of marks; an instrument used to measure weight

scale (on a graph): a system of marks at fixed intervals along a line for graphing numbers; a system of marks at fixed intervals along the axes for graphing ordered pairs on a coordinate plane

scale (on a map): the ratio of length used in a map to the actual length of the real distances depicted

scale drawing: a drawing that shows a real object smaller than (a reduction) or larger than (an enlargement) the real object; an accurate depiction of an object in which all parts are drawn using the same scale, such as 1 inch = 3 feet

scale factor: the value of a multiplier used to relate similar figures

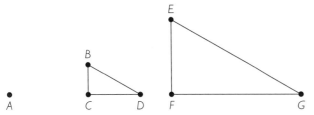

The scale factor for these two similar triangles is 2:5. Each side of triangle *BCD* is $\frac{1}{2}$ of the corresponding side in triangle *EFG*.

sector: a region of a circle enclosed by two radii and the arc joining their end points

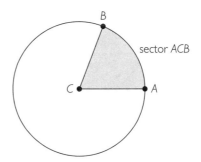

sector *ACB*

sighting an object: determining the angle between an artificial horizon and the top of an object to calculate its height

similar figures: figures that have the same shape but not necessarily the same size; in similar figures, all corresponding angles are congruent and all corresponding side lengths have the same ratio

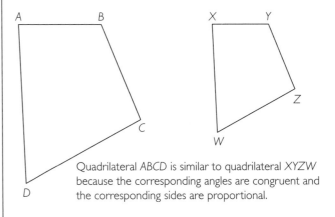

Quadrilateral *ABCD* is similar to quadrilateral *XYZW* because the corresponding angles are congruent and the corresponding sides are proportional.

slant height: the length of a lateral edge of a pyramid or cone

square pyramid: a geometric solid having a square base and triangular faces that meet at an apex

supplementary angles: a pair of angles containing a total of 180 degrees

surface area: the sum of the areas of all the faces or surfaces of a solid figure

transversal: a line that intersects at least two other lines

unit cost: the price for one unit of goods; for example, 3.5 cents per ounce

unit length: the distance between 0 and 1 on a number line or scale

unit rate: a rate having one unit as the second term (e.g., 50 mi./gal., 4.5 km/sec.)

vertical angles: a pair of nonadjacent angles formed by two intersecting lines; vertical angles are congruent

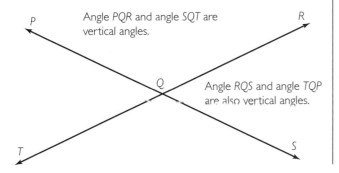

Angle *PQR* and angle *SQT* are vertical angles.

Angle *RQS* and angle *TQP* are also vertical angles.

volume: the measure of the amount of space taken up by a three-dimensional shape

weight: the vertical force exerted by a mass as a result of gravity

References

Bay-Williams, Jennifer M., Ann Bledsoe, and Robert Reys. 1998. "Stating the Facts: Exploring the United States." *Mathematics Teaching in the Middle School* (September): 8–14.

Bay-Williams, Jennifer M., and Sherri L. Martinie. 2004. *Math and Literature, Grades 6–8.* Sausalito, CA: Math Solutions.

Billstein, Rick, and Jim Williamson. 1999. *Math Thematics Book 1.* Boston: Houghton Mifflin.

Burns, Marilyn, and Cathy Humphreys. 1990. *A Collection of Math Lessons: From Grades 6 Through 8.* Sausalito, CA: Math Solutions.

Creech, Sharon. 1994. *Walk Two Moons.* New York: HarperCollins.

Ellis, Julie. 2004. *What's Your Angle Pythagoras? A Math Adventure.* Watertown, MA: Charlesbridge.

Jenkins, Steve. 1995. *Biggest, Strongest, Fastest.* New York: Ticknor & Fields Books for Young Readers.

———. 2004. *Actual Size.* Boston: Houghton Mifflin.

PBS. No date. "Fill 'er Up." The Middle School Math Project. Retrieved from www.pbs.org/teachersource/mathline/lessonplans/pdf/msmp/fillerup.pdf.

Schwartz, David M. 1999. *If You Hopped Like a Frog.* New York: Scholastic.

———. 2003. *Millions to Measure.* New York: HarperCollins.

Sundby, Scott. 2000. *Cut Down to Size at High Noon: A Math Adventure.* Watertown, MA: Charlesbridge.

Weibe, Arthur, ed. 1987. *Math and Science: A Solution.* Fresno, CA: AIMS Education Foundation.

Index